D1594662

Financialization in Crisis

Historical Materialism Book Series

The Historical Materialism Book Series is a major publishing initiative of the radical left. The capitalist crisis of the twenty-first century has been met by a resurgence of interest in critical Marxist theory. At the same time, the publishing institutions committed to Marxism have contracted markedly since the high point of the 1970s. The Historical Materialism Book Series is dedicated to addressing this situation by making available important works of Marxist theory. The aim of the series is to publish important theoretical contributions as the basis for vigorous intellectual debate and exchange on the left.

The peer-reviewed series publishes original monographs, translated texts, and reprints of classics across the bounds of academic disciplinary agendas and across the divisions of the left. The series is particularly concerned with encouraging the internationalization of Marxist debate and aims to translate significant studies from beyond the English-speaking world.

For a full list of titles in the Historical Materialism Book Series
available in paperback from Haymarket Books, visit:
www.haymarketbooks.org / category / hm-series

Financialization
in Crisis

edited by
Costas Lapavitsas

Haymarket Books
Chicago, IL

First published in 2012 by Brill Academic Publishers, The Netherlands
© 2012 Koninklijke Brill NV, Leiden, The Netherlands

Published in paperback in 2013 by
Haymarket Books
P.O. Box 180165
Chicago, IL 60618
773-583-7884
www.haymarketbooks.org

ISBN: 978-1-60846-237-7

Trade distribution:
In the US, Consortium Book Sales, www.cbsd.com
In Canada, Publishers Group Canada, www.pgcbooks.ca
In the UK, Turnaround Publisher Services, www.turnaround-psl.com
In Australia, Palgrave Macmillan, www.palgravemacmillan.com.au
In all other countries, Publishers Group Worldwide, www.pgw.com

Cover design by Ragina Johnson.

This book was published with the generous support
of Lannan Foundation and the Wallace Global Fund.

Printed in Canada by union labor.

10 9 8 7 6 5 4 3 2 1

Library of Congress Cataloging-in-Publication data is available.

Contents

Part One
Domestic Financialisation and the Roots of the Crisis

Part Two

International Financialisation and the Global Impact of the Crisis

Notes on Contributors

GARY DYMSKI is founder and Executive Director of the University of California Center Sacramento (UCCS), and professor of economics at the University of California, Riverside. Gary received his Ph.D. in economics from the University of Massachusetts, Amherst in 1987. He has been a visiting scholar at the Bangladesh Institute for Development Studies, Tokyo University, the University of Sao Paulo, the Federal University of Rio de Janeiro, the Federal University of Minas Gerais, Newcastle University, and the University of Athens. Gary's most recent books are *Capture and Exclude: Developing Nations and the Poor in Global Finance* (Tulika Books, New Delhi, 2007), co-edited with Amiya Bagchi, and *Reimagining Growth: Toward a Renewal of the Idea of Development*, co-edited with Silvana DePaula (Zed, London, 2005).

NURAY ERGÜNEŞ teaches economics at the Maltepe University, Turkey. She has written extensively on political economy of banking and finance, corruption and gender. Recent publications are *Banks, Accumulation, Corruption: the Banking Sector of Turkey after 1980s*, SAV Publications, 2008; 'Marxism and Women', in *Actuality of Marxism at the 160th year of Manifesto*, edited by Yüksel Akkaya and Irfan Kaygısız, EPOS Publications, 2008; 'Understanding of Intraclass Conflicts on Banking Capital', *Praksis* 19, 2009.

MAKOTO ITOH Emeritus Professor at the University of Tokyo; and a member of the Japan Academy. He has taught widely at many Universities including New School for Social Research, London University, Greenwich University, Thammasat University, and the University of Sydney. His books in English are; *Value and Crisis, The Basic Theory of Capitalism, The World Economic Crisis and Japanese Capitalism, Political Economy for Socialism, Political Economy of Money and Finance,* and *The Japanese Economy Reconsidered.*

CostAs LaPAVITSAS teaches economics at the School of Oriental and African Studies, University of London. He has done research in the political economy of money and finance, the Japanese economy, history of economic thought, economic history, and the contemporary world-economy. He has published widely, and his books include *Political Economy of Money and Finance* (with M. Itoh), MacMillan, 1999, *Development Policy in the Twenty-first Century* (with B. Fine and J. Pincus), Routledge, 2001, *Social Foundations of Markets, Money and Credit*, Routledge, 2003, and *Beyond Market-Driven Development* (with M. Noguchi), Routledge, 2005.

CarLos MorERA is Professor at the Economic Research Institute of the National Autonomous University of Mexico (UNAM). He has also taught in several Mexican universities and was a guest researcher at Oxford University and the Federal University of Bahía. He is the author and co-author of several books and chapters of books, among them *El capital financiero en México y la globalización*, Era Mexico City 1997; *Globalización inserción de México y alternativas incluyentes para el siglo XXI*, Porrúa-UNAM-IIEc; Mexico City, 2001; 'Mexico: Work Process, Oil Revenue and Financial Restructuring in World Economy', published in the proceedings of the international symposium held in Beijing, China. Morera has been a speaker at seventy national and international seminars.

Juan Pablo Painceira is currently carrying out research in the political economy of money and finance at SOAS, University of London, focusing on the role of central banks in middle-income countries. He has published work on financial instability, the South-Korean financial system, Brazilian external vulnerability and economic method in Brazilian annals and journals. He has worked as financial analyst for several years in the Brazilian financial sector, at the Banco Central do Brasil. He is also interested in the philosophy of science and macroeconomics.

DemoPHANES PAPADATOS works in the banking sector in Greece. He is also currently undertaking research in the political economy of money and finance at SOAS, University of London. His research interests include finance, economic development and macroeconomics.

JOSÉ ANTONIO ROJAS is Professor at the Academy of Political Economy and (until 1990) professor in postgraduate studies in the Energy Economics Programme in the UNAM Economics Department. He has also worked as a technical specialist at Mexico's Federal Electricity-Commission (CFE) since 1991. He has conducted research on energy economics since 1980, and received UNAM's 'Jesus Silva Herzog' Economy Award in 1986. He has also been a regular contributor to the national dailies *Uno más Uno* and, more recently, *La Jornada*.

PAULO L. DOS SANTOS lectures in capital-markets, finance and microeconomic theory at the School of Oriental and African Studies. His research focuses on the political economy of capital-markets, financial intermediation, and the internationalisation of banking.

List of Tables and Figures

Tables

Figures

Introduction: A Crisis of Financialisation

Costas Lapavitsas

1. An unusual and global crisis

In August 2007 international money-markets signalled that financial assets associated with the US
housing sector, particularly subprime mortgages,
had become illiquid. The significance of this event
was not immediately apparent to those who did not
regularly observe financial markets. During the following months, however, it gradually became clear
that something was badly wrong with global finance.
A year later, the US financial system suffered a massive shock as the Government Sponsored Enterprises, the backbone of the housing market, nearly
failed and then Lehman Brothers, one of the largest
investment-banks, went bankrupt.

Financial panic ensued in September–October
2008, one of those rare phenomena that can hold
the attention of economic historians for decades. In
the autumn of 2008, banks in the USA and much
of the developed world faced systemic collapse.
Disaster was avoided only through coordinated
and unprecedented state-intervention by Finance
ministries and central banks across the advanced
countries. Nonetheless, the world-economy went
into deep recession toward the end of 2008 and for
much of 2009.

The global crisis of 2007–9 is replete with uncommon characteristics. To begin with, it arose at the end of a gigantic housing bubble in the USA but also in other advanced countries, particularly the UK. The bubble of 2001–7 was fed mainly by domestic credit backed by lax monetary policy in the USA. During 2001–4 (following the burst of an earlier bubble in the New York Stock Exchange), the Federal Reserve lowered interest-rates to very low levels in order to forestall recession. Financial institutions took advantage of cheap funds to spur lending in the housing market, eventually creating a bubble. This sequence of events was a replay of the Greenspan 'put', a course of action that had been tried repeatedly in preceding years. In other words, the financial sector would blow a bubble; the state would deal with the aftermath; conditions would thereby be created for the next bubble.

The bubble of 2001–7 was also fed by loanable funds flowing into the USA from abroad. These international funds did not originate primarily in other advanced-capitalist countries, as would have happened in past incidents of financial excess. Rather, poor countries were the main outside source of loanable funds to the US-markets after 2004. The suppliers, moreover, were not private capitalists making commercial decisions but monetary authorities. After the Asian crisis of 1997–8, developing countries found themselves obliged to accumulate reserves of US-dollars as a precaution against exchange-rate crises. Monetary authorities bought huge volumes of US government-bonds in spite of low rates of interest in the USA. The global poor were compelled by global capital-markets to send their hard-earned surpluses to the USA, subsidising the US-government and earning low returns. Unfortunately for the USA, these flows also sustained and prolonged the bubble.

The main cause of the bubble, nonetheless, was domestic US-credit, which had still more peculiar features. The most heavily indebted economic agents during 2001–7 were not large capitalist corporations, or even small and medium enterprises. The heaviest borrowers were banks but also individual workers, including some of the poorest, previously 'unbanked', layers of the working class. The debt of US-households escalated enormously, exceeding 130% of disposable income in 2007. This was only surpassed by British households, whose debt fluctuated in the vicinity of 160% of disposable income.

The sudden turn of the banks toward the poor – the 'democratisation' of credit that presumably opened the path toward home-ownership for all – was combined with securities-transactions undertaken in open financial markets.

Banks 'securitised' the debt, or packaged it in marketable dollops and then sold it. Profits were made through fees and commissions on trading rather than by collecting interest on mortgages. Thus banks had an incentive continually to expand housing credit in order to securitise the fresh loans on their balance-sheets. To support securitisation, banks needed ever larger volumes of funds, which they sought in money-markets. The banks that were most aggressively involved in securitisation also relied most heavily on borrowing in money-markets.

During this period, banks systematically failed to undertake proper checks of the ultimate borrowers, that is, of the households acquiring mortgages. For one thing, securitised mortgages were sold as soon as they were made, and hence their quality hardly mattered to the lender. For another, banks relied systematically on new, computationally-intensive techniques of calculating securities-prices and managing risk, which lent a false air of scientific objectivity to bank-operations. Risk was, apparently, 'sliced and diced' through the new methods of financial institutions. It was presumed that those who eventually held the securities knew how much risk they were acquiring and had taken appropriate precautions. The traditional task of monitoring borrowers could thus be relegated to others, including to credit-rating organisations. Banks could concentrate on the pleasant business of borrowing in the money-markets, acquiring fresh mortgages, securitising the loans, selling the securities to recoup the initial advance, and making fabulous profits out of fees and commissions.

It is obvious with hindsight that the merry-go-round had to come to an end. US workers' wages, out of which mortgage-securitisation profits were ultimately to derive, had remained effectively stagnant throughout the bubble. Large groups of 'subprime' borrowers never had any chance of meeting payment-obligations. In reality, financial predators had descended on the poor in the USA by dangling the prospect of house-ownership and ever-higher house-prices. When interest-rates began slowly to rise after 2004, the poor came under increasing financial pressure and started to default in large numbers. By 2006, the US housing bubble was over.

The crisis that followed was induced primarily by the unravelling of the mechanisms of credit that had sustained the bubble in the first place. It is worth stressing that never before in the history of capitalism has a major global crisis been caused by the extension of credit to workers, including to the poorest. As the US-poor defaulted on mortgages, pressure mounted on the 'special-purpose vehicles' that collected interest which was to be distributed among those that held securitised debt. Consequently, the 'vehicles' turned to the 'mother'-banks for support. In effect, bad mortgage-loans returned to the books of the banks, losses mounted, and it became difficult for banks to borrow in the money-market.

The crisis thus began as a liquidity-shortage in the money-market, which is a typical way for capitalist crises to commence except that this particular shortage was caused by workers' housing rather than overstretched production and commodity-sales. It then became a solvency-crisis as the banks that were most heavily exposed to mortgage-securitisation looked incapable of withstanding the mounting losses. Eventually, the stock-market grasped what was at stake and exacerbated the solvency-problem through sharp falls in bank share-prices. This then fed back into liquidity-shortages, for by mid-2008 no-one would lend commercially to a housing-market buccaneer with a crumbling share-price, such as Lehman Brothers.

With liquidity drying up and solvency at stake, banks rapidly reduced their lending. As credit disappeared, large corporations and small and medium enterprises found it hard to finance even their wage-bills. Output was cut and inventories were eliminated, while workers were made redundant. The shock of the panic, furthermore, exacerbated falls in consumption and added urgency to workers' efforts to limit indebtedness. Collapsing consumer-demand impacted further on output but also on exports. And so the crisis was transmitted rapidly to major exporting countries – Germany, Japan, but also China and other developing countries. The synchronised fall of output across the world in late 2008 and early 2009 is remarkable for its rapidity. The burst of the US housing bubble had become a global recession.

The crisis of 2007–9 was global from the start, unlike the Japanese crisis of the early 1990s which had remained local. For securitisation had allowed the rest of the world to share in the fruits of the marvelous ingenuity of US-financiers. German banks were among the heaviest buyers of securitised paper, as was the benighted Union Bank of Switzerland, which had tried to go with the flow in the 2000s and ended up effectively bankrupt. When crisis-conditions spread across the world in late 2008, private capital-flows to developing countries collapsed, leading to balance-of-payments and exchange-rate crises. A raft of smaller countries was also drawn into the vortex despite having nothing to do with the earlier speculative orgy in US financial markets.

2. The state to the rescue

Complete catastrophe was averted through state-intervention, which took place decisively and across the board to rescue private capital and its markets. The ideological paradox that this development represents cannot be exaggerated. The dominant ideology during the decades of neoliberal ascendancy has been 'market good – state bad'. The presumed merits of free markets have been proclaimed most loudly in the sphere of finance. The crisis of 2007–9 showed that untrammelled financial markets lead to disaster. It also showed that, in the absence of state-intervention, contemporary capitalism would find it hard to function altogether. Behind the ideological smokescreen of free markets, liberalism, and the vaunted self-adjusting properties of private enterprise, modern capitalism remains managed capitalism.

State-intervention took a variety of forms in the course of the crisis. First, interest-rates were rapidly brought close to zero, minimising the cost of funds for banks. Second, huge volumes of public credit were made available though the central bank to assuage the liquidity-shortage. Third, large public funds were channelled to banks, allowing them to take mortgage-losses and lowering the risk of insolvency. Fourth, bank-deposits were guaranteed, eliminating the possibility of bank-runs. Fifth, large banks were assured that they would not face the danger of bankruptcy. Sixth, strong banks were encouraged to take over the weak in order to lessen pressure on the banking system as a whole. Seventh, but far from last, the state maintained fiscal expenditure in the face of collapsing private demand, thus softening the fall of output and the rise in unemployment.

State-intervention has relied heavily on central banks, which have emerged as the main arm of contemporary economic policy. The monopoly that central banks have over final means of payment (guaranteed by the state) allowed them to generate unprecedented volumes of liquidity, often in exchange for the least-creditworthy private assets. Thus, good public credit replaced bad private credit, shifting the risk onto the public sector. State-intervention, moreover, has also relied on the tax-resources and the borrowing ability of the treasury. Public stakes were acquired in several weak but large banks in order to strengthen solvency. Social resources were placed at the disposal of failed private banks which had engaged in speculative activities.

In that context, and for a brief period toward the end of 2008, the prospect of bank-nationalisation was seriously considered within powerful circles in Washington. But the day was won by those who advocated capital-injections as a temporary measure that would not disturb private property over banks even in the short term. A similar outlook prevailed in the highly concentrated UK-banking sector, leading to the absurd situation of the state owning majority-takes in important banks, but choosing not to exercise direct management-control.

In short, state-intervention deployed public resources and credit in order to rescue the banks but without fundamentally challenging private ownership and management within the banking sector. Meanwhile, ponderous debates took place about 'regulating' banks by means of tougher capital-adequacy, controls on bank-bonuses, and new methods of allowing large banks to fail. Banks had succeeded not only in receiving huge volumes of public help, but also in directing public debate about banking reform toward issues that would not disturb bank pre-eminence.

The results were soon apparent. Vast injections of public funds and public credit bolstered confidence in the financial sector. Low interest-rates reduced costs for banks and allowed them to raise profits. Realising that they had beaten back the threat of public takeover, banks became more confident. Financial markets gradually returned to life after March 2009, bank-profitability recovered, large bonuses returned, and securitisations made a modest reappearance. The Greenspan 'put' had been played once again but this time on a vast scale and literally at the last moment.

Yet, despite the stabilisation of finance by the middle of 2009, things had not returned to normal in several developed countries. Individual indebtedness remained enormously high; banks continued to carry bad loans deriving from previous securitisations; investment was weak; unemployment kept rising; and consumption showed no dynamism. Meanwhile, credit-creation by banks, although not falling, showed no signs of vigour. Free from risk of failure, private banks strove to make profits while cleaning up their balance sheets. They were not interested in extending credit to boost production and reduce unemployment. Above all, public intervention and the recession of 2008–9 had generated huge deficits for several states, thus encouraging adoption of austerity policies. In the Eurozone, rising public deficits among peripheral countries led to sovereign-debt crises that threatened to re-ignite the banking crisis in Europe. Consequently, Greece, Ireland and Portugal found themselves obliged to accept multilateral loans that were accompanied by IMF austerity-programmes.

State-intervention had succeeded in stabilising finance in developed econo-mies, but capitalist accumulation in developed countries looked set for low and precarious growth. The state had deployed its resources to rescue private banks without significantly altering the structure of the financial system, thus running the risk of indifferent accumulation-performance for years ahead. And the danger of further financial collapse remained present.

3. The theoretical conundrum

The crisis of 2007–9 caught mainstream-economics unawares. That is not to say that there were no warnings about the accumulation of debt by several economists, even from venerable institutions such as the Bank for International Settlements and a host of central banks. But the systemic dan-ger posed by securitisation of mortgages was not generally appreciated. This is not as surprising as it might seem at first sight. Mainstream-economics assumes that financial markets are 'efficient', that is, they use all available information to adjust supply, demand and prices appropriately. On these grounds, mortgage-securitisation might have increased rapidly, but the risk was spread by markets across the economy and was presumably held by those who had taken adequate precautions. Thus, it was possible even for the chairman of the Federal Reserve to imagine that there might have been some minor local difficulties but no bubble in the US-economy in 2001–7.

In contrast, post-Keynesian economists, particularly those influenced by Minsky, were far more alive to the systemic risk posed by the accumulation of debt, and repeatedly rang the alarm-bell. For a brief period after the crisis had erupted, Minsky-based theories stole the limelight. Unfortunately, this prominence did not last long and 'business as usual' reasserted itself within economic theory and policy. It did not help that the reform-proposals typi-cally inspired by Minsky's work appeared incommensurate with the charac-ter of the current crisis. If a 'big bank' and a 'big government' were necessary for economic stability, these tools seemed to be already in the possession of economic policy-makers, and were wielded vigorously.

For Marxist political economy, on the other hand, the crisis presented a different set of problems. Marxist theory stresses the systemic nature of capi-talist crises, ultimately emanating from the exploitative nature of capitalist production. Yet, this crisis has had an overwhelming financial aspect. And although Marxist economists were aware of the precarious nature of the bubble of 2001–7, they had no clear analysis of the ratcheting financial tensions in the world-economy. When the crisis burst in the money-markets in August 2007 few realised what was truly afoot.

A misplaced concern then gripped much Marxist political economy. If analysis of the causes of the turmoil stressed the role of finance, the crisis would somehow appear less real and profound. It seemed important to show that 2007–9 was another crisis of overproduction which had manifested itself in the sphere of finance. Parallels were sought with the epoch-making crisis of 1973–4 characterised by collapsing profitability and shrinking real accumulation. Unfortunately, the analogy between 1973–4 and 2007–9 carries very little conviction. There were signs of downturn prior to 2007, particularly as the housing bubble in the US ended in 2006, but there was no collapse in profitability comparable to the magnitude of the crisis that followed. And nor were there any signs of booming real accumulation during the period that preceded the crisis of 2007–9. What took place in 2001–7 in much of the developed world was a pure bubble.

A variation on the same theme was to argue that an incipient crisis of over-accumulation had been present in developed economies since the mid-1970s, but its actual outburst had kept being postponed by various devices, above all, through financial bubbles. When the bubble of 2001–7 burst, the underlying crisis was able to manifest itself. This extraordinary view, which might be called the 'crisis-in-suspension' theory of contemporary capitalism, carries even less conviction. There is no support at all in Marx, or other major economists, for the notion that the regular state of the capitalist economy is to be in crisis which just keeps getting postponed. On the contrary, capitalist economies are restructured continually thus placing accumulation on a new basis.

Much of the difficulty that Marxist political economy has faced arose from its tendency to treat financial turmoil as a 'surface'-event that presumably reflects the 'deeper' (hence 'real') causes of crisis. The point is, however, that the crisis of 2007–9 has had an irreducible financial aspect which emerged directly from the core of contemporary capitalism. This is not simply because of the conspicuous role played by financial mechanisms in both the bubble and its aftermath. More significantly, it is because the relation between finance and real accumulation has changed in recent years as advanced capitalism has become financialised. The financial activities of productive capital, but also of workers and state-institutions, currently involve much more than simply facilitating the underlying production and sale of commodities. The peculiarities of the crisis of 2007–9 have arisen precisely because it is a crisis of financialisation.

Grasping this point is important and not only for analytical purposes. The readiness to bypass the 'surface'-phenomena of finance in a forlorn search for the 'true' causes of the current crisis has in practice reduced the ability of Marxist political economy to intervene in ideological and political struggle since the outbreak of the turmoil. There is no doubt at all that capitalism as a 'system' is to blame for the crisis of 2007–9, and this obviously includes the productive sector. However, the particular configuration of the 'system' in recent decades has placed finance at the core of economic developments. It is not a distraction to focus the analysis of the crisis of 2007–9 on finance. On the contrary, it is to recognise the transformation of contemporary capitalism and to seek appropriate conclusions. By acknowledging the irreducibly financial aspect of the crisis, Marxist political economy is able to participate more effectively in the debates on the future direction of the capitalist economy.

This is the spirit in which this collected volume has considered the many-sided reality of the crisis of 2007–9. The roots of the crisis are to be found in the changed relationship between the sphere of production and the sphere of circulation, particularly finance. The prominent role of finance is far from a surface-phenomenon. On the contrary, it is an integral aspect of a crisis of financialisation.

4. Putting the book together

This book is a collective product of Research in Money and Finance (RMF), a network of political economists researching the development of contemporary capitalism, especially money and finance. Already in the summer of 2007 it was clear to us that the global-financial system was pregnant with extreme tensions. There was a pressing need for analysis that drew on Marxist political economy while remaining informed of mainstream-economics and the empirical development of finance. Above all, it was necessary to examine financialisation as a structural transformation of the capitalist economy during the last three decades.

The work began to take shape in conjunction with a proposal to hold a symposium on financialisation and crisis for the journal *Historical Materialism*. In March 2008, a workshop was held at Kadir Has University in Istanbul involving RMF and Turkish political economists. It became apparent that RMF arguments had considerable explanatory power over the events of the day, including the collapse of the US investment-bank Bear Sterns that occurred at precisely that time. RMF then organised an international conference at the School of Oriental and African Studies in London in May 2008. With broad participation by Marxists, post-Keynesians and other heterodox theorists, there was extensive discussion of financialisation and financial instability.

In the summer of 2008, it was evident that global finance was heading toward a major crisis, but no-one could have predicted the catastrophic eruption of September–October 2008. With financial systems facing complete collapse and the world-economy heading toward deep recession, the audience for Marxist and heterodox ideas expanded rapidly. A brief period of ideological tumult followed during which the hold of mainstream, pro-market ideas on organisations, workers and intellectuals appeared to be loosening. Unfortunately, by early 2009, the mainstream had recovered its poise. Reforms – if there were going to be any – would be dictated by the financial sector, and would not threaten financialisation. To be sure, neoliberal ideology had received a body-blow, but it still commanded all the major posts in policy-making, universities, and international institutions. Nonetheless, the extent and severity of recession made things difficult for neoliberal ideology. There was still room for Marxist and heterodox analyses of the crisis, but it was vital to place the turmoil within the broader parameters of financialisation.

This is the context in which *Historical Materialism* carried the symposium on financialisation and crisis in issue 17.2 comprising articles by Lapavitsas, Dymski and Dos Santos. The journal has kindly given permission for these articles to be used in the book. But a further five essays were also produced in short order dealing with further aspects of finance and contemporary capitalism. Thus, it became possible to put together a far fuller picture of the crisis as well as of the structural transformation of contemporary capitalism.

Accordingly, there are two parts to this collected volume. Part I focuses on the domestic aspects of financialisation and seeks the roots of crisis in the operations of the financial systems of developed countries. The essay by Lapavitsas argues that financialisation represents structural transformation of capitalist economies altering the balance of production and circulation in favour of the latter. Financialisation is characterised by a turn of capitalist enterprises toward open financial markets and a corresponding turn of banks toward lending to individuals and mediating in financial markets. Significant volumes of financial profits arise from direct extraction of profit from wages, comprising a form of financial expropriation. Dymski explores the extraction of financial profits from the income of the poorest in the USA in substantial empirical detail. Predatory practices with a racial aspect – directed at black and Latino borrowers – characterised the bubble in the USA in 2001–7. Dymski shows that the US-bubble and the crisis have had an exploitative and barely hidden racial undertow.

Dos Santos then examines in further detail the turn of banks toward individual workers in the course of financialisation. Focusing on a sample of large, internationally-active banks, he demonstrates the rising importance of personal lending for bank-profitability. Workers borrow for consumption and housing, transferring substantial parts of their money income to banks on terms reminiscent to – but not the same as – exploitation at the point of production. These processes are paramount to financialisation as structural change of the capitalist economy. In the same section, Papadatos turns to central banks that have emerged as the pre-eminent policy-making institution of financialised capitalism, and played a pivotal role in confronting the crisis of 2007–9. Papadatos shows that central-bank intervention has entailed abandoning the previous strategy of inflation-targeting in favour of managing financial disturbances flexibly. The result has been to socialise the losses created by finance, while protecting the private profits of financial institutions.

Part II then shifts attention to the international aspect of financialisation. Itoh considers one of the most pressing issues of the turmoil, namely the parallels with the crisis in Japan in the 1990s and the Great Depression of the 1930s. Itoh finds that the crisis of 2007–9 has resulted from a far bigger bubble than that of the Japanese crisis. The speculative explosion in the USA during 2001–7 exceeded that in Japan in the 1980s, even though the latter included both the stock-market and housing. But Itoh also argues that the crisis is unlikely to prove as severe as that of the 1930s, not least because the state currently plays a much bigger role in the economy.

Morera and Rojas turn to the most prominent international feature of financialisation, i.e., global capital-flows. Using a wealth of empirical material, they demonstrate the growth and complexity of international flows that pivot on the US-dollar. Dollar-hegemony has facilitated the consolidation of a world-financial sphere that connects national markets and financial systems. Of particular interest is the evidence Morera and Rojas present regarding the role of the oil-market. Painceira pays further attention to capital-flows, including the striking reversal of net capital-flows in the 2000s. Reserve-accumulation by developing countries has meant that the poor have been financing the rich in the world-economy during the last decade. Contemporary imperialism is characterised by a host of developing countries providing an implicit subsidy to the USA. This process has been pivotal to the bubble of 2007–9.

Finally, Ergüneş delves into the most recent but least researched aspect of financial development, that is, the emergence of domestic financialisation in middle-income countries. Spurred partly by international capital-flows and partly by the entry of foreign banks, domestic finance has been greatly altered in several developing countries during the 2000s. Focusing on Turkey, Ergüneş shows that bank-lending to individuals has been increasing rapidly since 2001. It appears that foreign and domestic banks are encouraging consumption rather than investment-credit in middle-income countries. The implications for development and domestic stability are likely to be profound.

Needless to say, financialisation and the crisis of 2007–9 are extremely complex phenomena and this volume covers only a fraction of the relevant issues. Still, the crisis has weakened neo liberal ideology while opening space for political economy. The contributions collected here will, we hope, act as a spur for further debate on the nature of financialised capitalism. There is little doubt that this is one of the most burning issues confronting political economy today.

Costas Lapavitsas
June 2011

Part One

Domestic Financialisation and the Roots of the Crisis

Chapter One

Financialised Capitalism: Crisis and Financial Expropriation*

Costas Lapavitsas

1. Introduction: Several dimensions of financialisation

The storm that has gradually engulfed the world-economy since August 2007 is a fully-fledged crisis of financialised capitalism. The crisis did not spring directly out of a malaise of production, though it has already caused major disruption of accumulation. It was precipitated by housing debts among the poorest US-workers, an unprecedented occurrence in the history of capitalism. Thus, the crisis is directly related to the financialisation of personal income, mostly expenditure on housing but also on education, health, pensions and insurance.

The crisis became global because of the transformation of banks and other financial institutions in the course of financialisation. Commercial banks have become more distant from industrial and commercial capital, while adopting investment-banking and turning toward individual income as source of profits. The combination of investment-banking

* Earlier drafts of this chapter were presented at a workshop at Kadir Has University, March 2008, as well as at a conference at SOAS, in May 2008. Thanks for comments are due primarily to members of Research in Money and Finance at SOAS. I am also grateful to several others, but far too many to mention individually.

and financialised personal income resulted in an enormous bubble in the USA and elsewhere during 2001–7, eventually leading to disaster.

During the bubble, it became clear that the sources of financial profit have changed significantly as mature capitalist economies have become financialised. Extracting financial profit directly out of the personal income of workers and others has acquired greater significance. This may be called financial expropriation. Such profits have been matched by financial earnings through investment-banking, mostly fees, commissions, and proprietary trading. To an extent, these also originate in personal income, particularly from the handling of mass-savings.

Profits from financial expropriation and investment-banking correspond to changes in social structure. They have accrued to managers of finance and industry, as well as to functionaries of finance, such as lawyers, accountants, and technical analysts. This trend appears as the return of the rentier, but modern rentiers draw income as much from position relative to the financial system as from coupon-clipping. Extraordinary payments take the form of remuneration for putative services, including salaries, bonuses, and stock-options. Contemporary rentiers are the product of financialisation, not its driving force.

Further, the institutions of economic policy-making have changed significantly in the course of financialisation. Central banks have become pre-eminent, buttressed by legal and practical independence. They have cast a benign eye on speculative-financial excess, while mobilising social resources to rescue financiers from crisis. But the limits to their power have also become apparent in the course of the crisis, requiring the intervention of the central state.

Financialisation has also deepened the complexity of imperialism. Developing countries have been forced to hold vast international reserves that have resulted in net lending by the poor to the rich. Private capital has flown into developing countries earning high returns, but was more than matched by reverse-flows to accumulate reserves by developing countries, which earn little. These anarchic capital-flows have benefited primarily the USA as issuer of the international means of payment, though they have also contributed to the US-bubble of 2001–7.

Financialisation, finally, has allowed the ethics, morality and mindset of finance to penetrate social and individual life. The concept of 'risk' – often nothing more than a banal formalisation of the financier's practices – has become prominent in public discourse. Waves of greed have been released by the transformation of housing and pensions into 'investments', dragging individuals into financial bubbles. To be sure, there has also been resistance and search for social alternatives. But finance has set the terms across the world.

This chapter is a step toward the analysis of financialisation and its attendant crises. Guidance has been sought in the work of Marx and the classical-Marxist debates on imperialism at the turn of the twentieth century. The chapter starts with a brief discussion of the US-financial bubble and its bursting in Section 2. It is shown that this was an unprecedented event, caused by the financialisation of personal income combined with the rise of investment-banking. To obtain a better understanding of the roots of the crisis, therefore, Section 3 briefly considers the historical and institutional background of financialisation.

On this basis, Section 4 analyses the process through which extraction of financial profit has led to global-economic turmoil. It is shown that interaction between financial expropriation and investment-banking has exacerbated the tension of liquidity and solvency for commercial banks. Several of the largest have effectively become bankrupt, thus crippling real accumulation. The focus of analysis is on the USA as the original site of the crisis, but broader structural trends are demonstrated across key-capitalist economies. Section 5 of the chapter then turns to the implications of financialisation for class-composition by discussing contemporary rentiers. Section 6 concludes by considering the relevance of the Marxist concept of finance-capital to the current period.

2. Brief anatomy of a crisis of financialisation

2.1. *Housing, securitisation and the swelling of the bubble*

The roots of the current crisis are to be found in the financialisation of workers' housing in the USA. Mortgage-lending increased rapidly from 2001 to 2003, subsequently declining but remaining at a high level until 2006:

Table 1   US Mortgage-Lending, 2001–6, $bn

Year	Originations	Originations Securitisation-Rate (%)	Subprime	Subprime Securitised	Subprime Securitisation-Rate (%)	ARM
2001	2215	60.7	160	96	60.0	355
2002	2885	63.0	200	122	61.0	679
2003	3945	67.5	310	203	65.5	1034
2004	2920	62.6	530	401	79.8	1464
2005	3120	67.7	625	508	81.3	1490
2006	2980	67.6	600	483	80.5	1340

Source: Inside Mortgage Finance; Mortgage Origination Indicators, Mortgage Originations by Product, Securitization Rates for Home Mortgages.

The explosion of mortgage-lending in 2001–3 met housing demand from households on significant income. When this demand was sated, subprime mortgage-lending rose rapidly (particularly during 2004–6) amounting to $1.75tr, or 19.5% of originations. Borrowers were from the poorer sections of the US working class, often black or Latino women.[1] They were frequently offered Adjustable-Rate Mortgages (ARM), typically with an initially low rate of interest that was subsequently adjusted upwards. Total ARM came to $4.3tr during 2004–6, or 47.6% of originations.

Thus, during the bubble, financialisation of personal income reached the poorest sections of the US working class. At the time, this appeared as a 'democratisation' of finance, the reversal of 'red-lining' of the poor by banks in previous decades. But solving housing problems through private finance eventually became a disaster, putting millions at risk of homelessness.

The subprime market, despite its growth, is not large enough directly to threaten US, and even less global, finance. But it has had a massive impact because of the parallel growth of investment-banking, particularly through mortgage-securitisation: $1.4tr of subprime mortgages were securitised during 2004–6, or 79.3% of the total. This was considerably higher than the average securitisation-rate of 63.9% for the whole of originations. Simply put, securitisation involved parcelling mortgages into small amounts, placing them into larger composites, and selling the lots as new securities. Particles of subprime debt, therefore, became embedded in securities held by financial institutions across the world.

---

1. See Dymski in this volume.

Table 2 US Mortgage-Refinance, 2000–7

Year	2000	2001	2002	2003	2004	2005	2006	2007
Originations ($tr)	1.1	2.2	2.9	3.8	2.8	3.0	2.7	2.3
Refinance (%)	20.5	57.2	61.6	66.4	52.8	52.0	48.6	49.8

Source: Mortgage Bankers Association; Mortgage Origination Estimates, updated March 24, 2008.

On the back of the housing boom, there was intensification of other forms of financialisation of personal income. As house-prices rose, home-owners were encouraged to re-mortgage and use the proceeds for other purposes. This so-called 'equity-extraction' was a key feature of the bubble.

A parallel result was collapse of personal savings, which approached zero as percentage of disposable income (Table 3). The decline in personal savings is a long-term aspect of financialisation, reflecting the increasing involvement of individuals in the financial system and the concomitant rise in individual debts. From 9–10% of disposable income in the 1970s and early 1980s, personal savings have declined steadily throughout the period. But the drop in the USA to 0.4% is remarkable, and historically unprecedented for a mature capitalist country.

As savings collapsed, the balance of trade deficit of the USA, already very large, expanded to an enormous $762bn in 2006. Such were the foundations of the apparent period of growth and prosperity in the USA during 2001–7.

Table 3 Personal Savings, USA, 2000–7

Year	2000	2001	2002	2003	2004	2005	2006	2007
Savings ($bn)	168.5	132.3	184.7	174.9	181.7	44.6	38.8	42.7
Savings as % of Disposable Income	2.3	1.8	2.4	2.1	2.1	0.5	0.4	0.4

Source: Federal Reserve Bank, Flow of Funds, various.

Table 4 Balance of Trade-Deficit, USA, 2000–7, $bn

Year	2000	2001	2002	2003	2004	2005	2006	2007
	379.5	367.0	424.4	499.4	615.4	714.6	762.0	708.6

Source: Federal Reserve Bank, Flow of Funds, various.

Table 5   Effective Federal Funds-Rate, 2000–7

Year	2000	2001	2002	2003	2004	2005	2006	2007
	6.24	3.88	1.67	1.13	1.35	3.22	4.97	5.02

Source: Federal Reserve Bank, Interest Rates, various.

Table 6   Excess of Savings over Investment as % of GDP

Year	2002	2003	2004	2005	2006	2007
USA	−4.2	−5.1	−5.5	−6.0	−5.9	−5.1
UK	−1.6	−1.3	−1.6	−2.5	−3.9	−4.9
Germany	2.0	1.9	4.3	4.6	5.0	5.6
Japan	2.9	3.2	3.7	3.6	3.9	4.8
Developing Asia	2.4	2.8	2.6	4.1	5.9	6.8
Commonwealth of Independent Countries (CIS)	6.4	6.3	8.3	8.6	7.4	4.5
Middle East	4.8	8.3	11.8	19.7	20.9	19.8
Africa	−1.7	−0.4	0.1	1.8	2.8	0.3

Source: IMF, World Economic Outlook 2008.

2.2. Credit feeding the bubble

Monetary policy contributed directly to the bubble and its burst. On the wake of the new-technology bubble of 1999–2000, the Federal Reserve cut interest-rates rapidly and kept them low, as is shown in Table 5. The gradual rise of interest-rates after 2004 eventually put an end to the bubble.

In addition to cheap credit from the Fed, several developed and developing countries found themselves with large trade-surpluses (excess of domestic savings over investment) around the middle of the 2000s. The counterpart was trade-deficits and a shortfall of savings relative to investment in the USA and the UK (and less so in France, Italy, and elsewhere), shown in Table 6.

To defend exchange-rates and as protection against sudden reversals of capital-flows, the surplus-holders sought reserves of dollars as quasi-world-money. The strategy of reserve-accumulation was also imposed on developing countries by international organisations, above all, the International Monetary Fund. The result has been accumulation of foreign-exchange reserves even by impoverished Africa, as is clear from Table 7.[2]

---

2. See Painceira in this volume. Rodrik 2006 has put forth a widely used estimate of the social cost of reserves.

Table 7   Reserve-Accumulation, Selected Developing Countries and Areas, $bn

Year	2000	2001	2002	2003	2004	2005	2006	2007
Total	800.9	895.8	1072.6	1395.3	1848.3	2339.3	3095.5	4283.4
of which:								
China	168.9	216.3	292.0	409.0	615.5	822.5	1069.5	1531.4
Russia	24.8	33.1	44.6	73.8	121.5	156.5	296.2	445.3
India	38.4	46.4	68.2	99.5	127.2	132.5	171.3	256.8
Middle East	146.1	157.9	163.9	198.3	246.7	351.6	477.2	638.1
Sub-Saharan Africa	35.0	35.5	36.0	39.9	62.3	83.0	115.9	144.9

Source: IMF, World Economic Outlook 2008.

Forming reserves meant that central banks bought US state-securities. Hence, a large part of the surpluses flowed to the USA, despite relatively low US interest-rates and the possibility of capital-losses, if the dollar was to fall. Developing countries thus became net suppliers of capital to the USA, keeping loanable capital abundant during 2005–6, exactly as the Fed started to tighten credit.

2.3. Burst of the bubble and shortage of liquidity

The crisis emerged after the exhaustion of the US housing boom in 2006. House prices fell by 5–10% in 2007, the fall accelerating throughout 2008. In the fourth quarter of 2007, 2.1 million people were behind with their payments. The epicentre of this collapse was subprime ARM: 7% of total mortgages but 42% of all foreclosures. Prime (better-quality) ARM were also vulnerable: 15% of total mortgages but 20% of foreclosures. In the second quarter of 2008, foreclosure-rates rose to unprecedented levels: 6.63% on subprime and 1.82% on prime ARM.[3] Thus, the housing-market crisis started in subprime mortgages but then spread to the prime sector. The plain mechanics are clear: rising interest-rates and falling housing prices forced ARM-holders to default in increasing numbers.

The most important feature of the burst of the bubble, from an analytical perspective, was the mutual reinforcement of the problems of liquidity and solvency for banks, which made the crisis progressively worse. This was a direct result of the financialisation of personal income combined with the spread of investment-banking. The tension between liquidity and solvency

---

3. Mortgage Bankers Association; National Delinquency Survey, various issues.

became severe for commercial banks due to widespread adoption of investment-banking practices. Independent investment-banks, meanwhile, succumbed *en masse* to the pressures.

Financial turmoil began as a liquidity-shortage in the inter-bank money-market in August 2007 and gradually became a solvency-crisis.[4] The reason was that US and other banks held large volumes of mortgage-backed securities, or were obliged to support financial institutions that held them. As mortgage-failures rose, these securities became progressively unsaleable, thus also putting bank-solvency in doubt. Banks preferred to hoard liquid-funds instead of lending them to others.

Liquidity-shortages can be captured as the divergence between the three-month LIBOR (interbank-lending) and the three-month Overnight Indexed Swap rate (risk-free rate key to trading financial derivatives among banks). These are normally very close to each other, but, after August 2007, they diverged significantly, the LIBOR exceeding OIS by 1% and even more in late 2007 and early 2008.[5] But this was as nothing compared to the size reached by the spread in September/October 2008.

The burst of the bubble thus led to an apparent paradox, much exercising the economic weather-experts of the press: markets were awash with capital but short of liquidity. Yet, this phenomenon is neither paradoxical nor new. In financial crises, money becomes paramount: the capitalist economy might be replete with value, but only value in the form of money will do, and that is typically not forthcoming due to hoarding.[6] This condition prevailed in the global-financial system in 2007–8. Loanable capital was abundant but there was shortage of liquid means to settle obligations – i.e. money – because of hoarding by financial institutions.

2.4. Bank-solvency and state-intervention

Central banks have led state-efforts to confront the persistent liquidity-shortage. Extraordinary methods have been used by the Fed and other central banks, including 'Open Market Operations', discount window-lending,

---

4. For analysis of the money-market from the standpoint of Marxist political economy, see Lapavitsas 2003, Chapter 4, and Lapavitsas 2007.
5. Mishkin 2008.
6. Marx 1976, Chapter 1.

'Term Auction Facilities', direct lending to investment-banks, swapping mortgage-backed for public securities, and purchasing commercial paper from industrial and commercial corporations. Weak collateral has been taken for some of this lending, thus shifting credit-risk onto central banks. At the same time, central-bank interest-rates were progressively cut throughout 2008, approaching 0% in the USA. Lower rates operate as a subsidy to banks by lowering the cost of funds.

But liquidity-injections alone were incapable of dealing with the aggravated malfunctioning of financialised income and investment-banking. The crisis went through two peaks in 2008 resulting from the tension between liquidity and solvency, while also showing the limits of state-intervention. The first was the collapse of Bear Sterns in March, a giant investment-bank that held $12.1tr of notional value in outstanding derivatives-instruments in August 2007.[7] The bank found it impossible to borrow in the money-market, while its mortgage-backed assets made it insolvent. The Fed, together with the US Treasury, managed its collapse by forcing a takeover by JP Morgan, which received a loan of $29bn for the purpose. Crucially, bondholders and other creditors to the bank received their money back.

Bear Stern's bankruptcy typified the failure of combining investment-banking with financialised personal income. The US-state controlled the shock-waves of its collapse, but failed to appreciate the deeper failure of the mechanisms of financialisation. Compounding the process was the steady decline of stock-markets after December 2007, as share-buyers eventually realised what was afoot. The Dow Jones stood at roughly 11,300 in August 2008, down from 13,300 in December 2007. As their shares collapsed, banks found it increasingly difficult to obtain private capital to support losses in mortgage-backed and other securities. The combination of liquidity- and solvency-problems proved fatal for banks.

The second peak occurred in September–October 2008, a period that has already found its place in the annals of capitalist banking. Rising defaults in the US housing market led to the near collapse of Fannie Mae and Freddie Mac. These government-sponsored agencies partake of roughly half the annual transactions of mortgage-backed securities in the USA, and typically buy only prime quality. But, during the bubble, they engaged in riskier

---

7. Bear Sterns 2007, p. 55.

investment-banking, including subprime mortgages, thus forcing the state to nationalise them. Barely a few days later, Lehman Brothers, another giant US investment-bank, found itself in a similar position to Bear Sterns. This time, the Treasury, with the connivance of the Fed, allowed the stricken bank to go bankrupt, both shareholders and creditors losing their money.

This was a blunder of colossal proportions because it removed all remaining vestiges of trust among banks. Money-market participants operate under the tacit premise that what holds for one holds for all. Since Bear Sterns' creditors received their money back but Lehman Brothers' did not, the grounds for interbank-lending vanished. Worse, the collapse of Lehman confirmed beyond doubt that combining investment-banking with the financialisation of personal income had failed irretrievably. Lehman might have been very aggressive, but it had done nothing qualitatively different from other banks.

The aftermath of the Lehman shock was not surprising, but its magnitude was historic. Liquidity disappeared completely, bank-shares collapsed and genuine panic spread across financial markets. The divergence between LIBOR and OIS even approached 4%, making it impossible for banks to do any business. The remaining US investment-banks, Merrill Lynch, Goldman Sachs, and Morgan Stanley, ceased to exist in an independent form. Forced bank-rescues and takeovers occurred in the USA and across Europe. For once, it was not an exaggeration to say that the global-financial system was peering into the abyss.

The Lehman shock showed that state-intervention in finance is neither omnipotent nor omniscient. The state can make gigantic errors spurred by wrong theory as well as vested interests. Faced with disaster, the US-state rapidly altered its stance and effectively guaranteed banks against further failure. This involved the advance of public funds to deal with the problem of bank-solvency. By the end of 2008, the USA had adopted the Troubled Asset Relief Program (TARP), committing $700bn, while similar plans had been adopted in the UK and elsewhere.

By then, however, it had become clear that a major recession was unfolding across the world. Contraction of credit by banks and markets forced enterprises to cut back on output and employment. Consumption declined as worried and over-indebted workers rearranged their expenditure. Export-markets collapsed, particularly for automobiles and consumer-electronics. Developing countries also suffered as capital-flows became problematic, necessitating emergency-borrowing. A crisis that had began as a financial shock had mutated into a global recession.

To recap, a fully-fledged crisis of financialisation commenced in 2007. Unlike major capitalist crises of the past, it arose due to the financialisation of personal income, particularly mortgage-lending to US-workers, even the poorest. This was combined with the spread of investment-banking practices among financial institutions, above all, securitisation. The crisis paralysed the financial system and progressively disrupted real accumulation. Central-bank intervention has been pervasive but not decisive, forcing governments to intervene to rescue banks and ameliorate the recession.

To go beyond the proximate causes of this crisis, therefore, it is necessary to consider the transformation of the financial system in the context of capitalist development, thus also specifying the content of financialisation. To engage in this analysis, Marxist political economy needs to develop its concepts and broaden its approach. The preceding discussion has shown that the crisis did not emerge because of overaccumulation of capital, though it is already forcing capital-restructuring on a large scale. Rather, this is an unusual crisis related to workers' income, borrowing and consumption as well as to the transformation of finance in recent decades. In short, it is a crisis of financial expropriation and associated financial mechanisms. The subsequent sections analyse the relevant trends and economic relations.

3. Financialisation in historical perspective

Financialisation has resulted from the epochal changes that followed the first oil shock of 1973–4. That crisis signalled the end of the long postwar-boom and ushered in a long downturn punctuated by repeated economic crises.[8] During this period, there has been a technological revolution in information-processing and telecommunications, with a pronounced effect on the sphere of circulation.[9] Furthermore, during the same period, there has been profound

---

8. There is extensive political-economy literature on this issue. The most recent, and widely discussed, contribution is by Brenner 1998 and 2002, who argues that the downturn is due to intensified global competition keeping profitability low. For a critique, see Fine, Lapavitsas, and Milonakis 1999.
9. The political-economy literature on these issues is extensive, including the debate on flexible specialisation as well as the debate on post-Fordism associated with the French regulation-school.

institutional and political change, above all, deregulation of labour-markets and the financial system, while neoliberalism has replaced the Keynesianism of the long boom.[10]

Three aspects of these processes are particularly relevant to financialisation. First, productivity-growth has been problematic from the middle of the 1970s to the middle of the 1990s, most significantly in the USA.[11] New technology did not generate significant gains in productivity-growth for two decades. After 1995, there were significant gains in the microprocessor-industry and eventually a broad basis was created for faster productivity-growth across the US-economy.[12] Productivity-growth picked up even in the services-sector, including in financial trading (though not in banking).[13] During the bubble of 2001–7, however, productivity-growth appears to have slowed down again. Moreover, other major capitalist economies, including the UK, have not registered similar gains. The relationship between new technology and productivity-growth, therefore, remains unclear.

Second, the process of work has been transformed, partly due to technological and regulatory change, and partly due to bouts of unemployment at key-junctures of the period. Casual labour and entry of women into the labour-force have had a strong impact on work-practices.[14] It is likely that there has been a rebalancing of paid and unpaid labour, while information-technology has encouraged the invasion of private time by work, as well as growth in piece-work and putting-out practices. In Marxist terms, it is probable that labour has been intensified, and unpaid labour stretched. From the extensive literature on job-satisfaction, for instance, it transpires that work-intensification

---

10. Two recent prominent political-economy contributions that discuss the rise of neoliberalism are Duménil and Lévy 2004 and Glyn 2006.

11. The measurement of productivity is a conceptual minefield, particularly in services. In this article, mainstream-measurements are used as reference-points for discussion.

12. There has been intense debate on this issue but a consensus has emerged along these lines. See Oliner and Sichel 2000, 2002; Jorgenson and Stiroh 2000; Gordon 1999, 2004.

13. Mainstream-literature on this is less extensive. See Triplett and Bosworth 2001, 2003.

14. There is sizeable mainstream-literature on the relationship between new technology and work. See, very selectively, Brynjolfsson and Hitt 2000, 2003; Autor, Levy and Murnane 2003.

associated with new technology is a key-reason for dissatisfaction with work in developed countries, together with loss of discretion over work-choices.[15]

Third, global production and trade have come to be dominated by multinational enterprises created through successive waves of mergers and acquisitions. The bulk of foreign-direct investment (FDI) takes place among developed countries, but there were also substantial flows to developing countries since the mid-1990s, rising significantly after 2000.[16] Competition has intensified globally, but without formal cartels or zones of exclusive trading and investment-rights. The rise of the multinationals has been accompanied by a shift of the most dynamic sites of production-growth away from the West – above all, toward China. There have even appeared sizeable South-South flows of FDI.[17] To be sure, Germany and Japan continue to earn large manufacturing surpluses. Nonetheless, in the West, typically in the USA and the UK, there has been a general shift of capitalist activity toward financial and other services.

Financialisation should be understood against this background of hesitant productivity-growth, altered work-practices, and global shifts in productive capacity. Since the late 1970s, real accumulation has witnessed mediocre and precarious growth, but finance has grown extraordinarily in terms of employment, profits, size of institutions and markets. There has been deregulation, technological and institutional change, innovation, and global expansion. Finance now penetrates every aspect of society in developed countries while its presence has grown strongly in the developing world. While real accumulation has been performing indifferently, the capitalist class has found new sources of profits through the revamped mechanisms of finance. Perhaps the most significant development in this respect has been the rise of financial expropriation of workers and others.

The economic aspects of this complex transformation are examined below, focusing primarily on commercial banks, the pivot of the credit-system. Analysis proceeds within the framework of Marxist political economy, deriving fundamentally from the work of Marx. Nonetheless, the output of subsequent Marxist political economy, especially Hilferding, is at least as important, and, in some respects, superior.

---

15. Green 2004a, 2004b; Green and Titsianis 2005.
16. World Bank 2006.
17. UNCTAD 2006.

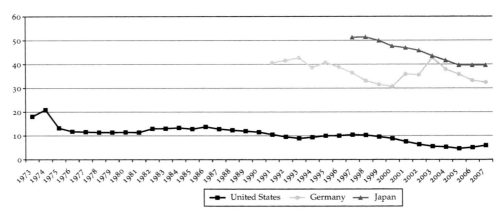

Source: Flow of Funds Accounts, USA, Japan and Germany.

Figure 1   Bank-Loans as Percentage of Corporate Financial Liabilities

4. Economic aspects of financialisation: financial expropriation and investment-banking

4.1. *Commercial banks turn to the individual: the rise of financial expropriation*

Commercial banks have been greatly transformed in the course of financialisation. The driving force of this transformation has been declining reliance of large corporations on bank-finance. Corporate enterprises in developed countries have been financing investment (on a net basis) primarily through retained profits.[18] As far as external finance is concerned, they have relied increasingly on direct borrowing in open markets. Consider the following for the USA, Japan and Germany.

There are differences among countries in this respect. US-corporations, for instance, rely more heavily on issuing bonds. These differences reflect the bank-based character of the German and Japanese financial systems as opposed to the market-based character of the US-system, briefly discussed in Section 6. But the trend is not in doubt, as is shown in Figure 1.

Put in Marxist terms, monopolies have become less reliant on banking credit to finance fixed capital. Circulating capital, on the other hand, continues to draw on trade and banking credit. Even there, however, monopolies

---

18. See Corbett and Jenkinson 1996, 1997.

have gained direct recourse to financial markets, particularly by issuing commercial paper. Monopolies, therefore, have become increasingly implicated in finance, even to the extent of maintaining separate departments for operations in trade-credit and financial securities. In short, they have become financialised, while relying less on banks.

The deeper reasons for this fundamental development are probably associated with the nature of information- and telecommunications-technology, and the corresponding lumpiness (or not) of fixed capital. Also important are changes in the internal organisational structure of modern corporations as well as variations in turnover-time. Irrespective of these deeper reasons, traditional opportunities for banks to lend to corporations have shrunk.

The process of financial deregulation since the late 1960s has drawn on the increasing distance between large corporations and banks. Large corporations have boosted open financial markets, actively by-passing controls over interest-rates and quantities of credit, thus preparing the ground for deregulation. Once deregulation occurred, commercial banks lost the captive-deposits that had previously sustained their activities. The scope for conventional commercial banking narrowed even more.

The responses of banks to narrowing profit-opportunities have been manifold, but two stand out. First, banks turned to the personal revenue of workers and others as source of profit. Second, banks focused on financial-market mediation, i.e. increasingly acquired investment-banking functions. These are closely related to each other; the former is analysed in this section, the latter in the next.

The turn of banks toward personal revenue as field of profitability exhibits significant variations among advanced countries according to their own historical and institutional development. But the general trend is beyond dispute, shown in Figures 2, 3 and 4.

This fundamental trend presupposes increasing involvement of workers in the mechanisms of finance in order to meet elementary needs, such as housing, education, health, and provision for old age. Only then would banks be able to extract significant profits directly from wages and salaries. Once again, there are major differences among developed countries in this respect, reflecting history, institutions, and plain custom. Still, the increasing 'financialisation' of individual worker-income is clear, in terms both of liabilities (mostly borrowing for housing) and assets (mostly pensions and insurance), as can be seen in Figures 5 and 6.

Source: Flow of Funds Accounts, USA, Federal Reserve.

Figure 2   Lending to Consumers and Real Estate as Proportion of Total Bank-Lending, USA

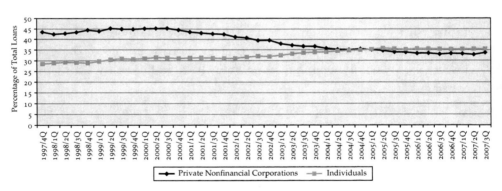

Source: Bank of Japan, Assets and Liabilities of Financial Institutions.

Figure 3   Lending to Individuals as Proportion of Total Bank-Lending, Japan

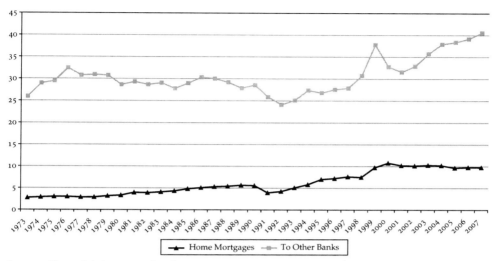

Source: Financial Accounts for Germany.

**Figure 4   Bank-Lending for Home-Mortgages and to Other Banks as
Proportion of Total Lending; (West) Germany**

Widespread implication of workers in the mechanisms of finance is the basis
of financial expropriation. However, the proportion of worker-income that
accrues to banks and other financial institutions is hard to measure on an
aggregate scale. Yet, from the perspective of large banks, there is no doubt at
all that lending to individuals has become increasingly important for bank-
profits.[19] Moreover, the USA offers some evidence about recent trends at the
aggregate-level, as is shown in Figure 7.

   Financial expropriation, then, is a source of profit that has emerged systematically during the recent decades. It should be clearly distinguished from
exploitation that occurs systematically in production and remains the cor-
nerstone of contemporary capitalist economies. Financial expropriation is an
additional source of profit that originates in the sphere of circulation. In so far
as it relates to personal income, it involves existing flows of money and value,
rather than new flows of surplus-value. Yet, despite occurring in circulation,

---

19. See Dos Santos in this volume.

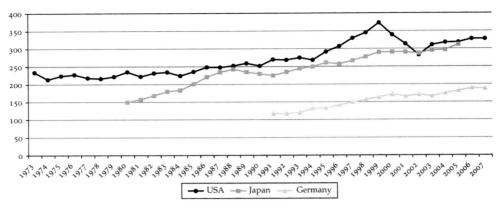

Source: Flow of Funds Accounts of the USA, Financial Accounts for Germany, OECD.

Figure 5   Household Financial Assets as Proportion of GDP;
USA, Japan, Germany

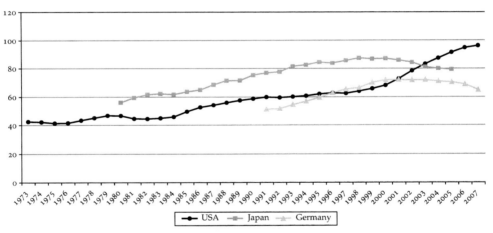

Source: Flow of Funds Accounts of the USA, Financial Accounts for Germany, OECD.

Figure 6   Household-Liabilities as Proportion of GDP;
USA, Japan, Germany

it takes place systematically and through economic processes, thus having an exploitative aspect.[20]

In Marxist theory, the sphere of circulation is not natural terrain for exploitation since commodity-trading is typically premised on *quid pro quo*. Only if traders happened to be misinformed about values, or if extra-economic force was applied, could exploitation arise. That would differ in kind from regular capitalist exploitation, which is both systematic and economic in character. The point is, however, that, financial transactions are about dealing in money and loanable money-capital, rather than in produced commodities. They typically involve the exchange of promises and obligations based on trust, instead of direct *quid pro quo*. The final transfer of value between finance-counterparties depends on institutional framework, legal arrangements, information-flows and even social power.

Advantages in information and power make it possible for financial institutions to deal with individuals differently from capitalist enterprises. The latter have reasonable access to information and are not inferior to financial institutions in social and economic power. The financial services they obtain are necessary for the production and circulation of value and surplus-value. Charges for these services generally fall within limits that are determined in every period by the availability of loanable capital and the profitability of real accumulation. If it were otherwise, capitalist enterprises could in principle bypass existing financial mechanisms, for instance, by relying more on trade-credit or by setting up alternative mechanisms *ab ovo*. To put it differently, capitalist users of finance engage in economic calculus that is dictated by the logic of the circuit of their own capital. As a result, and on average, the remuneration of financial enterprises in their dealings with productive and commercial enterprises complies with the dictates of the total social capital.

In contrast, finance directed to personal revenue aims to meet basic needs of workers and others – housing, pensions, consumption, insurance, and so on. It differs qualitatively from finance directed to capitalist production or circulation. Individuals focus on obtaining use-values, while enterprises aim at

---

20. In draft versions of this article, financial expropriation was called 'direct', or 'financial', exploitation. However, the term 'financial expropriation' better conveys the pivotal role of financial mechanisms, while avoiding confusion with exploitation at the point of production. This does not preclude the existence of exploitative processes in circulation.

the expansion of value. Consequently, the financial actions of individuals are driven by different objectives, motives, information, access to alternatives, and ability to 'economise' compared to enterprises. Moreover, individual workers and others who seek to meet basic needs through finance – particularly in the context of limited social provision – have few options in by-passing, or replacing, the mechanisms of the financial system. Hence individual income can become a target for financial expropriation.

Profit from financial expropriation is reminiscent of usurer's profit. The latter typically arises as production becomes commercialised, thus making (non-capitalist) producers dependent on money as means of payment.[21] It also arises as consumers (especially of luxury-commodities) come to depend on money as means of payment. Interest received by the usurer derives from monetary returns accruing to both producers and consumers, and can even eat into the minimum necessary for reproduction. It is different from interest received by financial institutions for lending to productive capitalists, which derives from profit systematically generated in production. By the same token, advanced financial institutions differ from usurers. But, in times of crisis, the former can become usurious, extracting interest out of the capital of the borrower, rather than out of profit.[22]

In financialised capitalism, the ordinary conditions of existence of working people have come increasingly within the purview of the financial system. Individual dependence on money as means of payment (not only as means of exchange) has become stronger as social provision has retreated in the fields of housing, pensions, consumption, education, and so on. Access to money increasingly dictates the ability to obtain basic goods, while also rationing supply. Thus, the usurious aspect of advanced financial institutions has been re-strengthened, except that financial profits are now generated not only by interest but also by fees.

The more that individual workers have been forced to rely on financial institutions, the more the inherent advantages of the latter in information, power, and motivation have allowed them to tilt transactions to their

---

21. Marx discussed usurer's profit in several places. See, for instance, Marx 1991, pp. 14–19, and Marx 1981, Chapter 36.
22. Marx 1981, p. 734.

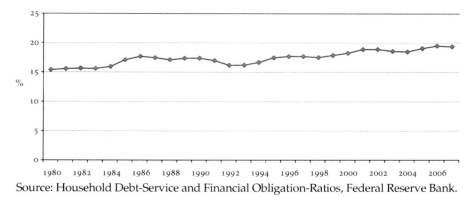

Source: Household Debt-Service and Financial Obligation-Ratios, Federal Reserve Bank.

Figure 7   Mortgage, Consumption, Auto and Other Loan-Payments plus Insurance and Other Housing-Related Payments as Proportion of Individual Disposable Income, USA

own benefit. Elements of supremacy and subordination are present in these relations, though there is no direct analogue with exploitation in production.[23] Still, financial expropriation draws on a fundamental inequality between financial institutions and working people accessing finance.

4.2. Banks turn to financial-market mediation: the advance of investment-banking

The growth of open financial markets, involving primarily shares, bonds and derivatives, has presented banks with further opportunities for profit-making. Share- and bond-prices result from discounting future payments, using the rate of interest (adjusted for risk) as benchmark.[24] Marx called this process the formation of 'fictitious capital', thus capturing its distance from value-creation in production.[25] Derivatives-markets allow participants to make bets aimed at managing risk, or simply speculating.[26] Their prices have a fictitious element,

---

23. Marx 1976, p. 1027, thought of these as fundamental to exploitation.
24. Hilferding 1981, Chapter 8, advanced the original, and still most powerful, analysis of share-prices within Marxist political economy.
25. Marx 1981, Chapter 29.
26. Very little guidance on derivatives can be found in the corpus of Marxist political economy. Some steps in forming an analytical framework were taken by Bryan and Rafferty 2007, though they erroneously treat derivatives as money.

but that derives from institutional practices and norms of trading. The rise of the Black and Scholes model (or variants) in the course of financialisation has given to derivatives-prices an air of objective reality.[27]

Open financial markets are natural terrain for investment-banks, which differ substantially from commercial banks.[28] Investment-banks are financial-market mediators that mobilise short-term funds to invest in securities. They do not take small deposits and their liabilities do not function as money. By the same token, they lie outside the regulatory framework of commercial banks, including deposit-insurance and capital-adequacy. Investment-banks derive profits from fees and commissions to facilitate securities-transactions (providing information about counterparties, placing securities with buyers, reducing transactions-costs, underwriting securities, and so on) as well as from proprietary trading. These activities can be called financial-market mediation.

Investment-bank profits pose difficult problems for political economy. Hilferding suggested that they are part of 'promoter's' or 'founder's' profit, that is, of the value of shares discounted at the rate of interest minus their value discounted at the (higher) rate of profit.[29] This difference, he postulated, is the future profit of enterprise accruing as a lump-sum to the seller of equities at the time of an Initial Public Offering. But Hilferding's analysis needs to be rethought, since different rates of discount could hardly be applied to the same flow of expected returns without financial markets becoming segmented. Moreover, the future profits of enterprise are likely to accrue to those who continue to run the enterprise, not to the sellers of shares.

It is more plausible that investment-bank profits result from the division of loanable money-capital (and plain money) mobilised through open financial markets. The stock of available idle money is mobilised either indirectly through banks, or directly through open financial markets.[30] But direct mobil-

---

27. Penetrating sociological analysis of this process has been provided in a series of papers by MacKenzie 2003, 2004, for instance, and MacKenzie and Millo 2003.

28. They are also natural terrain for insurance-companies, money-trusts, unit-trusts, money-funds, hedge-funds and pension-funds. These intermediaries differ critically from banks since their liabilities are not money, and nor do they lend directly for production-purposes. They have grown in recent years, partly because the state has retreated from welfare-provision, particularly pensions. Their growth has been felicitously called 'pension fund capitalism' by Toporowski 2000.

29. Hilferding 1981, pp. 128–9.

30. For further analysis of this see Lapavitsas 2000.

isation is still facilitated by banks and other financial institutions, which are remunerated through a share of the sums traded. Since this process takes place on the basis of fictitious prices, it is susceptible to sentiment, rumours, and manipulation.

Two fundamental trends have encouraged the adoption of investment-banking functions by commercial banks since the late 1970s. First, successive waves of mergers and acquisitions have taken place among 'financialised' corporations. Stock-markets have not been significant sources of finance for fixed investment in recent years, but they have certainly facilitated the concentration and centralisation of capital through IPOs, leveraged buy-outs and similar transactions.[31]

Second, the savings of workers and others have been directed toward open financial markets through state-policy. The introduction of regulation 401K in the USA in 1978 made pension-savings available for stock-market investment. Similar processes have occurred in the UK through Personal Equity Plans (PEP), Tax-Exempt Special Savings Accounts (TESSA), and Individual Savings Accounts (ISA). These are integral elements of the 'financialisation' of workers' income.

The turn of commercial banks toward financial-market mediation in the USA was confirmed and promoted by the abolition of the Glass-Steagall Act in 1999. The Act had been in place since the great crisis of the 1930s, preventing commercial banks from formally engaging in investment-banking. The formal separation of functions reflected the inherent difference in liquidity- and solvency-requirements between the two types of banking. Commercial banks rely for liquidity on a mass of money-like deposits, while investment-banks borrow heavily in open markets. Analogously, commercial banks need capital to confront losses from lending on production-projects, while investment-banks typically need less since they invest in securities held for relatively short periods of time.

Mixing the two types of banking could result in disaster, particularly as deposit-holders could be scared into withdrawing their funds from

---

31. This has raised important issues of corporate governance and 'shareholder-value', see Lazonick and O'Sullivan 2000. This debate has a long pedigree and originates partly in Marxist literature, particularly Marx 1981, pp. 512–14, and Hilferding 1981, Chapter 7. But since the focus of this article is on banks, there is no need to consider it further.

commercial banks that have engaged in investment-banking. This was one of the contributory causes of the Great Depression of the 1930s. In a related way, discussed below, it has contributed to the current crisis.

4.3. *The lethal mix of financial expropriation and investment-banking*

The destructive interplay of liquidity and solvency that has marked the current crisis has its roots in the trends outlined above. Commercial banks are intermediaries that essentially borrow short to lend long – they are heavily 'leveraged'. Hence, they need to keep some reasonably liquid-assets to deal with deposit-withdrawals; they must also maintain a steady inflow of liquid-liabilities to finance their own lending; finally, they must hold significant own capital to take losses on lending and avoid default. These requirements are costly, forcing commercial banks to walk a tightrope between liquidity and solvency.[32] Financialisation profoundly disrupted this process.

Consider first the lending, or asset, side of banking. For commercial banks, engaging in financial expropriation means primarily mortgage- and consumer-lending. But, since mortgages typically have long duration, heavy preponderance of mortgages would have made bank balance-sheets insupportably illiquid. The answer was securitisation, i.e. adoption of investment-banking techniques. Mortgages were originated but not kept on the balance-sheet. Instead they were passed onto Special-Purpose Vehicles (SPV) created by banks, which then issued mortgage-backed securities.

The creditworthiness of these securities was ascertained by ratings-organisations, and they were also guaranteed ('credit-enhanced') by specialist credit-insurers. Once they were sold, banks received the original mortgage advance and could engage in further lending afresh. Mortgage-payments accrued as interest to securities-holders, while all other parties, including the originators of mortgages, earned fees.

---

32. This is as old as banking itself and has concerned classical political economists. Steuart, for instance, 1767, Book IV, Part I, Chapter 1, stressed solvency because he advocated banks making long-term, largely illiquid-loans. Smith 1789, Book II, Chapter 2, on the other hand, stressed liquidity because he saw banks as suppliers of short-term circulation-funds. The balance is determined in each historical period by the needs of real accumulation, institutional structure, law, and customary bank-practices.

For commercial banks, therefore, the adoption of investment-banking practices turned lending (to earn interest) into mediating the circulation of securities (to earn fees). Securitisation was naturally extended to other assets, such as credit-card receivables, automobile-loans, home-equity loans, and so on. In this vein, independent investment-banks created 'Collateralised Debt-Obligations' (CDOs) by securitising a broad mix of underlying assets, including mortgages, consumer-credit, regular bonds, and even mortgage-backed securities. Banks appeared to have found a way of keeping the asset-side of their balance-sheet permanently liquid, while constantly engaging in fresh lending. This wonderful discovery was called the 'originate-and-distribute' banking model.

Commercial and investment-banks might have been spared the worst had they been able to keep away from the witches' brew they were concocting and selling to others. But, during the bubble, mortgage-backed securities paid high returns and credit was cheap. Thus, banks began to set up 'Structured Investment-Vehicles' (SIVs), that is, financial companies that raise funds in the money-market to purchase securitised assets, including CDOs. Banks also lent (or set up) a host of other financial institutions (including hedge-funds) for the same purpose.

Bank assets, finally, grew through the investment-banking practice of trading in 'Credit-Default Swaps' (CDS). These are derivatives in which one party (the seller) promises fully to reimburse the other (the buyer) for the value of some underlying debt, provided that the buyer pays a regular premium. At the peak of the bubble, their growth was astonishing, as is shown in Table 8.

CDSs are similar to insurance contracts, thus appearing to offer banks cover for their expanding assets. But they are also excellent vehicles for speculation if, say, the underlying debt is the bond of a company which a bank thinks might go bankrupt. Speculation became the prime purpose of trading in CDSs, adding to the destructive force of the crash.

Table 8 Credit-Default Swaps, Notional Amount Outstanding, $bn

Jun 2005	Dec 2005	Jun 2006	Dec 2006	Jun 2007
10211	13908	20352	28650	42850

Source: BIS various.

Consider now the implications of these practices for the liability-side of bank balance-sheets. To sustain expansion through securitisation, banks needed access to wholesale liquidity, that is, borrowing in the money-market. Independent investment-banks led the trend through ever-greater reliance on issuing paper in the money-market. Inevitably they were joined by commercial banks.[33] This was why the crisis first burst out in the money-market.

The implications for solvency were equally profound. Investment-banks have traditionally operated with lower capital-requirements than commercial banks owing to the different nature of their business. During the bubble, they drove their capital to extremely low levels, falsely believing that their expanding assets were safe for reasons explained in the next section. This was very profitable while it lasted, but ultimately contributed to their downfall as they could not take the eventual losses.

Commercial banks, on the other hand, typically keep higher capital-ratios, which are also closely regulated. Basle I regulations, formalised in 1988, stipulated that internationally-active banks should maintain own capital equal to at least 8% of their assets. Basle II, which began to take shape in the late 1990s, allowed banks that use modern risk-management methods (discussed in the next section) to have a lower ratio, if certain of their assets had a lower risk-weighting. The aim of the regulations evidently was to strengthen the solvency of banks. The actual outcome was exactly the opposite.

For, capital is expensive for banks to hold. Consequently, commercial banks strove to evade the regulations by shifting assets off the balance-sheet as well as by trading CDSs, which lowered the risk-weighting of their assets. Therefore, Basle II effectively promoted securitisation. By engaging in investment-banking practices, commercial banks could continually 'churn' their capital, seemingly keeping within regulatory limits, while expanding assets on and off the balance-sheet. In this marvellous world, banks appeared to guarantee solvency while becoming more liquid.

When the housing bubble burst, it became clear that these practices had created widespread solvency-problems for banks. As mortgage-backed assets became worthless, independent US investment-banks were rendered effec-

---

33. Japanese banks were very fortunate in that they had only just started to engage in the new practices when the bubble burst. Hence they have maintained a large flow of deposits relative to their assets.

tively bankrupt in view of extremely low capital-ratios. For the same reason, commercial banks found themselves in a highly precarious position. Even worse, as the crisis unfolded, Basle regulations forced banks to restore capital-ratios precisely when losses were mounting and fresh capital was extremely scarce.

The roots of the disaster that has befallen the world-economy are now easier to see. The ultimate bearers of mortgages in the USA were workers, often of the poorest means. Real wages had not risen significantly throughout the bubble even for workers on higher incomes. Thus, the source of value that would ultimately validate both mortgages and mortgage-backed assets was pathetically weak. On this precarious basis, the financial system had built an enormous superstructure of debt, critically undermining its own liquidity and solvency.

Once defaults on subprime mortgages started in full earnest in 2006, securitised assets became very risky. They could not be easily sold, and their prices declined. For SIVs and hedge-funds, this meant that their assets worsened in price and quality, making it impossible to borrow in the money-market. Confronted with bankruptcy, they had to call on the banks that had funded them. Consequently, banks began to take losses, making it necessary to replenish their capital as well as restricting their credit. Naturally, they also became extremely reluctant to lend to each other in the money-market, further tightening liquidity. Fear led to falling stock-markets, which made bank-solvency even more precarious. The destructive interplay of liquidity and solvency led to bankruptcy, collapse of credit, shrinking demand, and emerging slump.

4.4. *The mismanagement of risk, or what role for banks in financialised capitalism?*

The disastrous performance of banks in the course of the bubble poses broader questions regarding their role in financialised capitalism. The classics of Marxism thought that banks play an integrating role in the capitalist economy by collecting information, transferring resources across society, and facilitating the equalisation of the rate of profit.[34] But financialisation has changed things significantly.

---

34. Lenin 1964, p. 223, thought that banks had become institutions of a truly 'universal character' in capitalist society, while Hilferding 1981, p. 368, imagined that the German economy could be controlled through 'six large Berlin banks'.

Banks evidently need information about their borrowers in order to assess risk and keep appropriate levels of capital. Mainstream-economics postulates that banks acquire information in qualitative ('soft') and quantitative ('hard') ways.[35] The former involves regular contact with borrowers, personal relations, visiting the site of borrower-operations, and placing staff on company-boards. The latter involves analysis of quantitative data on companies as well as on markets and the economy as a whole.

Financial expropriation combined with investment-banking has changed the focus of banks from 'soft', 'relational' methods towards 'hard', statistically-driven techniques. More specifically, to advance mortgages and consumer-loans, banks have adopted 'credit-scoring'. These are 'arms-length' techniques that collect numerical information (income, age, assets, etc.) that produces an individual score and can be manipulated statistically.[36] Loans are advanced if the individual clears a given threshold. Subprime mortgages were precisely loans for which the threshold was low.

Banks have also begun to estimate the risk of default of their assets by applying mathematically-based models that utilise historical rates of default. These estimates are largely extrapolations from past trends, stress-tested within limits indicated by data. Banks have similarly learnt to apply 'Value at Risk' methods, which rely on correlations between asset-prices (estimated historically) and on volatility (estimated from stock-market prices).[37]

On this basis, banks estimate their 'Daily Earnings at Risk' (DEAR), that is, the probability that the value of their assets would decline below a certain level on a daily basis. Consequently, they can re-adjust the mix of their assets to bring DEAR within acceptable bounds. To this purpose, bank-assets must reflect current market-valuations, rather than historical prices. For this reason, the accounting practice of 'marking to market' has prevailed in the course of financialisation.

Inference-based computationally-intensive techniques of risk-management appear 'hard' and have a scientific air. They also fit well with the investment-

---

35. These are clumsy terms, but their meaning is clear. See Berger and Udell 1995; Berger, Klapper and Udell 2001.
36. Mester 1997.
37. For standard analysis see Saunders and Allen 2002, pp. 84–106; Duffie and Singleton 2003, pp. 31–42.

banking functions acquired by commercial banks.[38] During the bubble, it was universally claimed that banks had become experts in 'slicing, packaging and pricing' risk. Through securitisation, they apparently allowed risk to be held by those who truly wanted it, thus increasing financial stability.[39]

Inference-based management of risk by banks has been calamitous. For one thing, it uses past prices to calculate correlations, which hardly works in times of the unprecedented co-movements of prices that characterise crises. Furthermore, these techniques may have increased the homogeneity of decision-making by financial intermediaries, thus exacerbating price-swings and general instability.[40]

More fundamentally, the techniques appear to have led to failure by the whole of the financial system to collect necessary information properly to assess risk.[41] Mortgages were advanced on the basis of 'credit-scoring' and on the understanding that they would be rapidly securitised. The mortgage-backed securities were assessed by credit-rating organisations, which were paid by banks and thus had a vested interest in awarding excellent grades to securities to ensure rapid sales. Moreover, their assessment of risk was also based on inference-based techniques. The buyers then acquired the new securities on the blind assumption that all was fine.

At no point in the process was there genuine due diligence done on the original loans and subsequent securitisations. Banks imagined that they were shifting risk onto others through securitisation. In effect, they were simply giving a different form to risk as loans to SIVs, hedge-funds and so on. When mortgage-defaults started, the true extent of risk became apparent, and banks were ruined.

Put differently, the turn of banks toward financial expropriation and financial-market mediation has resulted in loss of capacity to collect information and assess risk on a 'relational' basis. Banks have acquired some of the

---

38. Allen and Santomero 1998 and 1999 argued that these changes showed that the deeper function of banks in contemporary capitalism is to manage risk in formal ways.

39. It goes without saying that the change would have been impossible without the widespread adoption of information-technology by banks. See Lapavitsas and Dos Santos 2008.

40. Persaud 2002.

41. To call this 'mispricing of risk' is uncharacteristically lame of Goodhart 2008. The real issue is systemic failure to apprehend risk altogether.

character of the broker, while partially losing that of the financial intermediary. This has created problems in assessing borrower-creditworthiness in a socially valid way. For, in a capitalist economy, this task has traditionally been undertaken through partly 'relational' interactions of banks with other institutions and markets in the financial system.[42]

The picture that emerges for commercial banks is bleak. They are no longer major providers of investment-finance to corporate enterprises; their capacity to collect information and assess risk has been compromised; and their mediation of workers' needs has been catastrophic. But, then, what is their future in the capitalist economy? To be sure, they still play a vital role in creating money and operating the payments-mechanism. Yet, this is not a specifically banking activity, and could be taken over by other institutions, such as the post-office. Is there a future banking role for the enormous banks of financialised capitalism? This is one of the most complex problems posed by the current crisis, and the answer is far from obvious. Needless to say, it immediately raises the issue of public ownership and control of banks, a long-standing socialist demand.

5. Social aspects of financialisation: the return of the rentier?

It was shown above that the current crisis is a result of financialisation, which is a systemic transformation of the capitalist economy pivoting on the financial system and involving new sources of profit. In the rest of this article the preceding analysis is placed in a broader context by considering social and political aspects of financialisation. This section, then, considers the renewed prominence of rentiers, who are often associated with income and wealth accruing through the financial sector and have contributed to the rise of inequality during this period. Is financialisation a new era of the rentier and, if so, in what way?

Much of the literature on financialisation assumes (sometimes tacitly) that the ascendancy of the idle rentier characterises contemporary capitalism[43] This is, at heart, a Keynesian approach arguing that the rentier slows down

---

42. See Lapavitsas 2003, Chapter 4.
43. Very selectively, Stockhammer 2004, Crotty 2005, Epstein and Jayadev 2005, Pollin 2007, Orhangazi 2008.

the rhythm of accumulation either by depriving the active capitalist of funds, or by raising interest-rates. It is shown below that there are significant problems to analysing financialisation by counter-posing idle rentier to functioning capitalist.

Analysis of the rentier can be found in Marxist political economy, with the occasional reference coming directly from Marx.[44] The strongest impact was made by Lenin's discussion of 'parasitical rentiers' in his classic theory of imperialism.[45] Lenin took the idea from Hobson, the liberal critic of imperialism.[46] The bulk of Lenin's economic analysis, on the other hand, drew on Hilferding, in whose work there is no mention of the 'parasitical rentier'. Hilferding did not relate finance to rentiers but – basing himself on Marx – argued that the financial system emerges necessarily out of real accumulation. Informed by German capitalism, he also had no truck with the notion that real accumulation runs into difficulties because idle rentiers constrain active industrialists.

Underpinning Marxist views on the rentier is the concept of interest-bearing (or loanable) capital.[47] However, there is some ambiguity in Marx's analysis of the sources of interest-bearing capital, which matters for the analysis of rentiers. At times, Marx treats interest-bearing capital as belonging to 'moneyed' capitalists, who are a subsection of the capitalist class.[48] 'Moneyed' capitalists lend capital to others, and are satisfied with interest which is a share of profits. Though Marx did not use the term in this context, 'moneyed' capitalists are essentially rentiers, in contrast to active capitalists who borrow capital to generate profits.

At other times, however, Marx suggests that loanable capital arises out of idle money generated in the normal course of the operations of industrial and commercial capital.[49] Thus, loanable capital does not belong to a distinct subsection of the capitalist class, but is constantly recreated in the course of real accumulation. The main function of the credit-system is to mobilise idle funds, transforming them into loanable money-capital and channelling them back

---

44. For instance Marx 1981, Chapter 22.
45. Lenin 1964, pp. 276–85.
46. Hobson 1938, Chapter 4.
47. Introduced by Marx in 1981, Part 5.
48. For instance, Marx 1981, Chapters 21, 22, 23, 24.
49. For instance, Marx 1978, pp. 165, 203, 248–61, 355–9, 423, 569, and Marx 1981, Chapters 30, 31, 32.

to accumulation. Along these lines, Hilferding specified the sources of idle money as well as the complex ways in which it becomes loanable capital.[50]

One merit of the latter approach is that it cuts through some of the confusions surrounding the current debate on rentiers and financialisation. For, the income of those who might be categorised as contemporary rentiers does not arise merely from possession of loanable capital. The managers of hedge-funds, for instance, draw extraordinary incomes typically from fees and large shares of the annual profits. These incomes derive from using the money of others to speculate on financial assets. Remuneration often takes the form of further financial assets, bringing capital-gains and evading taxation. Similarly, industrial managers draw incomes in the form of stock-options and other financial mechanisms, often masquerading as salaries. Substantial incomes, finally, accrue to accountants, lawyers and others who provide the technical support necessary for financial operations.

Such incomes are due in part to position and function of the recipient relative to the financial system, rather than simply to ownership of loanable money-capital, or even of idle money. Modern rentiers, in other words, are not plain money-holders who avoid the grubby business of production. They frequently own loanable capital, but their ability to command extraordinary income is also mediated by position relative to the financial system. Indeed, they do not even have to function within the financial system, for instance, as industrial and commercial managers.

The rentier as owner of loanable capital at loggerheads with the industrial capitalist is of limited relevance to contemporary capitalism. This is even more apparent in relation to institutional investors. Pension-funds, insurance-companies, investment-funds, and so on, collect idle money leaked from the income of broad layers of working people. They provide scope for financial intermediaries to generate profits out of handling such funds. But they also generate returns for 'financialised' individuals across social classes. They certainly do not distribute their earnings to a well demarcated social group of rentiers.

Similarly, it is erroneous to treat the aggregate profits of financial institutions as a measure of rentier-income. Financial institutions – above all, banks – are not parasites subsisting on the profit-flows of industrious productive capital-

---

50. Hilferding 1981, pp. 70–81.

ists. In principle, they are capitalist enterprises offering necessary services in the sphere of circulation. They are thus subject to competition and tend to earn the average rate of profit. Financialisation has entailed a turn toward financial expropriation and financial-market mediation. But there are no grounds for treating financial institution profits as proxy for rentier-income.

To recap, insofar as a rentier-layer can be identified today, it has resulted from the development of the financial system. It draws income from position relative to the financial system as well as from ownership of loanable capital. More broadly, the ability to extract rent-like income through financial operations is a by-product of the transformation of finance rather than its driving force. The ascendancy of finance has systemic origins and its outcomes are far more complex than industrialists being presumably squeezed by rentiers. By the same token, confronting financialisation does not mean supporting hard-working industry against idle finance.

6. Instead of a conclusion: is financialisation a new era of finance-capital?

The final issue to be considered in this article is the analogy between financialisation and the ascendancy of finance at the turn of the twentieth century. The latter was, of course, analysed in the classical-Marxist debates on imperialism.[51] Hilferding put forth the pivotal concept of finance-capital, capturing the epochal change that resulted from the altered relationship between industrial and banking capital.[52] For Hilferding, as the scale of production grows, monopolistic industrial capital relies increasingly on monopolistic banks for investment-finance, until the two become amalgamated, with banks in the ascendant. This is finance-capital, which dominates the economy, progressively restricting competition and 'organising' the economy to serve its interests.

Hilferding analysis provided foundations for Lenin's subsequently canonical formulation of imperialism. Bauer had already established that cartels demanded aggressive tariffs to create exclusive trading areas for themselves.[53]

---

51. Including Hilferding 1981, Lenin 1964, Luxemburg 1951, Bauer 2000, Bukharin 1972.
52. Hilferding 1981, p. 225.
53. Bauer 2000.

Hilferding argued that cartels also exported money-capital to less developed countries to take advantage of lower wages. This was the end of British 'laissez-faire' capitalism, replaced by German and US finance-capital. The late developers relied on the power of the state, hence spurring militarism and imperialism, with attendant racism. Lenin's theory stressed monopoly more strongly, also introducing parasitical rentiers and the territorial re-division of the world among imperialist powers. But the underlying economics came from Hilferding.[54]

Hilferding's and Lenin's analysis of finance-capital and imperialism is a masterpiece of political economy, shedding light on the ascendancy of finance and its implications for economy, society and politics. It looked somewhat frayed during the long postwar-boom, since finance was strongly regulated, the USA had subsumed imperialist divisions under its struggle against the Soviet Union, and a wave of liberation-movements had destroyed the old empires. But the rise of financialisation appears to have injected fresh life into it. Does financialisation represent a return of finance-capital? The short answer is no, but the analogy casts light on the current period for the following reasons.

First, as was shown above, banks and large industrial or commercial enterprises have not come closer together in recent decades, and nor is there evidence that banks hold the upper hand in relations with industry. Large corporations have become more distant from banks, while independently engaging in financial transactions. Banks have sought profits in 'financialised' personal incomes as well as in mediating transactions in open financial markets.

Second, the character of financial systems has changed in ways incompatible with the theory of finance-capital. All financial systems have common elements but the balance between them depends on stage of development, history, institutional structure, law and politics. A typical distinction is between market-based, or Anglo-American, and bank-based, or German-Japanese financial systems.[55] Broadly speaking, in market-based systems, the weight of open financial markets is greater, while banks and industry have arms-length relations. In contrast, bank-based systems have prominent

---

54. In contrast to Luxemburg 1951, who ignored finance-capital in her analysis of imperialism.
55. Also used in mainstream-economics, for instance, Allen & Gale 2001.

credit-systems and close relations between banks and industry, often involving exchange of personnel and mutual share-holding.

Hilferding's theory of finance-capital is one of the earliest analyses of bank-based financial systems. Implicit in his theory is that financial systems become progressively bank-based as finance-capital emerges. However, the rise of open financial markets, and the transformation of banks in recent decades are not consistent with such a trend. On the contrary, there has been a global shift toward market-based systems, drawing on the US-model, though bank-based systems have not disappeared by any means.

Third, for both Hilferding and Lenin, exclusive trading zones are vital to the emergence of territorial empires. But financialised capitalism has not produced phenomena of this type; instead there have been pressures for lower tariffs and a homogeneous institutional framework of trading. To be sure, the process has been uneven and contradictory, typically involving discrimination against less-developed countries. States have also created trading blocs (above all, the European Union and NAFTA), though these are not generally exclusive. In all, there has been nothing comparable to the competitive imposition of tariffs that characterised the era of finance-capital.

Fourth, Hilferding's theory has little to say on the systematic intervention of the state in the sphere of finance, despite his predilection for 'organised' capitalism.[56] But the state has been pivotal to the rise of financialisation. For one thing, the state has pursued financial deregulation. For another, the state is the power behind the central bank both through supplying it with bonds and through declaring central-bank liabilities to be legal tender. Without the state's backing, central banks would have been much less effective during crises of financialisation. More broadly, the state has emerged as the ultimate guarantor of the solvency of large banks and of the stability of the financial system as a whole.

Finally, fifth, financialisation has been accompanied by extraordinary turbulence in the international-monetary system. Gold – the world-money of Hilferding's and Lenin's day – has become marginal to the international monetary system, a reserve of last resort. In the absence of a genuine anchor, the US-dollar has gradually emerged as quasi-world-money. It was shown above

---

56. The same holds for Bukharin 1972, despite his strong emphasis on 'organised' capitalism.

that developing countries have been forced to accumulate enormous dollar-reserves in recent years. This has benefited primarily the USA, since poor countries have supplied it with loanable capital, thus allowing it to sustain substantial trade-deficits. But the leading imperialist country has also paid a price as the housing bubble was enlarged, leading to the current crisis.

Financialisation, in short, does not amount to dominance of banks over industrial and commercial capital. It stands, rather, for increasing autonomy of the financial sector. Industrial and commercial capitals are able to borrow in open financial markets, thus becoming heavily implicated in financial transactions. Financial institutions have sought new sources of profitability in financial expropriation and investment-banking. Meanwhile, workers have been increasingly drawn into the realm of private finance to meet basic needs, including housing, consumption, education, health and provision for old age. This has been an era of unstable and low growth, stagnant real wages, and frequent financial bubbles. The current crisis represents a gigantic concatenation of the imbalances, tensions and exploitative aspects of financialised capitalism. The need for alternative economic organisation that is crisis-free while serving the interests of working people is apparent.

Chapter Two

Racial Exclusion and the Political Economy of the Subprime Crisis

Gary A. Dymski*

I. Introduction

Most economists' explanations of the roots of the 2007–9 global financial crisis have focused on greed, myopia, and overreach by financial firms and homeowners, and on credit-rating agencies' moral hazard.[1] These diagnoses suggests that this crisis has the same root-causes as the 1982 Latin American crisis, the 1980s savings and loan crisis, and the 1997 Asian crisis: moral hazard due to flawed institutional design, combined with regulatory failure.[2] So, this latest crisis apparently demonstrates that,

* The author gives special thanks to Mariko Adachi, Philip Arestis, Glen Atkinson, Dean Baker, David Barkin, Etelberto Cruz, Jim Crotty, Silvana De Paula, Shaun French, Masao Ishikura, Tetsuji Kawamura, Costas Lapavitsas, Noemi Levy, George Lipsitz, Andrew Leyshon, Tracy Mott, Jesus Munoz, Anastasia Nesvetailova, Ronen Palan, Yoshi Sato, Tokutaru Shibata, Jan Toporowski, Thomas Wainwright, Michelle White, Clyde Woods, and two anonymous referees of the journal *Historical Materialism* for their insightful comments on the work presented here, and he acknowledges the useful feedback he received from participants in the January 2008 Association for Evolutionary Economics conference, in the 2008 conference on *Structural Change and Development Policies* at the National Autonomous University of Mexico, and in seminars at Denver University, the University of Nevada-Reno, Nottingham University, and the University of Tokyo. The author is especially grateful to CEDEPLAR/Federal University of Minas Gerais for supporting the completion of this research.
1. See, for example, Krinsman 2008, Shiller 2008, and Tully 2007.
2. For representative analyses of these crises, see respectively Eaton, Gersovitz, and Stiglitz 1986, Kane 1989, Kaufman 1990, and Krugman 1998.

when incentives and information are asymmetrically distributed, and when financial markets are inadequately unsupervised, then myopic, risk-taking, or incompetent borrowers and lenders can generate huge economic and social losses.[3] This implies that policies to offset loan-losses would be counterproductive: financial markets have to be taught about down-side risk yet again.[4]

Admittedly, financial crises are a hardy perennial in the capitalist garden. But the depth of the still-evolving economic meltdown that has resulted from this crisis suggested that its history should be interrogated carefully, not written out of the story.

This chapter argues that a key element in the 2007–9 subprime crisis was the transformation of racial exclusion in US mortgage-markets. Until the early 1990s, racial minorities were systematically excluded from participation in mortgage-finance due to banks' practices of redlining and discrimination. From that point forward, however, racial exclusion in credit-markets was transformed. Racial minorities were no longer denied mortgage-credit altogether. Instead, they were increasingly given access to housing credit under terms far more adverse than were offered to non-minority borrowers.

The emergence of these subprime loans is linked, in turn, to banks' strategic transformation of banking in the 1980s in response to their own difficulties at the dawn of the neoliberal era. Banks, having shed their traditional roles as risk-absorbers, were seeking out ever more ways to generate net income. They created financial assets designed to provide services to different segments of their customer-base in different ways, generating substantial fee-based income along the way. Their successful direct and indirect forays into higher-risk loans for lower-income and minority-markets, together with the emergence of new outlets for higher-risk debt, opened up the subprime mortgage-markets. Boom regional housing markets in the US then created opportunities to spread subprime instruments to new homeowners well beyond the boundaries of segregated urban neighbourhoods. The apparently endless supply of low-cost liquidity, linked to the US's unique global

---

3. Reinhart and Rogoff 2008.
4. Allen Meltzer 2007 wrote: 'Capitalism without failure is like religion without sin. The answer to excessive risk-taking is "let 'em fail".... Bailouts encourage excessive risk-taking; failures encourage prudent risk taking'.

macroeconomic position, provided the fuel for the large-scale manufacture and distribution of mortgage-based investment-vehicles.

As long as subprime loans were fully collateralised by underlying housing assets, banks could use loans to boost their profits with little increase in risk. From the viewpoint of the capitalist accumulation-process, these loans increased the depth of the financial expropriation of the working class by financial capital. The conditions for crisis emerged when lenders began issuing subprime loans on an under-collateralised basis. This happened when subprime loans were increasingly used to cover over the growing gap between median earned incomes and housing prices. As this happened, these housing loans became not just extortionary but speculative. Mortgage-brokers and lenders heightened this shift, because so doing maximised their fee-based income. Finally, crisis emerged when the housing price/credit-pyramid grew larger than the income-flows of financially fragile homeowners could support.

The approach developed here emphasises that economic crises unfold in particular historical and institutional conjunctures of global capitalist processes. Financial processes are understood here as key sources of contemporary capitalist crises. Instability and accumulation-problems can arise from financial dynamics both due to fundamental uncertainty in financial processes and due to the emergence of speculative credit-flows within the economy.[5] Banks and financial relations are not passive elements in accumulation-processes, simply facilitating exploitation in production; they are active elements that independently impact the trajectory of crises. In the case examined here, lenders' innovation of providing minority-households with access to mortgage-finance via predatory loans was an independent root of the current crisis.[6]

---

5. Dymski 2006.
6. Throughout this chapter, we refer to subprime loans as being predatory and involving financial exploitation and expropriation. These terms all refer to the fact that these loans require higher-than-average interest rates and fees to be paid. Exploitative relations in the credit-market should not be confused with the exploitation of labour from labour-power. The question of the relationship between these lender-borrower relations and Marxian exploitation-theory is addressed in Lapavitsas's chapter in this volume. On the links between racial exclusion and exploitation-theory, see also Dymski 1992, and 1996a.

2. Racial exclusion in US credit-markets

The postwar-period is often celebrated as a period of generalised prosperity for the working class in the US[7] and in Europe.[8] In this Fordist era, the real wage rose for many categories of worker, permitting a substantial increase in living standards. Previously scarce consumer-goods became widespread and residential homes became larger and more comfortable. This increased housing consumption was accomplished in the US (not in every country) largely through expanded homeownership.[9] The rise in homeownership-rates from the 1950s through the mid-1980s, then, provides one measure of relative household-prosperity. Of course, linking increased housing and domestic-appliance consumption to home-building and homeownership also opened up important new venues to market-competition. Housing construction became even more pro-cyclical than durable and non-durable investment-expenditures.[10] Further, those workers who were homeowners gained an interest in the maintenance of regulatory and economic-stabilisation policies that generated higher home-prices.

But it must be emphasised that this generalised prosperity existed alongside substantial racial inequality.[11] Until the 1970s, most cities in the US had *de facto*, and sometimes *de jure*, prohibitions on where racial minorities could live. Most minorities moved to urban areas from the rural South and the fields in the labour-shortage periods accompanying World-Wars I and II. They were prohibited from home-ownership in most areas of cities by racial covenants – contractual agreements between prospective home-buyers and home-sellers that the homes in question would neither be sold nor resold to minorities. These social arrangements forced minorities to crowd into available, largely rental, housing in restricted portions of the city. Landlords could charge higher rents than would otherwise have been possible, and to expropriate an extra share of minorities' wages and salaries.

So the Golden Age never crossed the race line: African-Americans and other minorities largely functioned as a labour buffer-stock, spatially seg-

---

7. Bowles 1982, and Bowles and Gintis 1982.
8. Glyn et al. 1988.
9. Dymski and Isenberg 1998.
10. Dymski 2002.
11. Dymski 1996b.

regated in lower-income neighbourhoods with low home-ownership rates.[12] Federal housing policy was partly to blame for these patterns of spatial segregation and low home-ownership. Since its founding in the 1930s, the Federal Housing Administration's guidelines precluded the funding of homes from minority- or mixed neighbourhoods. This reinforced segregation and racial wealth-disparities. Depository institutions were also to blame: they did not locate branches in minority-neighbourhoods or make loans there. In reaction, African Americans and other minorities established minority-owned banks in many cities.[13] However, most financial services and credit were provided in these areas by local stores and informal providers – check-cashing stores, finance-companies, and pawn-brokers. Some were franchises and some were locally owned; virtually all charged exploitative fees. The political momentum of the Civil-Rights movement forced some changes in this situation. Two new laws, the 1968 Fair Housing Act and 1974 Equal Credit Opportunity Act, extended the anti-discrimination principles of civil rights law to housing and credit-markets, respectively.

Then a new trend emerged: the emergence of 'white flight' from some urban neighbourhoods, in the 1960s and 1970s. This destabilised racial boundary-lines, as minority-households began to move into formerly all-white areas. Banks and thrifts reacted by reducing mortgage-lending throughout the inner city. Ironically, this led to the creation of a multi-racial community-based movement opposing lenders' 'redlining'.[14] This movement created the political pressure that led to the Home Mortgage Disclosure Act (HMDA) of 1975 and the Community Reinvestment Act (CRA) of 1977. Respectively, these acts provided a mechanism for monitoring bank loan-making, and precluded 'redlining' – the implicit or explicit refusal of lenders to make mortgage-credit available to neighbourhoods with large minority-populations.

The CRA required banks to meet the credit-needs of their entire market-areas, and prevented banks from claiming market-areas that excluded minority and low-income populations. HMDA required all depository institutions to report annually on the distribution of their mortgage-loans by census-tract. Academics and community-activists used HMDA data to prove in city

---

12. Baron 1985.
13. Ammons 1996.
14. Squires 1993.

after city that bank home-ownership loans were made much less frequently in minority- and lower-income areas than elsewhere. For example, a 1991 study of banking, race, and income in Los Angeles found that banks made home-mortgage loans five times more frequently in low-minority than high-minority census-tracts, controlling for income.[15]

Community-advocates used the leverage provided by such studies to frame their demand for 'reinvestment'. Mortgage-finance was central to these advocates' demands, as it would permit more minorities to engage in wealth-accumulation through homeownership. Depository institutions argued that they did not redline: there was low demand for home-purchases in these areas, which were, in any event highly risky. These assertions were supported by economists, and by logic: insofar as the mortgage-market is competitive, lenders in that market would not leave 'money on the table'.[16] In any event, HMDA-data were not rich enough to resolve this dispute.

The crisis of the savings-and-loan (thrift) industry in the 1980s made it clear that lenders in the mortgage-market had not performed optimally in deciding on which mortgages to make and under what terms. The locally-based thrift-industry was perceived as having failed in large part because moral hazard had dominated profit-and-loss considerations in its loan-making. In exchange for the federal assistance provided to clean up the mess, the mortgage-market was opened to new lenders. And, to permit new entrants into the supply-side of the mortgage-market, rules on bank-holding company purchases of non-bank lenders were loosened. Due to pressure from CRA-advocates, the 1989 bailout-bill also required more extensive reporting by mortgage-lenders under HMDA.

From 1990 on, lenders had to report annually on mortgage-loan applications, denials, and loans made, including information about applicants' race, gender, income, and loan-size. These data permitted researchers to test econometrically for racial discrimination in mortgage-markets. These tests almost uniformly found minority-applicants to have a systematically lower probability of loan-approval than white applicants. What such results meant was

---

15. Dymski, Veitch, and White 1991. For other studies, see the references in Squires 1993.
16. See, respectively, Benston 1981, and Holmes and Horvitz 1994.

contentious.[17] For some, this racial disadvantage demonstrated that lenders' racial animus toward borrowers outweighed other factors. For others, it represented 'rational discrimination' based on the greater risks associated with loans made to minorities and to minority-areas.[18]

From the perspective of capital-accumulation, the result that minority-status per se affected loan-market decisions represented a paradox: why would profit-seeking firms not set aside racial bias and make profitable loans? This racial exclusion would reduce profits, all things equal. Two responses suggest plausible explanations of this paradox. First, while lenders seek profits, most lending institutions and lending officers are non-minority, and thus susceptible to perceptual racial bias (despite their commitment to profit-maximisation). Second, the perceived risks associated with lending in minority-areas and to minorities are sufficiently great to deter lending.

This situation was about to change. To understand how, we need to review the strategic transformation of US-banking.

3. US-banking from the Golden Age to the neoliberal age

After being reorganised during the 1930s Depression-era, the US-banking system consisted of a tightly controlled set of specialised institutions that provided different categories of credit to different economic sectors. Housing credit was provided primarily by savings and loan companies and savings banks ('thrifts'), which attracted longer-term consumer-savings.

The evolution of US housing finance in the postwar-period reflected the federal government's commitment to expanded homeownership. The Federal Housing Administration provided almost half of all US mortgage-funding in the 1949–59 period, and guaranteed a portion of the remaining mortgages. Further, federal deposit-insurance underwrote the deposit-holdings that supported most outstanding mortgages. The homeownership-rate climbed from 44 per cent in 1940 to 61 per cent by 1960, to 63 per cent a decade later, and then to 66 per cent in 1980.

---

17. Dymski 2006 reviews the theoretical discrimination-models and these extensive econometric debates.

18. Calomiris, Kahn, and Longhofer 1994, for example, characterise rational discrimination as appropriate lender-behaviour.

After having been a source of economic instability in the Great Depression,[19] the segmented US banking system – including the housing-finance subsystem –, was very safe. Bank-failures virtually never occurred from the 1940s until the 1980s. Consequently, the Federal Reserve used the banking system as a key lever in stabilising the macroeconomic growth-path. In the 1950s and 1960s, the Federal Reserve would reduce inflationary pressure by engineering credit-crunches whose point of impact was the banking system.[20] This would slow economic growth; expanding the availability of reserves, in turn, would stimulate more economic activity by way of increased housing finance (and other forms of lending).

Because of its susceptibility to credit-crunches, and because potential home-buyers' incomes vary pro-cyclically, housing finance is highly sensitive to the business-cycle. Housing-construction outlays are more volatile over the cycle than durable or non-durable investment spending.[21] Figure 1 shows that fluctuations in mortgage-debt outstanding were more volatile than fluctuations in real GDP. Further, Figure 2 demonstrates that the ratio of unsold houses relative to home-sales varies over the cycle as well – this ratio rises when the economy slows.

Until the mid-1970s, banks and thrifts navigated these chronic cyclical downturns without significant institutional stress. But then stresses started to emerge. The trigger was a shift in the global position of the US macro-economy. A decade of instability in the 1970s undercut the stable, low-inflation, high-growth period that had prevailed under the Bretton Woods system. By the late 1970s, macroeconomic turmoil had broken out: stagflation and interest-rates well above banks' regulatory maxima led to systematic dis-intermediation – the loss of depositors to innovative savings-outlets, such as money-market instruments. Banks' credit-supply to non-financial businesses was threatened; large non-financial corporations responded by creating the modern commercial paper-market and vastly expanding the scope of corporate bond-markets.

Depository institutions, short of sufficient deposits to cover their asset positions, were forced to borrow at high nominal rates. The inverted yield-curve

---

19. Fisher 1933.
20. Wojnilower 1980.
21. Leamer 2008.

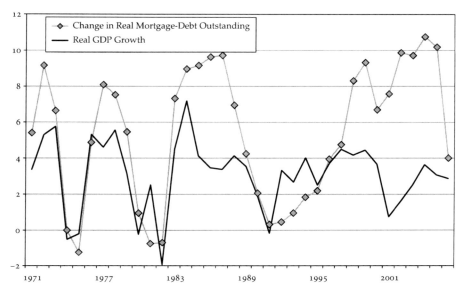

Source: Office of Policy Development and Research, US Department of Housing and Urban Development

Figure 1   Growth-Rates of Real GDP and Mortgage-Debt Outstanding, US, 1971–2006 (%)

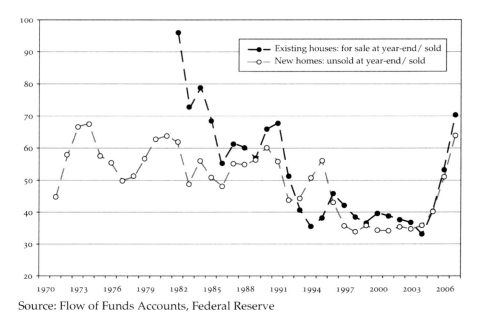

Source: Flow of Funds Accounts, Federal Reserve

Figure 2   Homes on the Market at Year-end as a Percentage of Homes Sold, Existing and New Homes, 1970–2007

caused substantial losses from realised liquidity-risk, especially in the thrift industry. Thrifts, originators of most US-mortgages, were hit especially hard, because their asset-portfolio was dominated by fixed-rate, illiquid mortgages.

These banking and thrift-crises led to the passage in 1980 and 1982 of federal legislation designed, respectively, to deregulate commercial banks' liability instruments and to free thrifts to undertake more asset-side activities. This legislation unleashed a period of competitive deregulation between federal and state-regulators of thrifts. This led some states' thrifts to undertake ill-advised speculative investments in the mid-1980s, including equity-participation in speculative housing development. As a result, the problem of thrift-illiquidity was transformed into a pandemic of failed investments and non-performing assets.

Consequently, some of the post-deregulation thrifts crashed, often spectacularly. Federal legislation in 1989 then provided the funding for cleaning up the savings-and-loan crisis. The size of the thrift-sector was vastly reduced: many insolvent thrifts were merged into commercial banks. The macro-instability in the early 1980s also precipitated the Latin-American debt-crisis and a crisis of commercial-bank solvency in several 'oil-patch' states. These events led to substantial commercial-bank losses, and to several US money-centre bank-failures.

Banks' survival was threatened. Banks reacted in part by developing new business-strategies. Banks' first strategic shift involved the creation of upscale retail-banking strategies, which focused on selling financial services to consumer- and business-customers with stable incomes and positive wealth-positions. These strategies saw banks concentrating in upper-income areas, and systematically avoiding lower-income, African-American and Latino areas. These new strategies shifted the balance from net earnings based on interest-margin to net earnings based on fees for financial services.

These shifts toward desirable up-market customers and fee-based services were mutually reinforcing: the customers most sought by banks are targeted for the marketing of standardised financial services – credit-cards, specialised deposit- and investment-accounts, and mortgage-loans. Both strategic shifts led to bank-mergers aimed at market-expansion: so, over time, a shrinking number of ever-larger banks were serving ever more of the US banking market.

4. Securitisation and the mortgage-market

As Figure 3 shows, the overall homeownership-rate in the US, which had risen secularly in the 1970s, began a decline from a 1980 peak of 65.6 per cent to a 1986 level of 63.8 per cent. However, the early-1980s thrift-collapse did not lead to a meltdown of mortgage-finance in those years. Mortgage-debt outstanding did turn negative (Figure 1). But this 1980s event was no deeper a downturn than the mid-1970s recession, and GNP-growth slowed even more. One factor in this downturn was the sensitivity of mortgage-backed securities-rates to balance-sheet risk – a characteristic of the market until a 1989 federal act bailed out savings-and-loan depositors and owners.[22] As Figure 2 above shows, the ratio of unsold-to-sold new homes rose, but to a slightly lower peak than in the mid-1970s.

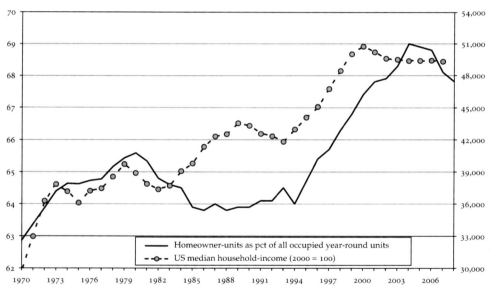

Source: Office of Policy Development and Research, US Department of Housing and Urban Development. US Department of Commerce, Bureau of Economic Analysis.

Figure 3   US Homeownership-Rate and Real Median Household-Income, 1970–2008 (% of All Housing Units Occupied All-Year-Round)

---

22. Brewer III and Mondschaen 1992.

This profound institutional crisis had a muted effect for two reasons. First, the housing market adjusted rapidly to the income-downturn. Between 1974 and 1979, real household median income grew modestly (0.84% annually), while real median housing prices climbed 3.6 per cent per annum; see Table 1. When real incomes were declining 2 per cent annually in the 1980–2 period, real housing prices fell almost as fast. When real incomes began rising significantly again in 1983 and 1984 (2.3 per cent per annum), housing prices remained stable, so that housing affordability (measured by the housing-price/income ratio) declined. For the remainder of the 1980s, both variables rose, housing somewhat faster than income.

Second, the 1980s thrift-crisis had such a restrained impact because it only accelerated a trend already in motion for US housing finance: from an intermediary-based to a securities-market based system. As noted, lenders previously held mortgages to maturity, exposing them to both default and liquidity-risk. The new norm involved making mortgages so as to sell them to the securities-markets. The process of originating, servicing, and holding mortgages was split into its constituent parts, with each part priced and performed separately. One immediate implication is that commercial banks, mortgage-companies, and others could compete for fees from originating mortgages and from bundling and servicing them.

Securitising housing finance depended on the commodification of mortgages. In the 1980s, securitisation necessitated standardised eligibility-criteria. The criteria that emerged privileged customers with minimal default-risk. This risk-aversion had several sources. First, the computational challenges embodied in combining multiple dimensions of riskiness – and especially in calculating default-risk on a given bundle of mortgages that were also subject to pre-payment risk –, required that default-risk per se be standardised to the extent possible. Second, two federally-chartered agencies, FNMA (the Federal National Mortgage Association) and FHLMC (the Federal Home Loan Mortgage Corporation) were buying an increasing share of mortgage-debt. These entities accounted for just 16 per cent of all mortgage-debt outstanding in 1979; but their share surpassed 25 per cent by 1986, and grew steadily until it reached a peak of 43 per cent in 2003. Most agency-bought debt was then at least implicitly guaranteed and sold onto the market.[23] The agencies then insisted on low-

---

23. What governmental guarantee exists for FNMA-paper is unclear; see note 10.

risk ('plain vanilla') mortgages, which set minimal levels for down-payment/ loan ratios and for mortgage-payment/income ratios. This leads to the third factor: a large share of the customers for agency-backed mortgage-securities were overseas wealth-holders, who were relatively risk-averse.

These changes rescued the mortgage-finance system by transforming it, from a system with localised savings circuits provided by numerous thrifts making decisions autarchically, to an increasingly national market dominated by lenders using market-wide criteria. The 'relationship'-lending at the heart of the postwar-system was replaced: credit-allocation no longer relied on lenders deciding which borrowers' micro-characteristics and motivations warranted risk-taking, but instead involved identifying which prospective borrowers met globally-established thresholds. These thresholds marked dividing lines among borrowers with different generalised default-risk profiles. In effect, growing macro-uncertainty and institutional and technological innovations resulted in the repositioning of risk-assessment on the basis of standardised macro-parameters, not micro-decisions.

With a growing population of mortgage-originators generating standardised credit and a growing demand to hold this mortgage-debt, loan-making was separated from risk-bearing. And, as this market was initially structured, both default- and liquidity-risk would be reduced. Depository institutions could make long-term mortgages without absorbing liquidity-risk. In turn, the funds and firms buying mortgage-debt could, if they held longer-term payout-commitments (such as insurance- or pension-funds) turn, match the maturity-dates of these liabilities with those of their assets (the mortgages they bought). So, liquidity-risk could be transferred and substantially ameliorated. And, given a stable interest-rate environment and cautious lending criteria, the default rate would remain low and predictable.

From the mid-1980s to the mid-1990s, most mortgages were conforming conventional loans, underwritten by the quasi-governmental agencies, FNMA and FHLCC, and held in these agencies' portfolios until, in most cases, they were sold off.[24] These agencies accommodated the need for more securitised

---

24. Whether these agencies have implicit governmental backing is, and remains, contentious. FNMA was removed from the federal budget in 1968; and FHLCC was created as a separate entity to facilitate secondary-market sales of mortgage-backed securities in 1970. Both now operate as independent, wholly-private entities. However, the notion that these entities are implicitly backed by the US-government is widely held. See, for example, *The Economist* 2007a.

mortgages by creating more pass-through securities, that is, securities whose share-holders have claims on the underlying mortgage cash-flows. These agencies' efforts were supplemented by the expanded efforts of private mortgage-insurers; these private companies specialise in loans that are 'non-conforming' because they exceed FNMA loans – 'jumbo'-loans larger than are allowed under FNMA. In any case, the upward limit for FNMA-qualifying loans was increased by 63 per cent between 1989 and 1985, after rising just 22 per cent in the previous four years. In sum, maintaining the strength of US housing finance did not require the invention of new institutions in the 1980s – only an adjustment of these institutions' parameters, and a market for the financial paper these institutions had to sell.

This returns us to a key-point. What kept mortgage-flows relatively resilient was the unique position of the US within the global neoliberal régime. As noted, a crisis in the global economy – and in the position of the US within it – spurred the change in banking strategy, and necessitated a transition to a new housing-finance mechanism. What made this transition relatively seamless vis-à-vis US housing finance (Table 1) was that much of the rest of the world was caught in low-growth traps or crises. Since the US was the principal global source of reserve-currency and had huge current-account deficits, it needed systematic capital-account inflows.

The fact that the US appeared to be a global safe haven was then triply fortuitous. Mortgage-backed securities responded to the needs of offshore-investors: securities implicitly backed by the government, paying more than treasuries, and denominated in the world's reserve-currency during a period of global financial disorganisation.[25] Further, the US macro-economy needed overseas-buyers for its securities, so as to maintain cross-border balances. And, finally, these savings inflows permitted the US to re-establish low nominal interest-rates. Low rates minimised the implicit financial risks on the mortgages being packaged and traded in secondary markets. In time, these risks would be exposed.

This triple global financial conjuncture was eventually unwound, in part because this safe-haven situation invited excessive risk-taking. To understand

---

25. Dymski 2008 develops the argument about the US-role within the international system at length.

how this happened, we must first unfold the next step in the evolution of racial exclusion in US credit-markets.

5. Racial exploitation from redlining to predatory lending

As we have seen, the 1980s forced the rethinking of long-established banking processes: *how* housing is financed and *how* banks generate earnings finance mechanism and banking strategies were in transition. The steady deepening of wealth- and income-inequality, combined with strong competition for upscale customers, led banks to develop strategies to capture and hold business from lower-income and minority-customers. One magnet for banks was the astronomically growing market for cross-border remittances, of which banks had a tiny share (about 3% in the early 2000s).[26]

A particular challenge in accessing lower-income financial markets was the high proportion of unbanked people in that market-segment. According to the General Accounting Office (2002), 28 per cent of all individuals and 20 per cent of all households lack bank-accounts, and thus were 'unbanked'. Minorities are overrepresented among the unbanked; but more than half of unbanked US-households are white. This segment offered large potential profits. Underbanked and unbanked households generate $6.2 billion in fees – an annual average of $200 per household, even for the very poor.[27]

So, racial exclusion – the refusal to make loans to minority credit-applicants – was partly replaced by extortionary racial inclusion – providing access to credit to those formerly excluded from it, but only at terms and conditions that are predatory, that is, which involve far higher costs and penalties for non-compliances than 'normal' loans. Banks have moved into these markets by acquiring subsidiaries and then designing special instruments aimed at lower-income and minority-customers they had previously overlooked. These banks then marketed, originated, and distributed these predatory loan-instruments. Since the mid-1990s, these instruments have been growing at a frenetic pace in neighbourhoods historically subject to financial exclusion. These loans often have led to excessive rates of household and firm non-payment, and thus to foreclosures and personal financial distress – well

---

26. Orozco 2004.
27. Katkov 2002.

before the 2007 mortgage-market meltdown. There are two principle categories of these loans: income-based payday-loans and housing-based subprime loans.

The payday-loan: lower-income US-households have more volatile incomes than do other households, and hence need credit to close income-expenditure gaps more frequently than other households.[28] But, in obtaining credit, many such households lack the financial track-record to be fundable for credit-cards or loans.[29] This volatility provides the payday-loan market with its rationale.

The practice of advancing workers a portion of the money they stand to earn from their paychecks has become a common check-cashing service. This form of credit has spread very fast, as has the infrastructure of lenders disbursing it. Unheard of in 1990, now some 22,000 store-locations offer payday loans. These loans have a market-volume of $40 billion in the 37 states that allow this practice.[30] The average fee for a $100 check is $18. In 2001, there were 15,000 stores in the US offering payday-loans, with 70 million transactions and $2.6 billion in fees – $37 per transaction, on average, with $173,310 in fees per store location. Fees from this market reached $4.4 billion in 2005.

Some financial firms are now developing new sources of information which could qualify households for higher levels of credit, over longer time-frames. However, the absence of this information has not inhibited the growth of these credit-markets. The reason it has not is the structural transformation of the markets for lower-income – and ultimately for lower-income and higher-risk – collateralised loans in the US-economy.

Why has the payday-loan sector grown so rapidly? On the credit-supply side, financing is often provided by large bank-holding companies, by investment-banks and hedge-funds (through intermediaries) interested in bringing structured investment-vehicles (see below) to market. On the demand-side, several factors have converged. One is the falling real value of workers' wages, and the increased volatility of wage-earnings. Among payday-customers, some 29 per cent earn less than $25,000 per year, and 52 per cent earn $25–50,000 per year. African Americans and military families are overrepresented. Some 41 per cent are homeowners. There is recurrent use; most customers use

---

28. Gosselin 2004.
29. Information Policy Institute 2005.
30. The payday-lending statistics in this subsection are drawn from Bair 2005.

payday-loans 7–12 times per year. A second, related factor is the ready availability of credit in recent years; this has encouraged even lower-wage workers to take on debt to meet living expenses or to acquire durable consumables.

A final demand-factor concerns changing banking practices. Note that the customer-base for payday-loans does not include the unbanked: payday-loans require checking accounts. Banks are charging increasingly high fees for returned (not sufficient funds or NSF) checks. Combined with these charges are the increasingly high late fees for rent, credit-card, and utility-payments. Some $22 billion in NSF fees and $57 billion in late fees were collected in 2003.[31] That is, the increasing probability of very high fees for being late due to an overdrawn checking account pushes workers toward payday-loans.

Subprime lending: this originated when lenders created predatory mortgages – that is, mortgages with excessively high fees, penalties, and interest-rates – and began to market them to higher-risk households who had restricted access to other sources of credit, especially low-cost credit. Lenders' marketing of these loans focused on redlined areas, and on households that had traditionally been denied access to credit.[32] Initially, most subprime loans were second mortgages. These were attractive to borrowers because they permitted owners of modest homes to gain access to money for whatever financial contingencies were being faced. Funds that could be pulled 'out of a house' ameliorated the deteriorating economic fortunes of worker households, especially the minority-households hit disproportionately hard by deindustrialisation.

Soon, subprime loans were marketed to those seeking to acquire homes. From the viewpoint of community-advocates, these loans' terms and conditions were predatory; for bank-apologists, they were legitimate responses to some home-seekers' special risk-characteristics. In any case, many households formerly excluded from access to longer-term credit – especially lower-income and minorities – were now offered credit on exploitative terms. In 1998, for example, subprime and manufactured housing lenders accounted for 34 per cent of all home-purchase mortgage-applications and 14 per cent of originations. In this same year, subprime and manufactured housing lenders made a fifth of all mortgages extended to lower-income and Latino borrowers, and

31. Bair 2005.
32. See, for example, California Reinvestment Committee 2001.

a third of all those made to African-American borrowers.[33] Subprime lending grew 900 per cent in the period 1993–9, even while other mortgage-lending activity actually declined.[34] A nationwide study of 2000 HMDA data found that African Americans were more than twice as likely as whites to receive subprime loans, and Latinos more than 40–220 per cent more likely.[35]

A set of specialised – and often predatory – lenders emerged, using aggressive business-practices to sell loans. This new class of lenders reflected the drastic changes in this sector. The largest subprime lender, Ameriquest Mortgage Company, began life as Long Beach Savings in 1979. It moved to Orange County, California in 1991, and gave up its banking licence in 1994 and focused instead on retail and wholesale sales of subprime mortgages. In 1999, Long Beach Savings split into two: a public subsidiary, which was sold to Washington Mutual in 1999, becoming that bank's subprime trading arm; and a privately-held subsidiary, Ameriquest, which was forced to settle a consumer-protection lawsuit for $325 million in January 2006 (based on practices in 49 states).[36] A *Washington Post* account of this settlement indicates the character of abuses under subprime lending:

> Under the agreement, Ameriquest loan officers will be required to tell borrowers such things as what a loan's interest rate will be, how much it could rise and whether the loan includes a prepayment penalty. Loan officers who do not make that disclosure will be subject to discipline. The company would also be forbidden from giving sales agents financial incentives for pushing consumers into higher-interest loans or prepayment penalties.[37]

The subprime mortgage-loans and payday-loans already had some common structural features that later opened the door to the broader subprime markets of the 2004–6 period: (1) they were based on some collateral (homes and paychecks), which had value no matter the income-based cash-flows of the economic units to whom these loans were made; (2) they represented higher-risk assets, whose holders could anticipate higher returns in compensation

33. These statistics are drawn from Canner et al. 1999.
34. ACORN 2000.
35. Bradford 2002. See also Staten and Yezer 2004 and McCoy and Wyly 2004.
36. Gittelsohn 2007.
37. Downey 2006.

for these risks; (3) the lenders originating these loans needed to move this paper systematically off their balance-sheets.

What this new set of financial market needed to grow precipitously were customers that would readily buy securities comprised of highly risky loans. The requisite customer-growth would soon come.

6. Pressures and strategic adaptations in 1990s consumer-credit and housing markets

For banks, doing business systematically with lower-income and previously-excluded households required a new consumer-banking business-model. The core concept in this model is that riskier customers can be supplied with credit if the combination of fees and attachable assets is sufficient to permit the overall transaction to pencil out. Since equity in homes represents most households' primary asset, the logic of subprime mortgage-lending is readily grasped. The logic underlying the payday-loan industry is similar – next month's paycheck serves as a guarantee against loss. The success of this new model is evident in the Survey of Consumer Finances: data for the period 1989–2004 shows that households in the two lowest-income quintiles have had surging levels of debt, not paralleled by proportionate increases in asset-levels.

Much of the pressure for debt build-up in this period stemmed from forces in the housing market. The trajectory of federal housing policy for lower-income households was increasingly biased toward home-ownership. The central public-housing programme in the 1980s and 1990s was Section 8 housing, which provided housing rental vouchers to selected qualifying households but did nothing for the supply of affordable rental housing. After 2000, the Bush Administration pushed the idea of universal home-ownership, in part through converting formerly public rental housing into owner-occupied units. The scale of both public low-income rental and homeowner-programmes was far less than the potentially eligible populations. Both the creation of new lower-income credit-channels and the absence of federal programmatic capacity led US-households toward market-based innovations in homeownership-practices.

This growth in the demand for homeownership is evident in the empirical evidence. As Figure 3 shows, after the crisis years of the 1980s, US median household-income rose until 1990; it then declined through 1994, and then grew rapidly again until 2001. Housing prices were also rising; but as Figure 4 shows, the ratio of median home-purchase price-to-median income rose only slightly between 1983 and 2000. Table 1 shows that, as in the 1980s, aggregate real housing prices were at least partially responsive to real income-trajectories. In the 1991–4 period, real median household-incomes fell; real median housing prices rose, but by less than 1 per cent per annum, must more slowly than in the later 1980s. When real incomes grew again in the 1995–9 period, housing prices did too, but a somewhat lower rate.

The US homeownership-rate grew from 64 to 69 per cent between 1994 and 2004 (Figure 3). Figure 5 illustrates, in turn, that while whites' homeownership-rates increased systematically from the mid-1980s onward, African-American and Latino homeownership-rates grew at slightly faster than that for whites. Trends in new home-construction moved the entire market upscale in the 1980s: Figure 4 shows that new-home prices, which were almost at parity with existing-home prices in 1982, rose rapidly to a premium of 28 per cent by

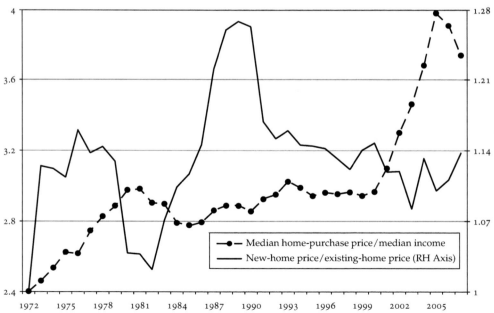

Source: Office of Policy Development and Research, US Department of Housing and Urban Development. US Department of Commerce, Bureau of Economic Analysis.

Figure 4   Housing Price-to-Income Ratio and New-Home/Existing-Home Price-Ratio, 1972–2008

1990. After the early-1990s recession – that is, during the period of minorities' homeownership-rate rising as fast as whites' – the new-home premium fell below 10 per cent.

The increasing strength of housing demand – spurred into hyperdrive by the extortionary inclusion of African-American and Latino homeowners – is traced out in Figure 2. The percentage of existing-houses-for-sale to existing-houses-sold fell systematically from a peak of 68 per cent in 1991 to a low of 33 per cent in 2004; that for new homes fell from 64 to 35 per cent in the same time-period. Subprime mortgages shaped this ever-hotter market: the rise of minority homeownership-rates coincided with a declining new-home premium; and the housing shortage created an environment in which it became as easy to sell an existing home as a new one. The construction-industry boomed, and existing homeowners experienced rapid equity gains.

So much for the demand side. But how about supply? The subprime lending sector has grown so explosively in the past several years precisely because the links required to connect loan-making with the securitisation of diverse,

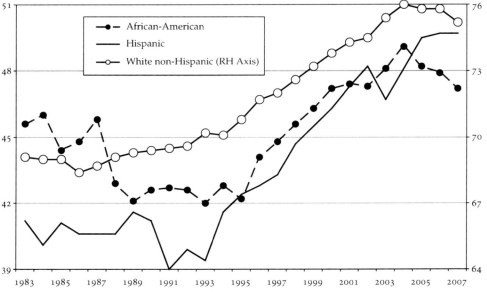

Source: Office of Policy Development and Research, US Department of Housing and Urban Development.

Figure 5   US Homeownership-Rates by Race/Ethnicity, 1996–2007
(Percentage of All Households Who Are Homeowners)

and often risky, credit-claims were put into place. This riskiness, due to ever more adventurous house-price-to-income ratios, paled in comparison with the apparently ceaseless upward rise of housing prices. Wall Street investment-banks channelled an ever-increasing amount of funds to subprime lenders: securitisations in this market already averaged $80 billion annually by 1998 and 1999. Further, Wall Street insurers backed the mortgage-backed securities that subprime lenders sold off into the markets.[38]

The large fees to be made in the loan-origination and securitisation-process, and the ready availability of low-interest money-market funds – linked, in turn, to the macro-economic capital-account dependency of the US-economy – attracted many supply-side players to these markets. This supplier-influx has led to ever more interpenetration between major banking corporations, finance-companies, and subprime lenders. Major banking corporations have undertaken or attempted numerous acquisitions. Some bank holding companies purchased subprime lenders. Citicorp acquired Associates First Capital Corporation, which was then under investigation by the Federal Trade Commission and the Justice Department. In another case, First Union Bancorp bought the Money Store in June 1998 – and then closed it in mid-2000 after it generated massive losses.[39] In 2003, HSBC bought Household International, parent of Household Finance Company, after settling charges that it had engaged in predatory lending. Associates First represented a step toward Citi's goal of establishing its Citifinancial subsidiary as the nation's largest consumer-finance company.[40] In any event, this consumer-lending subsidiary helped to stabilise Citi's cash-flow during a period in which most megabanks' earnings slumped.[41]

So, the 1990s prepared the way for the subprime crisis a decade later. The initial premise of securitisation was the homogenisation of risks. Securitisation centred on borrowers whose risk was low and who were expected to pay. Federal agencies' underwriting underlay a large share of the market. Then, due to heightened financial competition, more relaxed attitudes about risk-taking, and increases in computability, this premise was systematically punctured. Lenders originated and sold off heterogeneous housing-based

---

38. Henriques and Bergman 2000.
39. Berman et al. 2006.
40. Oppel and McGeehan 2000.
41. Sapsford et al. 2001, *Business Week* 2007.

loans, sometimes to borrowers whose longer-term payment prospects were doubtful. The combination of high fees and penalties, along with sufficient pledged collateral, made these loans profitable.

But what the 1990s brought was not just a new housing-finance instrument, the subprime loan, but an increasingly efficient pipeline for originating and distributing risk. Subprime lenders at one end of this pipeline made mortgage-loans and then sold them to banks, which, in turn, manufactured securities that could be held or sold to investors. Before, the mortgage-backed securities built from 'plain vanilla' mortgages had attracted buyers more interested in risk-aversion than return-maximisation. But the structured investment-vehicles (SIVs) into which subprime mortgages were made created higher-risk, higher-return options.[42]

Many different types of collateralised debt, not just subprime mortgages, were combined on the asset side of SIVs. The relative transparency associated with pass-through securities was replaced by opacity. This provided banks an opportunity to move diverse types of debt off their balance-sheets – with fees to be made each step of the way. SIVs found ready funding in the money-markets. High profit-rates left many corporations awash in funds; and the prospect of sustained low nominal interest-rates – linked, as noted above, to the US capital-account surplus – made it seem quite natural to fund SIVs with commercial paper. Indeed, 'asset-backed commercial paper' became com-monplace. Ignoring liquidity-risk, SIVs seemed a sure-fire way to generate interest-margin-based income with minimal – or even no – equity-investment. The next step, soon taken, was for hedge-funds and private-equity funds to get into the game. Whether such SIV-investors were taking on the default-risks implicit in the assets underlying these securities was unclear; indeed, as opacity replaced transparency in the mortgage-backed securities-market, SIV-investors lost track of what risks they were bearing. Further, credit-risk derivatives were often used to shift risks onto third parties.[43] In any case, SIVs quickly became a $400 billion sector. As the *Wall Street Journal* put it, SIVs 'boomed because they allowed banks to reap profits from investments in newfangled securities, but without setting aside capital to mitigate the risk'.[44]

---

42. According to Mollenkamp et al. 2007, the first SIVs were created for Citigroup in 1988 and 1989.
43. *The Economist* 2007b.
44. Mollenkamp, Solomon, Sidel, and Bauerlein 2007.

The third significant shift in the 1990s lay in banks' direct or third-party lending practices in inner-city areas. Previously, banks' reluctance had led to credit starvation in minority and lower-income neighbourhoods. Now, cities were awash with credit. Banks set up or contracted with intermediaries to make and securitise huge volumes of subprime and payday-loans. The same lender might make exploitative loans in some portions of a city, while making prime loans elsewhere. Lenders, banks, and markets came to regard aggressive and even expectationally unsustainable terms and conditions for a subset of their borrowers as normal business-practices. And these practices soon migrated from inner-city areas to the broader markets.

7. The subprime explosion and crisis in the 2000s

Once securities-markets accepted heterogeneous assets not backed by iron-clad underwriting, these markets were set to absorb ever riskier mortgages and other financial claims.[45] As noted above, the demand for residential real estate began to take off in the late 1990s. This asset-boom soon blossomed into a mania: homeowners who had homes wanted bigger ones; those who were not homeowners yet wanted to get into the housing market, even at premium-prices. The fact that many potential home-buyers had neither the income nor savings to support 'plain vanilla mortgages' – which prescribed that no more than 30 per cent of income spent on housing, and 20 per cent down on any mortgage-loan – fed a feeling of desperation, of 'now or never', especially in markets experiencing the fastest price-appreciation.

Lenders' and brokers' successful experience in creating loans for borrowers with very risky parameters suggested the required solution: to create loans tailored to the special risks of those whose income and down-payment profiles had not kept pace with many cities' white-hot housing markets. Since housing prices were rocketing upward, buyers could be given loans for amounts more than 80 per cent of their new homes' prices; or they could be given two loans, one for the 80 per cent – making the loan potentially sellable to FNMA –, and another for the other 20 per cent of the price.

---

45. The failure of Franklin National Bank in 1974 due to incautiously gathering non-homogeneous risks into real-estate investment-trusts, should have served as a warning. See Sinkey 1981.

At the level of macro-aggregates, what triggered the housing market's bubble-phase was the continued expansion of real housing prices even while real incomes stagnated. Table 1 shows that real median household-income declined by 0.21 per cent per annum from 2000 to 2005, while real housing prices rose 5 per cent per annum. Consequently, as Figure 5 shows, the median-housing-price-to-median-income ratio rose rapidly as of year 2000. However, as Figure 3 shows, while median household-income peaked in 2000, the homeownership-rate peaked only in 2004. As Figure 4 shows, African-American and white homeownership-rates both peaked in 2004 (that for Latinos peaked prematurely in 2002 and then rose steadily). The bubble began bursting by 2005: after 2004, unsold inventories of both existing and new homes rose precipitously (Figure 2).

In effect, the concept of subprime was stretched along a different dimension of the mortgage-instrument. Previously, subprime loans went primarily to borrowers who had been shut out of mainstream credit-markets, as Section 5 showed. As of the 2000s, however, subprime also referred to loans made to homeowners unable to support 'plain vanilla' mortgage-packages. These borrowers might be permitted to take on loans at special discount-rates for limited periods of time. To get potential buyers 'into' a home, a loan could be made at a below-market 'teaser'-rate for the first year or two of the mortgage. Any gap between market- and 'teaser'-rates could be amortised, and the entire mortgage refinanced at a risk-adjusted market-rate after the 'teaser'-rate expired. Housing-price appreciation would eventually negate the risks of a 100–per-cent-financed housing purchase; and anticipated income-growth and/or anticipated housing-price growth could, in turn, offset overly burdensome home-payments. Fees and penalty-clauses could be attached as warranted to such paper.

As housing prices and as euphoria about housing-price increases intensified, especially in some regional hot-spots, buyers were more and more forced into 'teaser'-rates, hybrid-ARMs, and so on.[46] But housing-price appreciation so dominated the consciousness of buyers and sellers that the high fees and high expected payments associated with getting into a loan seemed merely what was necessary to get in while the window of opportunity remained cracked open. For certainly, reasoned buyers, future price-increases would

46. Wray 2007, p. 9.

allow the renegotiation of non-viable terms and conditions in two years, when one's 2/28 mortgage-loan 'flipped' from below-market entry-level rate to fixed market-rate.

The rising housing-price/income ratio explains some but not all of the growing demand for subprime mortgage-loans. Mortgage-brokers manufactured some of it themselves. A survey of 2005 and 2006 experience found that 55 and 61 per cent of those acquiring subprime mortgages, respectively, had credit-scores high enough to obtain conventional loans.[47] This study also found that the mortgage-brokers selling these claims earned fees far higher than conventional mortgages would have netted.

On the supply-side of the housing-finance market, funds were plentiful. Macro-structural circumstances remained favourable – the US's current-account remained strongly negative, so that savings continued to flow into the US. The market for mortgage-backed securities, which had been the largest financial securities-market in the world for two decades, was familiar to foreign investors. In particular, many UK and European banks rushed to acquire subprime paper.[48] A strong dollar and low nominal interest-rates negated liquidity-risk.

Other factors spurring supply were banks' strategic shifts toward fee-based income and risk-shedding, analysed above, and hyper-competition among lenders. For example, a recent *Wall Street Journal* article highlighted the 'once-lucrative partnership' between Wall Street and subprime lenders, which according to one insider, involved '...fierce competition for these loans.... They were a major source of revenues and perceived profits for both the investors and the investment banks.'[49] In this article, Jeffrey Kirch, president of a firm that buys home-loans, is quoted as saying: 'The easiest way to grab market share was by paying more than your competitors'. At stake were large prospective income-flows for investment-banks, as well as lucrative management-bonuses. Managing directors in investment-banks averaged total compensation in 2006 of $2.5 million. These inducements led many firms to continue aggressively in these markets even as warning signs loomed.

---

47. Brooks and Simon 2007.
48. See, for example, Mollenkamp, Taylor and McDonald 2007.
49. Anderson and Bajaj 2007.

Subprime-loan volumes exploded in 2004–6, even as the housing boom peaked. In 2001–3 period, mortgage-originations totalled $9.04 trillion, of which 8.4 per cent were subprime loans; and 55 per cent of subprime origina-tions, or $418 billion, were securitised. In the 2004–6 period, total mortgage-originations were the same in nominal terms, $9.02 trillion. However, 19.6 per cent of all originations consisted of subprime loans, of which 78.8 per cent – some $1,391 billion – were securitised.[50] Further, as noted above, the opaque character of SIVs and other vehicles for securitisation led to more types of credit being included on these instruments' balance-sheets. Among these were private-equity funds' bridge-loans for leveraged buyouts, real-estate acquisition-loans, construction-finance, credit-card receivables, and so on.

The onset of the subprime crisis

Like the Asian crisis in 1997, the subprime credit-crisis built momentum through a domino-effect involving interconnected events over a large geo-graphical area. Some 80 subprime mortgage-companies failed in the first seven months of 2007. The big credit-ratings agencies came under pressure to overhaul their methods of assessing default-risk in the US subprime mar-ket.[51] As they did so, banking firms in the US and abroad were affected. On 20 June 2007, Bear Stearns was forced to shut down two subprime funds it operated for its investors.[52] Six weeks later, American Home Mortgage closed its doors.[53] Meanwhile, Countrywide Financial, which had originated about one-sixth of recent US mortgage-loans, descended more and more visibly into crisis.[54]

In August, the German bank IKB was bailed out by Deutschebank and other banks when it could no longer access the money-markets to finance Rhineland Funding, an offshore-vehicle containing $17.5 billion of collateralised debt-obligations, including some US subprime mortgages.[55] Some of the largest banks, such as Goldman Sachs, added fuel to the crisis by continuing to

---

50. These data, from the Mortgage Market Statistical Annual, appear as Table 1 of Wray 2007, p. 30.
51. Pittman 2007.
52. Kelly, Ng, and Reilly 2007.
53. Dash 2007.
54. Hagerty and Richardson 2007.
55. *The Economist* 2007c.

package and sell securities backed by subprime mortgages, even while reducing their exposure to subprime debt on their own balance-sheets.[56] By September, between 16 and 24 per cent of the subprime securities packaged by global banks in 2006 were at least 60 days in arrears – a total of $73.7 billion of 60-day delinquent loans in these securities alone.

In 2008, the situation got successively grimmer. Many homes went into foreclosure. Many of these had been marketed to the formerly racially excluded and built in close proximity to areas historically subject to mortgage-market redlining. That is, even when subprime lending had expanded beyond the inner city in the bubble-period, racial dividing lines in urban land-use had remained in place. So, when the crisis hit, it had a disproportionate impact on minority and lower-income neighbourhoods;[57] minority-households, the most likely to be targeted by subprime lenders, were also most likely to live in neighbourhoods in which subprime-based foreclosure-cycles would cause terrible losses.[58]

Further, short-term credit for subprime paper and SIVs dried up. Consequently, ever more global banks, in the US and abroad, were forced to take subprime paper back onto their balance-sheets, declaring losses in the tens of billions. These banks had to seek out capital-injections even while drastically tightening credit-supply.

8. Conclusion

The meltdown in global banking and credit-markets began when the end of the US housing bubble in 2007 precipitated a rapid increase in mortgage-delinquencies. These mortgages were held in securitised form in portfolios around the world. So payments-difficulties at the base of the financial food-chain led to seismic financial-market eruptions at the top.

One root of the still-unfolding subprime crisis, then, is banks' transformation of their revenue-generation strategies due to macro- and micro-distress

---

56. Anderson and Bajaj 2007. Goldman's new originations equalled $6 billion in the first 9 months of 2007; by December, 15 per cent of these loans were already delinquent by more than 60 days.

57. California Reinvestment Committee et al. 2008.

58. Housing and Economic Rights Advocates and California Reinvestment Coalition 2007.

at the onset of the neoliberal age. This involved separating loan-making from risk-taking, that is, the creation of risk from its absorption. These strategic adaptations, which apparently reduced the overall riskiness of financial intermediation, had a huge collateral impact: banks no longer had to balance the profit potential from loan-making with the default- and liquidity-risks to which loan-making gives rise: a key brake on finance-based expansion was removed.

This strategic re-orientation of banks then transformed the landscape of racial and social exclusion in US credit-markets. A scenario of financial exclusion and loan-denial became a scenario of financial expropriation and loan-making. Households previously denied mortgages were now awarded high-cost, high-risk loans. As direct markets' institutional capacity grew, non-bank lenders joined banks in providing – for a high fee – high-risk, high-cost loans. And, when practices pioneered in predatory loan-making to socially excluded communities were generalised and introduced into the broader housing market, the conditions were created both for the unsustainable explosion of US housing prices and for the unsustainable stretching of the limits of financial-market liquidity.

The third root of the crisis is the long decline in wages of the US working class. As the possibilities of a dignified life based on the wages of labour faded, US-workers' desire to share in the 'American dream' came to include homeownership. But the gap between housing prices and incomes has been widening for two decades (Figure 4). Our analysis of the 1980s showed how US median household-income rose in the 1980s after the crisis then. But analysis of the post-peak subprime period indicates that US median income remains flat (Table 1) even while housing prices have fallen.

Table 1 Percent Changes in US Median Housing and Income, 1974–2007

	Real Median Household-Income	Real Housing Price (New & Existing)	Housing-Price to Income Ratio
1974–1979	0.84	3.55	2.71
1980–1982	−2.02	−1.81	0.22
1983–1984	2.28	0.25	−1.96
1985–1990	1.75	2.15	0.39
1991–1994	−0.19	0.93	1.15
1995–1999	3.08	2.77	−0.30
2000–2005	−0.21	4.97	5.20
2006–2007	0.04	−3.05	−3.09

Source: Department of Commerce, Bureau of Economic Analysis.

This made homeownership more costly and more desirable at the same time. For housing seemed to gain market-value at rates faster than even subprime borrowing rates. In effect, it became workers' means of participating in the speculative gains to which the US-economy had become addicted in the postindustrial age. Ironically, the growing gap between housing price and income was moderated in part through adaptations that both represented and worsened the working class's positional weakness – more two-wage or three-wage households, the perfection of mass housing production-techniques, and the use of non-union labour on construction-sites: all so that working-class households could move into 'affordable' units ever more distant from work-sites and urban centres.

The fourth structural root of the subprime crisis emphasised here is the US macro-economic context. After the chaotic early 1980s, the US's current-account deficit and its status as a global 'safe haven' created ready liquidity for the securitisation-machine. This situation, based ultimately on the unique circumstances of US monetary hegemony, was unsustainable.[59] Here, a second irony emerges. Subprime lending and opaque high-risk securitisation, which was rooted in part in the ready availability of liquidity, reached its high point at precisely the time – June 2004 to July 2006 – in which the Federal Reserve was making a sustained effort to restrict liquidity. The Fed's efforts were over-whelmed by the continuing inflows on the US capital-account; linked to the US's current-account deficit, these inflows seemed out of the central bank's control. When overseas wealth-holders became leery of dollar-based assets generally in the wake of the gathering subprime crisis, the Federal Reserve similarly faced limits in its ability to manage the damage.

In sum, the subprime crisis originates in the perverse interaction between America's legacy of racial discrimination and social inequality, its unique and ultimately uniquely fragile global position, and its hyper-competitive, world-straddling financial sector. To put it provocatively, America's racial chickens have come home to roost in the subprime crisis.

The racial roots of this crisis have also drawn attention in the extended and vigorous debate regarding policy-responses to this crisis. *New York Times* columnists Bob Herbert and Paul Krugman have asserted that racial exclusion underlies the subprime crisis. Other experts have turned this argument on

---

59. Dymski 2008.

its head, by arguing that the Community Reinvestment Act – which, as we have seen, was passed into law in response to banks' racial redlining – forced banks into speculative loan-making.[60] The analysis in this chapter lets us see how profoundly this latter line of reasoning twists the trajectory of history. It is banks' continuation of their historical – if contested – legacy of denying equal credit-market access led to the creation of new instruments of financial expropriation that, once generalised and transported into a raging home-purchase market, has led the banking system and the US-economy to the edge of a very high cliff.

60. See, for example, Calomiris 2008 and Liebowitz 2008.

Chapter Three

On the Content of Banking in Contemporary Capitalism

Paulo L. dos Santos[1]

1. Introduction

By many historical measures, the current financial crisis is without precedent. It originated from neither an industrial crisis nor an equity-market crash. It was precipitated by the simple fact that increasing numbers of largely black, Latino and working-class white families in the US have been defaulting on their mortgages. That this caused Bear Sterns and Lehman Brothers to collapse, bringing the entire financial system to the brink, and continues to generate losses for banking giants like Citibank and UBS, underscores the fundamental changes to the practices, class- and social content of banking that have taken place over the past twenty-five years.

Banking has become heavily dependent on lending to individuals, and the direct extraction of revenues from ordinary wage-earners. It has also become enmeshed with capital-markets, where banks mediate financial-market transactions involving bonds,

1. I would like to thank the participants of the International Workshop on the Political Economy of Financialisation at Kadir Has University in Istanbul, and the participants of the Crisis of Financialisation Conference at SOAS earlier this year. A special acknowledgement is owed to Professor Makoto Itoh for his detailed and prescient comments on this draft. All remaining errors and one-sidedness are my own.

equity, and derivative-assets, and where they increasingly obtain funding. And it increasingly relies on inference-based techniques for the estimation of risk of capital-market instruments and banks' own financial position. The current financial crisis is, in many ways, a crisis of banking as it has emerged through these dramatic changes. Identifying the origins, content and contradictions of contemporary banking is, consequently, an important part of understanding the current crisis, as well as the broader character of contemporary capitalism.

Contemporary banking is very different from the traditional business of taking deposits from corporations and the general public, making loans to enterprises, and making profits from the difference in interest rates between them. It is also different from the 'finance-capital' described within the Marxist tradition by Hilferding in 1910. Nevertheless, Marxist political economy has a unique and important contribution to make to the analysis of the social and historical significance of contemporary banking and its relationship to accumulation. This chapter seeks to make empirical and analytical contributions to this task.

Empirically, it considers macro-level data, centrally from the US, on banking and capital-markets. It also considers in detail the operations of nine of the largest international commercial banks, based on their annual corporate disclosures.[2] These are leading US, European and Japanese banks which, by the end of 2007 collectively controlled more than US$16 trillion in assets across every region of the globe. Even in 2007, when most of them took considerable losses, their average return on equity was still a relatively high 14.87 per cent.

Firm-level inquiry reveals how central lending to individuals has become for the world's largest banking organisations. It also reveals the relative importance of different financial-market mediation-activities, each of which

---

2. The banks examined are Citigroup, HSBC, Bank of America, RBS, Barclays, Santander, BNP Paribas, Dresdner Bank, and Sumitomo Mitsui Financial Group. The first two banks have the most prominent and extensive international operations. The list includes the top two US and top three British commercial banks. Santander is the top bank from Spain, with extensive international operations, notably in Latin America. Dresdner bank was chosen over Deutsche as a representative German bank as the latter is principally an investment bank. BNP Paribas and SMFG are leading French and Japanese banks. See appendix for details on extraction of data from corporate reports.

embodies different social relations. Notably, revenues from fund-management and profits on trading and proprietary accounts appear as important sources of bank-profits, particularly for European banks.

In order to characterise these activities, the chapter advances a series of analytical elements pertaining to the different major functions of contemporary banking, drawing on Marx, Itoh and Lapavitsas, and most directly from Hilferding.[3] Particular attention is given to the characterisation of financial-market mediation-functions. This includes advancing a distinctive appreciation of the social content of capital-markets and investment-banking, building critically on Hilferding's 1910 analysis.

On these bases, the chapter argues that contemporary banking centres, on one hand, on mutually beneficial, arms-length relationships with corporations based on investment-banking services. At the same time, banks have developed historically new, *exploitative* modes of appropriation from the independently secured income of wage-earners. Those have developed in the political climate created by significant class-defeats suffered by the working-class movement, in which the provision of a growing share of necessary goods and services became or remained private.

Private provision of education, housing, and health make access to money a growing requirement for present and future consumption. Against a setting of stagnant real wages and rising income-inequality, this has pushed wage-earners onto financial markets as an integral part of their basic reproduction. Banks mediate access to housing, durable consumer-goods, education, and increasingly health-care, though insurance, mortgage and other individual loans, drawing profits from wage-income that are increasingly central to their operations.

The gradual privatisation of pension-provision has also helped banks develop other avenues of appropriation founded on wage-income. Pension- and other investment-funds have generated rising fee incomes for banks. The associated unprecedented money-inflows into capital-markets have also enhanced the scope for various corporate 'financial-engineering' measures in which banks play a central role. In contrast to the relationship between corporations and banks, these activities bear the mark of the profound social inequality between wage-earners seeking to secure future consumption and

---

3. Marx 1909, Itoh and Lapavitsas 1999, Hiferding 1981.

banks seeking to maximise profits, as glaring and arguably systematic dis-advantages to the former. It may be usefully understood as possessing an exploitative content.

The rest of the chapter proceeds as follows. Section 2 lays out the broad changes to the composition and character of banking incomes and discusses the regulatory, technological and capital-market setting that has shaped them. Section 3 turns to the changes to conventional lending and money-dealing activities of banks. Sections 4 and 5 consider the significance and social content of financial-market mediation-functions performed by banks. Section 4 focuses on fund-management, derivative-assets and proprietary gains. Section 5 offers distinctive Marxist analytical elements for an approach to the social content of capital-markets and traditional investment-banking functions. Section 6 offers a brief concluding discussion.

2. New sources and types of bank income

A number of studies have documented and discussed the changes in banking over the past three decades.[4] The broad empirical contours highlighted by those studies are clear. The income banks receive from interest-rate spreads has steadily diminished in importance. Households have shifted their assets away from bank-deposits in favour of various investment-funds, and the importance of bank-lending to enterprises has fallen significantly. Banks have responded by developing new revenue-streams in fees, commissions and other non-interest gains from activities associated with 'financial-market mediation'. These involve facilitating the participation of others in financial markets through investment-banking services to corporations, brokerage and, increasingly, through the management of investment-, mutual, pension-and insurance-funds for retail-investors. Banks have also increased lending to individuals through consumption-loans and mortgages.

These trends are evident in macro-level data for advanced economies.[5] Bank non-interest income has increased in significance throughout the OECD-countries.

---

4. See Allen and Santomero 1997, 2001, Erturk and Solari 2007, Leyshon and Thrift 1999, Lapavitsas and dos Santos 2008, for instance.
5. The observations here also broadly apply to the other OECD-economies for which comparable data is available. See <www.oecd.org>.

Table 1   Non-Interest Income as Percentage of Total Bank Revenues

	1980	1985	1990	1995	2000	2005
United States	24.9	30.5	30.3	32.1	39.7	40.7
(West) Germany	20.4	20.6	26.8	21.0	35.8	34.2
Spain	14.9	15.6	18.2	23.1	35.8	33.2
France			22.6	45.5	60.9	62.2

Calculated from OECD Bank Income Statement and Balance Sheet Statistics

Bank-lending has correspondingly declined in importance. It has also changed in composition, shifting from lending to real-sector firms towards individual consumption- and mortgage-loans. In Germany, non-mortgage bank-lending to non-banks declined from 68.2 per cent of GDP in 1972 to 26.8 per cent in 2003. In Britain, resident banks' lending to individuals rose from 11.6 to 40.7 per cent of total lending between 1976 and 2006, with lending to financial intermediaries also rising from 20.3 to 32.4 per cent. In the US, bank-lending to commercial and industrial enterprises fell from 10.8 to 8.2 per cent of GDP. Although belated, the corresponding fall in Japan has been sudden, with bank-lending to non-financial enterprises moving from 61 per cent of GDP at the end of 1997 to 39.2 per cent in the autumn of 2007.[6]

2.1. *The rise of the institutional investor*

A number of interrelated processes and innovations have created the context for these changes. Technical innovation has been instrumental in the orientation of banks to individual credit. Credit-scoring methods have made mass retail-lending possible by yielding quantitative (and problematic) estimates of the creditworthiness of individual borrowers, and of large, securitised pools of loans to individuals. Technological change has also created new money-dealing services, such as ATMs and ebanking, whose costs banks appear to have been passed on to retail-depositors.[7]

State policy in favour of financial liberalisation, and secular changes in the financial behaviour of corporations and households, have been particularly important. Most directly, the relaxation and repeal of Glass-Steagall restrictions

---

6. Percentages calculated from Bank of England, US Flow of Funds, Financial Accounts for Germany, Bank of England and Bank of Japan data.
7. See Lapavitsas and dos Santos 2008.

in the US, and the acceptance of the provision of various insurance-services by banks in Europe have widened the scope for commercial-bank intervention into capital-markets.

More fundamentally, the rising importance of corporations' own retained earnings, and the gradual privatisation of pension-provision have had a major impact on both sides of capital-markets. On the demand-side, increased volumes of money have sought to buy securities. On the supply-side, the scope for capital-gains generated from various 'financial engineering' measures has increased. And, across both sides, the scope for fee and other income from financial-market mediation has been greatly enhanced.

As state-pensions have been eroded across the OECD-countries, trillions of dollars entered capital-markets in the form of various retirement-related investment-funds. The late 1970s and early 1980s saw a raft of measures that both degraded public pensions and encouraged private-retirement savings in the US. Access to tax-sheltered Individual Retirement Accounts was steadily broadened in the 1970s, and 401(k) plans were implemented in the early 1980s. The 1981–3 Greenspan Commission on Social Security endorsed these measures and led the charge against the quality of public pensions by imposing income-tax on benefits over a very low level.[8] As a result, the holdings of pension- and mutual funds by US-households exploded, from a post-war average around 40 per cent of GDP to the 120–140 per cent average of the last ten years.

Japanese households also accumulated significant financial assets over the same period, including a high level of insurance-reserves, which include pension-savings

Table 2 Japan Household Mutual-Fund Holdings and Insurance-Reserves, Percentage of GDP

1980	1985	1990	1995	2000	2005
21.8	36.2	54.6	72.3	83.5	88.3

Calculated from OECD Data

---

8. See Greenspan Commission 1983 and Investment Company Institute 2006, 2007.

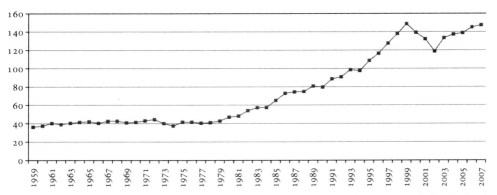

Calculated from Flow of Funds of the United States, Board of Governors of the Federal Reserve System

Figure 1   **US Household Holdings of Pension and Mutual Fund, Percentage of GDP (1946–2007)**

Similarly, across a range of OECD-countries, total holdings of open- and closed-end investment-funds and insurance-reserves rose from 41.9 to 73.4 per cent of GDP between 1995 and 2005.[9] By 2006, these increases had helped take the worldwide total of assets in managed funds to a total of US$63.8 trillion, more than twice the combined GDP of the US and EU for that year.[10]

The rise of these institutional funds created new 'buy-side' opportunities for banks. They could earn fees from directly managing investment-funds. In addition, they could earn fees by assisting independent insurance-, hedge- and other investment-funds in their securities-transactions.

2.2. Changes in corporate financial behaviour

The new funds also helped create new 'sell-side' revenues for banks by fueling a tremendous increase in capital-market issuance, particularly in the US. The issuance of US corporate liabilities, notably bonds, grew in tandem with new money-inflows, rising from a postwar-average of around four per cent of GDP to well over 30 per cent in 2001.

Evidence for US non-financial corporations suggests this increase in the issuance of marketable corporate liabilities signalled fundamental changes in

---

9. Figures calculated from OECD data for Belgium, Canada, Denmark, France, Germany, Italy, Japan, Netherlands, Spain and the United Kingdom.
10. Watson Wyatt 2007.

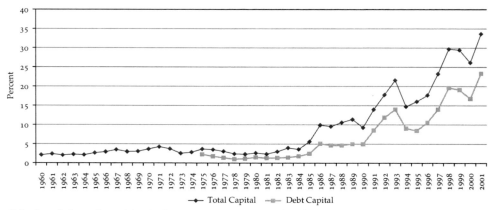

—◆— Total Capital —■— Debt Capital

Calculated from Securities Industry Association Factbook, 2002

Figure 2   US Corporate Capital Raised as Percentage of GDP (1960–2001)

their relationship with capital-markets. Since the early 1970s, their net fixed investment has tended to fall, with cyclical fluctuations, in relation to profits. In the 25 years to the end of 1984, the net fixed investment of US non-financial corporations averaged 23.7 per cent of their actual profits. In the 25 years that followed, they averaged 17.7 per cent, despite the dot.com investment-boom of 1995 to 2000. In this context, the increase in corporate-security issuance was not associated with increased productive investment, which could increasingly be funded with internal funds.

Instead, it was associated with a dramatic increase in 'financial engineering' operations aimed to secure capital-gains. As bond-issuance grew in importance for non-financial corporations,[11] its relationship with net equity-flows underwent a fundamental structural change. In pure statistical terms, bond-finance flows displayed a clear positive correlation with equity-finance flows between 1946 and 1983, suggesting they were alternative sources of funds. Since 1983, the correlation become negative, as did net equity-flows.

In words, the increased corporate bond-borrowing over this period appears to be closely related to the withdrawal of equity, which typically takes the form of 'financial-engineering' operations like share-buybacks, private-equity purchases, mergers and acquisitions. These operations have become increasingly

---

11. Rising from 46.7 per cent of their borrowing in 1983 to 70 per cent by 2007.

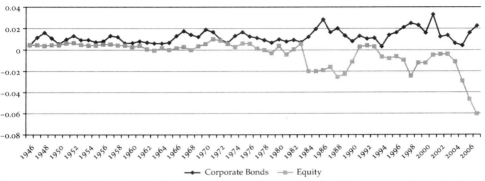

Calculated from Flow of Funds of the United States, Board of Governors of the Federal Reserve System

Figure 3   US Non-Financial Corporations' Net Finance-Flows Percentage of GDP (1951q1–2008q2)

important to the relationship of non-financial corporations and financial markets, at least in the US. As discussed in detail below, the potential capital-gains achieved by such operations are greatly enhanced in a setting of increasing volumes of money entering capital-markets. Commercial banks have developed significant revenue-streams by managing, advising, underwriting and financing these financial operations.

Through all these changes, banks have been able not only to maintain, but actually to increase the significance of their profits in the advanced economies.

3. Economic relations of bank-lending and money-dealing

Changes in banking operations and social relations have included important changes in bank-lending and money-dealing functions. Marxist political economy has long offered compelling accounts of the nature and social

Table 3   Bank-Profits as Percentage of GDP

Country	1980	1988	2005
United States	0.72	0.74	1.62
(West) Germany	0.53	0.81	1.35
Spain	0.84	1.42	1.77
France		0.96	1.53

Calculated from OECD Bank Income Statement and Balance Sheet Statistics

content of these banking activities.[12] Those can be readily extended to offer insights into the particular forms these activities take in contemporary banking: lending to individuals, and rising banking and credit-card account-fees paid by retail-bank clients.

Through both channels, banks have come to mediate increasing proportions of consumption, drawing revenue from the independently secured wage-income of their clients. As such, they constitute historically novel avenues for the financial expropriation of wage-earners. This section tackles these changes in bank-behaviour, offering an empirical and analytical discussion of the importance and distinct social content of these new channels of appropriation.

3.1. *Lending to enterprises*

Classical-Marxist analysis of bank-lending is founded on the distinctive concept of interest-bearing (or loanable) capital. Interest-bearing capital is a peculiar type of capital that is distinct from industrial and commercial capital. It originates from idle pools of money-capital that appear in the first instance over the course of the circuit of industrial and merchant-capital. Such pools are mobilised and transformed into loanable money-capital by the credit-system, which channels it back into circulation in the form of loans to capitalist enterprises.[13] Trading in interest-bearing capital involves credit-relations, that is, the advance of value against a promise of repayment with interest. In this light, banks are capitalist enterprises that specialise in all aspects of dealing in interest-bearing capital, accruing revenues from the difference in the price paid for deposits and that paid on loans.

Loanable money-capital receives not profits but repayments with interest. To Marx,[14] the level of the rate of interest contains an element of irrationality: it is the price – or expression of value in money – of a future flow of money. It also reveals no underlying socio-economic relationship or inherent material aspect of social reproduction, not least because it is not the price of a produced commodity. The rate of return on loanable money-capital is determined simply through the interaction of supply and demand. To Marx, competition

---

12. Best developed in Hilferding 1981.
13. See Itoh and Lapavitsas 1999.
14. Marx 1894. See Part 5.

between buyers and sellers, however, tends to maintain the rate of interest between zero and the rate of profit during ordinary periods. Their relative detachment from the material realities of production makes relations defined over loanable money-capital highly susceptible to the influence of broader patterns of socio-political power.[15]

In lending to capitalist enterprises, the payment of interest is generally a share of the profit generated by capital applied to production or circulation of commodities. At the broadest level, the systematic basis for the payment of interest in this context is the increased turnover of total capital achieved by the mobilisation of idle money and its application to functioning circuits of capital through lending. More concretely, individual firms will be able to increase the returns on their own capital by leveraging it through borrowing, so long as the return on applied capital exceeds the rate of interest. Finally, given that debt-holders must be paid in order to avoid bankruptcy, high levels of debt may be used as a lever to keep enterprise-costs down, most often by lowering or keeping down total wage-payments.[16]

Under normal conditions, loanable money-capital advanced to a capitalist enterprise will help generate the source of its own repayment with interest, by circulating in the borrower's circuit and expanding through the appropriation of surplus-value. Finally, the relationship between capitalist lender and borrower is at this level of abstraction one between social equals who both enter the transaction on the basis of a profit-maximising calculus. An important expression of this equality is the hiring of financial officers, whose very jobs are to ensure the firm secures outside finance on the most advantageous terms possible. The social relations defined by lending to individuals are fundamentally different in most of these regards.

3.2. *Lending to individuals*

Lending to individuals has became a major part of banks' overall lending activities. This is evident for the banks surveyed here, particularly the top two US-banks.

---

15. Lapavitsas 2003.
16. This appears to be an increasingly common practice, particularly in firms controlled by private-equity groups aiming for fairly quick gains in market-capitalisation.

Table 4   Loans to Individuals as Percentage of Total Loan-Portfolio, Dec 2006

HSBC	Citigroup	B of A	RBS	Barclays	Paribas	Dresdner	SMFG
40.5	77.7	76.3	24.0	44.0	33.0	20.1	26.8

Yet, even these figures understate the importance of this type of lending for the world's largest financial groups. The very organisation of Citibank, HSBC and Bank of America reveals their orientation to individual credit. Citibank's 'Global Consumer' business-segment generated profits of US$12.1 billion, or 56 per cent of all profits, in 2006. Revenues from credit-cards and consumer-lending stood at US$13.5 billion, or 31.6 per cent of all revenues. That same year HSBC's 'Personal Financial Services' segment, which focuses on consumption- and mortgage-credit, generated US$9.5 billion in profits, 42.9 per cent of the total, ahead of commercial and investment-banking divisions, which accounted for 27.3 and 26.3 per cent of profits respectively. Central to this performance is HSBC's credit-card network of over 120 million cards worldwide. Bank of America's 'Global Consumer and Small Business' segment, which focuses centrally on consumption- and mortgage-credit and retail-accounts, accounted for 65.6% of net interest income that year.

This type of lending has a distinctly *exploitative* social content. Money loaned out to individuals for consumption or mortgages does not ordinarily generate the value from which it is to be repaid with interest.[17] Interest-payments are generally made from subsequent wage-receipts by borrowers, representing an appropriation of value borrowers have secured independently of the loan. Recent innovations in consumer-lending involving the international operations of banks like HSBC and Citibank offer a congealed expression of this direct appropriation. Along with other banks across Latin America, these banks offer wage- and pension-linked loans that often include a legal agreement by the borrower's employer or the state to deduct loan-repayments directly from payroll.

At least two concrete factors condition the exploitative character of lending to individuals. First, the relationship is profoundly unequal. It involves on

---

17. The obvious and partial exception to this relates to residential real-estate bubbles, which open the possibility for temporary leveraged capital-gains in housing assets for some households. The instability, inequity and destructive power of this type of bubble needs no explanation at this point.

one hand a specialist in managing money flows trying to maximise profits, on the other an ordinary wage-earner trying to secure access to consumption. A range of patterns deemed 'irrational' by mainstream-economic analysis follow, including the tendency for consumers to continue using the first card they ever obtained, regardless of its comparative rates.[18] Also, lending rates are often 10 to 20 percentage-points above base-rates. The high relative profitability of this type of credit suggests high rates of interest do not arise from lower repayment-rates. HSBC, for instance, generated 42.8 per cent of its profits from lending to individuals and related fees in 2006, while allocating only 29.4 per cent of its total assets to such activities. Significant economies of scale in credit-scoring methods compound these effects, reducing the scope for competition.[19]

Second, the scope for exploitation through lending to individuals has increased in the past two decades. The privatisation of provision for a number of basic social necessities has increasingly forced ordinary individuals into debt, transferring growing shares of their incomes to banks and other financial enterprises. The most obvious example is housing, where provision for the working class and poor has become synonymous with facilitating private ownership through the development of mortgage-securitisation markets. As Table 5 shows, mortgage-lending accounts for a very high fraction of lending to individuals for these banks.[20]

Another significant item is education, where growing costs have increasingly fallen directly on individual students and their families across a range of countries. This has opened yet another avenue for direct exploitation by banks. In 2006, Citibank reported US$220 million in profits from its US student-loans division alone.

Credit-cards are another important part of this lending. And, here, banks in the US moved aggressively to concentrate the industry as it grew in size

Table 5 Mortgage-Loans as Percentage of Total Loans to Individuals, Dec 2006

HSBC	Citigroup	B of A	RBS	Barclays	Paribas	Dresdner	SMFG
53.6	33.1	59.1	72.9	73.0	N/A	33.3	98.1

18. Gruber and McComb 1997 point to evidence of this for the US-economy.
19. Mester 1997.
20. These figures include home-equity withdrawals, which are best understood as consumer-credit. Even in Britain, where such withdrawals were exceptionally high, they never amounted to more than 20 per cent of mortgage-credit.

and profitability in the 1990s. In 1995, they held no more than 25 per cent of credit-card receivables in the US.[21] As late as 1999, the top ten US-issuers controlled 55 per cent of the market; many of them were independent credit-card companies.[22] Since then, large banks bought their way into dominant market-share, acquiring Associates, Bank One, British-based MBNA, and Providian. After 2004, the top ten US-issuers controlled over 90 per cent of the market, and counted only one independent, non-bank enterprise.[23]

The broader significance of this orientation to individual lending cannot be overstated. In the US, against a background of stagnant real wages, the financial obligations of households is estimated to have increased from 15.36 to 19.35 per cent of disposable income between 1980 and 2007.[24] The volume of transfers from households to the financial sector on this account is unprecedented. And, as the current financial crisis shows, this lending has introduced a distinct, new source of instability to financial markets.

3.3. *Money-dealing fees*

Banks have always earned income from the plain handling of money, such as operating the payments-system, transmitting money abroad and undertaking foreign-exchange transactions. Banks are money-dealers, or commercial enterprises that specialise in managing money-flows and hoards.[25] Money-dealing and account-related fees are very important sources of income for contemporary banks. They have also generated considerable controversy, including in Britain, where the Office of Fair Trading has for a number of years been trying to curb overdraft- and related bank-fees widely perceived to be excessive and opaque. The figures for fee income from card- and account-services for the surveyed banks tell their own story, particularly for Bank of America and British banks.

---

21. Allen and Santomero 2001.
22. Land, Mester, and Vermilyea 2007.
23. JP Morgan, Citigroup, Bank of America, the independent Capital One, HSBC and Washington Mutual held the top seven spots at the time. See Akers et al. 2005.
24. See Federal Reserve, Household Debt Service and Financial Obligations Ratio.
25. See Lapavitsas 2007.

Table 6   Card and Other Account Service-Charges, 2006[26]

Bank	2006		2007	
	US$ billion	Revenue-Share	US$ billion	Revenue-Share
HSBC	9.00	12.8%	10.86	12.4%
Citigroup	6.78	7.6%	7.22	8.8%
Bank of America	22.51	30.5%	22.99	33.8%
RBS	9.1	17.7%	10.08	16.2%
Barclays	11.10	27.9%	12.73	27.6%
BNP Paribas	2.53	7.2%	3.07	7.2%
Dresdner	0.33	3.9%	0.35	4.7%
Santander	1.53	5.5%	1.95	5.7%
SMFG	1.58	9.6%	n/a	

Bank of America and Citigroup together received almost US$30 billion in fees from money-dealing services to individual accounts in 2007. In Britain, Barclays received more than a quarter of its revenues in 2007 from banking and credit-fees, a slight decrease in significance in relation to 2006, when the British Office of Fair Trading implemented rules limiting late and overdraft-fees.[27] Together with HSBC it made out with a total of US$23.607 billion in fees from money-dealing activities in 2007.

An important part of these revenues relates to credit to individuals. Overdraft-charges, late-payment fees, credit-card charges, etc are levied as fees but are part of consumer-lending. Bank of America attributed the significant rise in its non-interest income between 2005 and 2006 to its purchase of British-based credit-card issuer MBNA, which resulted in increases in excess-servicing, cash-advance, and late fees. Similarly, Furnace reports that total US late credit-card fees rose from insignificant levels in 1990 to over US$1 billion in 1996, and to almost US$9 billion in 2003.[28] As such, they should also be understood as exploitative.

Other account-related fees relate to account-management and other money-dealing services. Some of these are new and relate to new access-services,

---

26. See appendix for explanation of categories used in different corporate reports to obtain all data reported in this section. The figure given in this table for RBS also includes retail-fee revenues not associated with money-dealing.

27. Shareholders can be reassured that the ensuing losses in revenue were at least partially made up for with growth in Barclaycard International. See Barclays 2008, p. 30.

28. Furnace 2004.

such as ATMs, phone and internet-banking facilities. Banks have incurred significant fixed costs in establishing these new facilities, and their introduction is yet to translate into reductions in overhead-costs. Bank-clients have become heavy users of the new technologies, increasingly using cards and making frequent ATM-withdrawals to access consumption.[29] Growing money-dealing fees, thus, may in part amount to payments by ultimate users of new, expensive, technologies. But their persistence and opacity, the magnitudes involved, and their intrusion into the very process of consumption suggest the presence of exploitative elements in them.

While further research is necessary on this particular account, it is clear that, in both lending and money-dealing services, banks have re-oriented to private-wage income as a source of revenues. The resulting relations contain important exploitative elements. Significant as the resulting profits are, they do not exhaust the current scope for bank-appropriation of wage-earnings. The growing scope of financial-market mediation-activities have afforded banks additional avenues for bank-profits grounded on wages. The next two sections turn to those activities and the social content of contemporary capital-markets.

4. Financial-market mediation

Facilitating access to capital-markets has emerged as an important activity for commercial banks over the past twenty years. As Table 7 shows for 2006, revenues from these activities are very important for the surveyed banks, particularly European ones. The nine banks grossed US$113 billion on this account that year.

These revenues arise from a range of activities, from conventional investment-banking functions of underwriting, brokerage and corporate

Table 7 Revenues from Financial-Market Mediation as Percentage of Total Revenues, 2006

HSBC	Citi	B of A	RBS	Barclays	Paribas	Sant'dr	Dresd'r	SMFG
19.5%	14.6%	16.6%	30.5%	37.8%	58.1%	19.0%	50.8%	6.6%

---

29. See Berger and Mester 2003 and Lapavitsas and dos Santos 2008.

advisory services to investment- and insurance-fund management and the issuance and dealing in derivate assets. Associated with all these activities are the increasingly significant capital-gains made by banks on their trading and own accounts.

The view motivated in the next two sections is that, through these functions, banks appropriate fractions of existing loanable money-capital ultimately owned by the mass of all investors. As with ordinary lending, the social character of the relationship banks have with capitalist clients is fundamentally different from that of their relationship with retail-savers. In the current setting, there is scope for systematic mutual gains in arms-length relationships between investment-banks and corporations and other financial intermediaries. Those gains are ultimately funded by flows of loanable money-capital owned by the mass of investors, who are increasingly ordinary savers. In contrast, the relationship between banks and average retail-investors appears in the present context as exploitative, as banks systematically appropriate value by mediating future retirement-consumption.

In order to establish these points it is necessary to characterise the functioning of capital-markets and the intervention in them by banks. This requires the extension of existing Marxist theory. No significant Marxist contribution has been made to this analysis in the hundred years since Hilferding's 1910 seminal work. And despite its many insights, *Finance Capital* presents problems in its approach to the concept of *founder's profit* as well as in the contemporary relevance of its core concept of *finance-capital*, both of which lie at the heart of Hilferding's conceptualisation of the integration of corporations, capital-markets and investment-banks.

Section Five below offers initial analytical elements of a Marxist approach to the contemporary form of those social relations. Before that, this section documents the relative importance of revenues from fund-management, proprietary gains, and derivatives-trading for top international banks.

4.1. *Fund-management*

As already mentioned, managed funds held a total of US$63.8 trillion in assets at the end of 2006. Even small management-fees on such volumes can lead to appropriations of very large volumes of loanable money-capital. In the US alone, mutual-fund management-fees have grown considerably since 1980.

Table 8 Total Mutual-Fund Fees Paid by Holders in US, US$ billion

1980	1985	1990	2000	2001	2002	2003	2004	2005	2006
0.0	0.2	1.1	3.4	11.0	8.9	9.1	10.3	10.6	11.8

Source: Investment Company Institute

In the US, investment-banks and brokerage-houses were the first firms to profit from the new mass-retail investment-funds. In 1980, the top ten New York investment-banks earned less than one per cent of their revenues from asset-management fees. By 2004, top investment-banks earned 7.5 per cent of their revenues from such fees.[30] After the 1988 partial relaxation of Glass Steagall restrictions, US commercial banks were offering mutual-fund shares, albeit selling them for an 'administrative fee' and not an 'underwriting commission' or 'brokerage fee'.[31] In 1989, commercial banks already had 7 per cent of US mutual-fund assets under their management. By 1995, this had risen to 15 per cent.[32] Worldwide, the nine banks surveyed and their financial-group partners controlled at least 10.2 per cent of the entire managed-fund market in 2006, a share on par with the combined total for investment-banks UBS, Credit Suisse, JP Morgan, Goldman Sachs, and Deutsche.[33] The importance of these activities is evident in the banks' revenue-figures.

Table 9 Fund-Management Commissions and Fees

Bank	2006		2007	
	US$ billion	Revenue-Share	US$ billion	Revenue-Share
HSBC	2.98	4.2%	2.59	3.1%
Citigroup	1.44	1.6%	1.97	2.4%
Bank of America	4.21	5.7%	3.38	5.0%
RBS	9.1	17.7%	10.08	16.2%
Barclays	2.83	7.1%	3.58	7.8%
BNP Paribas	2.37	6.8%	2.91	6.8%
Dresdner	0.42	4.9%	0.45	6.1%
Santander	2.24	8.0%	2.59	7.6%

---

30. See Morrison and Wilhelm 2007
31. McGrath 1989.
32. Neely 1995.
33. Insurance companies and independent intermediaries controlled 50 per cent at the end of that year. Calculated from Watson Wyatt 2007.

The revenue-share is broadly higher for banks operating in Europe, where banks and insurance-companies overwhelmingly control the market. Independent funds still maintain a significant market-share in the US.[34]

Mutual-fund holdings, at least in the US, are widespread among middle-class professionals as well as ordinary working-class wage-earners. As of 2006, 53 per cent of households owning mutual-fund shares had a total annual income below US$75,000; 28 per cent earned less than the median of approximately US$50,000.[35] The attraction of mutual funds for small holders of loanable money-capital, for whom direct access to capital-markets is too costly, time-consuming, or complicated, is access to rates of return higher than those available through commercial bank-deposits or mostly safe government-securities. Yet the social realities of the relationship cannot be escaped. Retail-investors are various types of wage-earners approaching it on the basis of securing future (typically retirement-) consumption. Fund-managers are well-connected financial professionals seeking to maximise profits.

The results are startling. The *Economist* (1 March, 2008) has reported on research by top US fund-management firm Vanguard showing that, between 1980 and 2005, the S&P 500 share-index returned 12.3 per cent per year on average. Over the same period, the average equity mutual fund yielded only 10 per cent. The average investor gained only 7.3 per cent on average per year, largely due to the strong tendency of retail-investors to buy high and sell low. The return realised by the average equity mutual-fund investor is not much higher than rates available for long-term savings-deposits. Over the same period, US six-month T-bills yielded an average 6.00 per cent, while US municipal and local government 20-year bonds yielded an average 6.92 per cent.[36]

The significance of these differences can be illustrated by considering a hypothetical investment of $100 made in 1980.[37] If it were invested in safe T-bills, by 2005 the investor would hold $454.94. In contrast, had it been invested in

---

34. See BCG 2003.

35. Investment Company Institute 2007. For reference, in May 2007, a household with a full-time assembly-line worker and a full-time teaching assistant, each making average earnings, would have earned US$ 49,300. See Bureau of Labor Statistics, <www.bls.gov>.

36. Calculated with monthly data from Federal Reserve's Selected Interest Rates.

37. Assuming each instrument paid its average annual return over the period every year.

S&P index-securities, it would have grown to $2,041.14. The total premium for investing in equity over T-bills over this period stood, thus, at $1,559.20. Now consider a wage-earner hoping to save for retirement who tried to take advantage of those potential gains by investing $100 in an equity mutual fund in 1980. Earning only the average return received by equity mutual-fund investors over this period, her investment would have only grown to $624.59 by 2005. This represents a gain over the safe T-bill investment of $169.65, or a mere 10.9 per cent of the total potential gains from equity-investment!

The remaining 89.1 per cent were appropriated by fund-managers and other financial-market firms. This includes appropriation through commissions and fees on investment-funds as well as the trading and proprietary gains discussed below. Unsurprisingly, fund-management is remarkably profitable. In an international survey of money-fund managers' performance in the lean year of 2002,[38] Boston Consulting Group 2003 found that 64 per cent of the funds reported pre-tax profit-margins above 20 per cent. A full 42 per cent of the funds reported profit-margins higher than 30 per cent. Funds targeting retail-investors were reportedly the most profitable.[39]

Although the thought-experiment pursued here is no substitute for more comprehensive empirical study, its results suggest these activities have a strong exploitative element, particularly given the high profitability of fund-management. By providing pension-savings services that used to be provided by the state, fund-managers mediate future consumption and appropriate loanable money-capital originating in the wages of ordinary retail-investors. As discussed in Section 5 below, the bases for these systematic flows of value arising in the sphere of exchange in capital-markets ultimately lie in the fundamental class-differences between retail-investors on one hand, and banks and corporate managers on another.

4.2. Proprietary trading

Commissions and fees from fund-management are only one of the ways in which banks performing investment-banking and fund-management services can profit at the expense of investors, particularly retail ones. Investment-

---

38. Including seven of the top ten fund-managers by asset, plus another 33 who collectively controlled over one-fifth of the world-market.

39. Morrison and Wilhelm 2007 discuss extensively the significant economies of scale present in retail investment-fund management.

banking and fund-management activities naturally pose opportunities for banks to make capital-gains on securities. Underwriting requires banks to make investments in the securities being issued. Brokers often stand in as counterparty for client-transactions with volumes that could alter market-prices, in which case banks charge clients a margin on the security's current price. And banks increasingly invest in the companies they advise, on which they have intimate knowledge.[40] Finally, when retail-investors buy high and sell low, the counterparty to the transaction is the bank's trading account. To the extent that the bank possesses better knowledge about capital-markets and has the financial clout to withstand and take advantage of even moderate downturns, it will profit handsomely from such transactions.

This is a controversial issue, as it is rightly perceived to pose potential conflicts of interest between the bank and its clients, and to be fertile ground for the manipulation of markets at the expense of other investors.[41] Banks are generally reluctant to report which transactions are carried out for clients and which are carried on a principal basis. Further complicating matters, this type of gain can accrue not only on listed own investment, but also on securities held for trading as part of brokerage-services for both institutional and retail-clients. The combined figures for gains on those accounts gives a good sense of the importance of this type of revenue for commercial banks.

Table 10   Own and Trading Account-Gains

Bank	2006		2007	
	US$ billion	Revenue-Share	US$ billion	Revenue-Share
HSBC	8.86	12.6%	13.89	15.9%
Citigroup	5.76	6.4%	−8.00	
Bank of America	5.57	7.5%	−3.92	
RBS	11.48	22.2%	12.39	19.9%
Barclays	8.42	21.2%	9.96	21.6%
BNP Paribas	11.22	32.0%	14.17	33.4%
Dresdner	3.57	41.7%	−0.66	
Santander	2.70	9.6%	4.10	12.1%
SMFG	1.08	6.6%	n/a	
UBS	10.97	33.2%	−6.96	
Goldman Sachs	25.56	67.9%	31.23	67.9%

---

40. See Morrison and Wilhelm 2007.

41. See, for instance, Blackburn 2006 for accounts of a number of instances of market-manipulation.

Collectively, the nine banks surveyed made profits of US$58 billion in 2006 from such gains. For its part, Goldman Sachs made over US$25 billion on this account that year, more than enough to cover the employee-compensation bill of just over US$16 billion.[42]

The sub-prime crisis also highlighted the importance of these activities. While some of the surveyed banks suffered losses in outright mortgage and other consumer-loans, centrally in US-markets, the main impact on these banks took place through their trading-account holdings of subprime-mortgage CDOs. The 2007 trading-account losses in credit or structured products for Citigroup, Bank of America and Dresdner stood at US$ 21.806 billion, 5.176 billion, and 468 million, respectively. While posting net overall trading-account gains, RBS, Barclays, and HSBC registered net trading losses in credit-instruments amounting to US$2.861 billion, 823 million, and 419 million. Some of these losses were associated with holdings for trading, as these banks mediated purchases by many hedge-funds investing in subprime-mortgage CDOs.[43] But the sheer volume of losses suggests these holdings were to a significant extent proprietary in that they were motivated by the hope of returns on holding these assets.

4.3. *Derivatives*

Investment- and commercial banks have engaged heavily in issuing, trading, and market-making for derivative-assets. Markets for over-the-counter (OTC) interest-rate and foreign-exchange derivatives have grown tremendously in the past twenty years, reaching almost US$400 trillion in notional amounts outstanding in June of 2007, according to the Bank for International Settlements. Although insignificant as recently as the end of last century, the volume of credit-default swaps has also increased dramatically in the past seven years.

Table 11 Credit-Default Swaps, Notional Amounts Outstanding at Year-End, US$ Trillion[44]

2001	2002	2003	2004	2005	2006	2007
0.92	2.19	3.78	8.42	17.10	34.42	42.58

Sources: International Swaps and Derivatives Association Market Survey, BIS

---

42. For an average of just under US$622,000 per employee.
43. Dodd 2007.
44. Except in 2007, for which the end of June figure is given.

Banks were naturally placed to lead the way as derivative-markets developed. They were the first enterprises affected by the increased risks posed by interest- and exchange-rate liberalisation starting in 1973. They became pioneers in deploying hedging techniques with interest-rate and foreign-exchange derivative-contracts as part of their own risk-management. It is difficult to identify the revenues banks raise from issuing these assets and gains they make on their trading accounts as they are not reported separately. What is clear is that six of the nine commercial banks surveyed have prominent market-positions. According to Emm and Gay, Citigroup, Bank of America, BNP Paribas and RBS have been recently among the top seven dealers of derivative-assets worldwide. HSBC and Barclays also have a solid presence in US-markets.[45]

The investment-banking functions of these banks naturally placed them in a position to sell derivative-contracts to corporate clients. As discussed below, those assets may help improve capital-market perceptions of a corporation's liabilities, thus lowering their cost of capital and creating the basis for the payment of issuance-fees. Despite the fact that non-financial corporations make heavy use of these assets,[46] financial intermediaries account for the bulk of OTC-markets, particularly for credit-default swaps.

Table 12   Selected OTC-Derivatives Dealers in United States by Market-Share, June 2007

Bank	US, 2007	Ranking
JP Morgan	51.3%	1
Citigroup	20.7%	2
Bank of America	19.5%	3
HSBC	2.9%	4
Wachovia	2.7%	5
ABN Amro	0.8%	13
Barclays	0.4%	19

US Office of the Comptroller of the Currency, Quarterly Report on Bank Derivatives Activities

Table 13   OTC-Derivative Contracts with Financial Firms, Percentage of Total, June 2007

Foreign Exhange	Interest-Rate	Credit-Default Swaps
78.8%	86.9%	97.9%

Source: Calculated from BIS Semiannual OTC derivatives statistics

---

45. Emme and Gay 2005.
46. The International Swaps and Derivatives Association reports well over 90 per cent of the world's top 500 corporations regularly use over-the-counter derivatives.

As with corporations, financial intermediaries may acquire derivative-assets to improve market-perceptions of their position and liabilities. Banks increasingly use credit-default swaps, as part of holding and dealing in structured-debt products like CDOs, as well as to lower the regulatory capital-cost of holding debt-securities under Basle II capital-adequacy conventions.[47] Insurance-companies, investment- and hedge-funds regularly acquire derivative-assets from dealers in order to conform their positions with the expectations and requirements of customers and regulators. Gains made from these improvements provide the foundation for payments of fees for obtaining derivative-contracts. It should be noted here that the most important function of a derivative-asset in this connection is not necessarily to change the prospects of the buyer, but to change the *perception* of those prospects by other capital-market players.[48]

Whether bought for hedging or pure speculation, derivative-assets yield fees to issuing banks. Like good bookies, issuers generally maintain a neutral position to either side of all markets. Issuance-fees represent various appropriations of existing loanable money-capital, centrally from institutional investors drawing funds from the mass of retail-investors. As such, bank-profits from this issuance also represent systematic transfers of value from the mass of retail-investors to the financial sector.

5. Capital-markets, investment-banking and Marxist theory

The increasing significance of financial-market mediation to capitalism in general and for commercial banks in particular poses a considerable analytical challenge for Marxist political economy. These activities can be highly complex, and many of them are historically novel. Identifying their social content requires development and extension of Marxist theory.

Building on Marx,[49] Hilferding offers the best developed Marxist approach to capital-markets. Yet, despite its important insights, the book's approach

---

47. By reducing the measured risk of an asset-holding and, thus, lowering the corresponding risk-weighted capital-reserves.

48. Millo and MacKenzie 2007 eloquently emphasise this aspect of derivative-markets, particularly in relation to the prevalence of pricing models based on the basic models of Black and Scholes 1973 and Merton 1973 whose mathematical foundations yield easily authoritative prices, regardless of their empirical purchase on reality.

49. Marx 1909.

to the integration of corporations, banks and capital-markets is defined by the concepts of *finance-capital* and *founder's profit*. Subsequent developments in capitalism have pointed to empirical and analytical weaknesses in both concepts. As the discussion above suggests, contemporary capitalism is not characterised by the merger of banking and industrial capital.

The concept of *founder's profit*, as formulated by Hilferding, also poses difficulties. It refers to a peculiar capital-gain realised by a corporation's founders when equity is issued and sold because buyers expect and receive only the basic rate of interest as a return on their investment. In this, he followed very closely on the steps of Marx, for whom the rate of interest represented the general mode of appropriation for all holders of money-capital, regardless of the instruments employed.

Yet, historically, expected and realised equity-returns have exceeded returns on bills and bonds over long periods of time.[50] More importantly, this view makes it impossible to characterise the social content of relations defined by investment-banking activities.[51] Put most simply, if corporations can directly raise capital at the rate of interest, there is no reason for them to engage the costly services of investment-banks and little content to financial-market mediation.

Starting from these appreciations, and the most general and compelling foundations of Hilferding's approach to capital-markets, this section aims to make a modest and preliminary contribution to a Marxist theorisation of capital-markets, investment-banking and financial-market mediation. The discussion affords a general characterisation of the socially necessary and inherent contradictions of capital-markets and investment-banking in capitalism, as well as an elucidation of their parasitic class-content in the concrete historical setting prevalent since the early 1980s.

---

50. A wide literature documents the superior returns on equity over bonds in the US throughout the twentieth century. In the postwar-period, US equity-returns have yielded an average excess-return of 5.5 per cent over bills (DeLong and Magin 2007). Besser 1999 also presents evidence from Germany between 1870 to 1995 showing that equity-returns, while highly volatile, have been consistently higher than bond-returns over long investment horizons.

51. In Hilferding, these relationships are rather simple. Banks fused with and controlled industrial capital and the resulting *finance-capital* appropriated the totality of founder's profits, and increasingly dominated economic, social and political life within rival national-imperialist blocs.

5.1. *Capital-markets, risk and investment-banking*

Capital-markets are markets for securities: rights to different future cash-flows paid by corporations. In the first instance, corporations enter capital-markets to raise funds for investment. Loanable money-capital enters capital-markets seeking self-expansion through the future cash-flows associated with securities and possible capital-gains. Two broad types of securities are traded, bonds and equity. Bonds are debt-claims and holders are entitled to the payment of interest. Equity represents a claim on residual profits of enterprise in the form of dividends; it may also legally represent voting rights at corporate meetings. Capital-gains may be realised on any security when a holder sells it for a price higher than its purchase-price.

Capital-markets effect a socialisation *sui generis* of debt and of capital itself, with potential benefits for the capitalist class as a whole. In the purchase of any non-marketable enterprise-liability, the value advanced by the buyer loses the flexibility and general acceptability it had when it was in the form of loanable money-capital. Loanable money-capital is transformed into commodities in the enterprise's circuit of capital, and its transformation into more value hinges on the vicissitudes of that circuit over time. This loss of liquidity can be ameliorated through developed capital-markets. Liquid-markets for corporate securities allow security-holders readily to realise value into money, which is not only the most flexible, independent and socially recognised embodiment of value, but the very purpose of the advance of loanable money-capital. Increased liquidity will attract larger volumes of money seeking a security, generally reducing the cost of outside finance.

Bonds and equity give holders rights to uncertain future flows of money. As with ordinary loans, their prices are irrational, from the perspective of Marxist political economy, in that they are money-expressions of the value of future money. Prices are determined unanchored, through the competitive interaction of supply and demand. In the capitalist setting of competitive-individual appropriation, this relative detachment poses a range of difficulties, including problems of trust and confidence between parties in a setting of anarchic uncertainty about the economic future.

It is in relation to these difficulties that corporate 'financial engineering' and investment-banking acquire social significance by possibly assisting a corporation to reduce its financing costs or generate capital-gains. In general, all developments that increase the profitability of an enterprise will also increase equity-prices – higher rates of exploitation, leadership in the installation of new techniques of production, increased control of markets, and so forth.

But the detachment of capital-market prices from underlying realities of accumulation creates other potential sources of capital-gains (or losses) that have no direct relationship to underlying real investments or profitability. A generalised expectation of future security-price rises will often in itself increase demand, leading to further price rises that, for some time, yield considerable profits and appear to validate expectations. Sheer manipulation, including by investment-banks, has often been an integral part of such processes. Capital-markets and investment-banking inherently create the possibility of such speculative bubbles and their devastating consequences.[52]

Yet capital-markets also create a systematic foundation for investment-banking functions and profits that does not by itself involve swindles, bubbles or manipulation: potential improvements to the social perceptions of the risks associated with the self-expansion of value through a particular corporate security. These may lower the cost of raising capital and generate capital-gains that sustain investment-banking fees and profits.

As generally noted by Hilferding,[53] investors' perceptions of risks associated with security-returns play a defining role in the demand for securities. Specifically, security-buyers will try to assess the potential problems posed by its future cash-flows and its reconversion into money. Thus the perceived credit-worthiness and liquidity of a security are central determinants of demand.

The less creditworthy or liquid a security is perceived to be, *ceteris paribus*, the smaller demand for it will be. Resulting security-prices will be lower, and the expected future cash-flows accruing to holders will represent a higher yield on initial investment. Similarly, two securities with different expected potential future cash-flows, but with the same perceived creditworthiness and liquidity, will see their present prices move until both yield the same expected return. As a result, systematic 'risk-premia' arise in capital-markets: a general

---

52. Effects are often compounded by leveraging of investments made on the basis of such self-fulfilling expectations. Returns may be astronomical while the bubble lasts, making jumping into it very difficult in the context of general competition in capital-markets. See Kindleberger and Aliber 2005 for a good historical account of such crises.

53. Hilferding 1981, p. 108.

positive association between expected returns on a security and the perceived risks to the self-expansion of loanable money-capital it poses.

The potential benefits of investment-banking operations in this regard are most clear when considering the issue of a new corporate security. Neither its liquidity nor its creditworthiness can be guaranteed a priori. Investment-banks help redress this situation in the first instance through underwriting. They commit to buy the new security at a particular price, assuring buyers of its ready reconversion into money and signalling the bank's confidence in its creditworthiness.

As argued and historically illustrated by Morrison and Wilhelm, investment-banks are able to do this given their position and relations within social and business-networks of corporate managers, individual investors, and managers of institutional funds.[54] On the security-selling side, the banks are responsible for 'due diligence' on the issuer's conditions, making use of their specialisation in credit-enhancement. On the buying side, the bank engages in ongoing consultations with a network of close private and institutional investors, gathering knowledge of prices those buyers would pay for the issue, and any aspects of the issue and issuer they may wish to see changed. Buyers agree to discuss these issues with the bank on the understanding they will be offered preferential access to the resulting security-issue. Banks also advise corporations on a range of issue-related and broader corporate-finance matters that may increase improve market-perceptions of a corporation's securities. This often includes advising on the management of total security-supply, or selling derivative-assets to its corporate clients to reduce perceptions of risks associated with the issuer.

All insiders generally gain as a result of these activities. The initial buyers, who are individual or institutional clients of the bank, get a first shot at buying securities that, if the bank has done its job well, will likely appreciate significantly in the short run. The issuer faces a lower cost of capital. And the bank receives fees, typically in the form of a discounted price on the issued security in relation to the offer price.[55]

---

54. Morrison and Wilhelm 2007.
55. Chen and Ritter 2000 report this discount is usually around seven per cent of the listed price.

Corporate managers and investment-banks may also try to generate capital-gains on old issues of equity by employing similar methods. Whether the securities are new or old, all such gains are funded from the loanable money-capital of outside buyers. Those buyers accept higher security-prices because they come to *perceive* better prospects or fewer risks associated with ownership of the security in question.

The uncertainty, competitiveness and relative detachment of capital-market operations ensure they are directly shaped by historically concrete social conventions and sustained practices among market-participants.[56] This includes perceptions about securities, which may be generally shared and sustain transactions even while at considerable variance from the realities underpinning the value of securities.[57] This gives rise not only to potential instability, but also to possible systematic advantages to market-participants better able to shape and apply capital-market conventions and practices.

5.2. *Bonds, equity, and capital-market returns*

Capital-market competition imposes general constraints to potential gains from these activities, as well as certain tendencies in the quantitative relationship between capital-market and real-accumulation rates of return. It is useful to consider separately bonds and equity in this regard.

Bonds embody credit-relations, not fundamentally different from those created by bank-loans. Their rate of return is a rate of interest, which is a sharing of profits. Its level will depend on the quantity and characteristics of other bonds, the relative perceived risk of the individual bond, and the amount of loanable money-capital seeking self-expansion in bond-markets. Private bonds ordinarily pay higher interest-yields than state-paper regarded as safe. Bond-rates are typically measured as premia above returns on state-bonds.[58] The expected rate of return on a bond effectively demanded by

---

56. See MacKenzie 2003, for instance.
57. The current crisis has exposed a range of such cases in the credit-scoring models used in mortgage-lending, and in the estimation of future cash-flows associated with mortgage-backed CDOs. The methods used were adequate for convincing successive layers of security-buyers, but not for actually describing the objective characteristics of the security. See Lapavitsas and dos Santos 2008.
58. The existence of a large, liquid-market for state-securities generally deemed as risk-free is an important underpinning in the development of liquid private bond-markets. The rise in volumes of private marketable debt since the early 1980s was

buyers may account for expected capital-gains on the bond. Those could arise as the relative riskiness of the corporation's debt falls, or as overall demand for bonds increases. These are unlikely to be systematic as the management of corporations will not generally try specifically to increase the price of outstanding bonds.

Equity possesses a distinct relationship to the process of accumulation, returns realised through dividend-payments and capital-gains. Equity-capital (in Marx's words, 'fictitious capital') does not represent an aliquot of real circulating capital. It entitles the holder to a pro-rata claim on future streams of dividends drawing on the profits generated by the circulation of capital. This is clear from the divergence of a corporation's market-capitalisation and net asset-values. Capital engaged in industrial or merchant-circuits appreciates through the *rate of profit*, established through mediations involving struggles at the point of production, the composition of capital, and competition in input- and output-markets. Equity-capital appreciates according to the *rate of return*, established through competition in capital-markets. While related, each of these rates represents fundamentally different social relations.

At purchase, the expected rate of return on a corporation's equity will generally be higher than the rate of interest on its bonds. Debt-repayment is generally more secure than residual gains on equity. In this important regard, the position articulated here differs from that offered by Hilferding, who argued that competition among buyers of equity would take returns on equity down to the rate of interest. Hilferding understood quite well the existence of risk-premia across different securities. But in his approach to capital-market securities he followed closely on Marx's own exposition in Chapter 23 of Volume III of *Capital* on the returns to loanable money-capital.[59] And, while Marx's exposition on the matter elucidates the objective foundation of interest-payments in the generation of profits by real capital, it also advances the rate of interest as the *general* return on all loanable money-capital, regardless of the financial and social relationship between the buyer and the seller or the type of secu-

---

accompanied by an equally impressive rise in the volume of outstanding marketable US Treasury-bonds, notes and bills. Those rose from just over 20 per cent of GDP in 1980, to almost 45 per cent by 1997.

59. I owe this important observation on the origins of Hilferding's approach to Makoto Itoh.

rity in question. It is impossible to approach risk-premia, which inherently involve individual securities and their returns, on such a basis.

The rate of return expected by new buyers of equity will depend on their perceptions of present profitability, their confidence in the security, as well as on their expectations of the future evolution of these factors.[60] Investment-banking and 'financial engineering' operations can affect these perceptions and expectations, reducing the expected rate of return demanded by new equity-buyers, and thus generating price-rises and capital-gains for incumbent owners.

The scope for gains from such activities will generally depend on the evolution of demand for securities in relation to supply, and on the capacity of corporate managers and investment-bankers to devise ways to increase the confidence in the security by potential buyers. This will hinge on historically specific practices and conventions that have acquired general acceptance in shaping capital-market perceptions,[61] as well as on the specific composition of investors seeking to make gains from securities.

The steady privatisation of pension-provision and other necessities since the early 1980s created a unique setting in capital-markets. It not only greatly increased demand for securities, but also added a growing mass of ordinary savers onto capital-markets. The class-implications have been dramatic. On one side, we have seen corporate managers and investment-bankers nestled in extensive social and business-networks of capitalist investors and managers, organised professionally with the explicit purpose of maximising returns by shaping market-perceptions. On the other side, we have seen atomised individual savers whose engagement with capital-markets is primarily dictated by trying to access consumption – retirement, a child's education, a down payment on a house, and so on.

It should not be surprising that the results of this encounter have proven systematically unfavourable to retail-savers. The relative detachment of

---

60. Earlier versions of this text considered the simple case of equity issued by a corporation not expected to experience capital-gains and paying out all profits as dividends. In that case, returns on equity will not normally be higher than the corporation's rate of profit. Market-capitalisation will typically be much lower than the price of the corporation's assets. Eventually, either the corporation will buy back cheap equity, or it will be bought up and liquidated. Either way, the situation is unlikely to last very long.

61. Such as derivative-assets. See Milo and MacKenzie 2007.

capital-market operations from underlying realities of production, and their susceptibility to perceptions, conventions and – more recently – highly technical practices, tend to favour the well-connected capitalist relative to retail-savers. The dramatically different outcomes of capital-market trading for retail-investors and for financial intermediaries are not usefully understood as the product of the 'irrationality' of retail-investors. After all, financial intermediaries have amply proven their own capacity for 'irrationality'. Systematically uneven capital-market outcomes are simply an expression of the class-content of contemporary capital-markets.

While more analytical and empirical work are needed in this regard, it is clear that the foundation of the recent astronomical profits associated with investment-banking activities have ultimately been funded from the investments of ordinary savers. In a setting where these activities have not been generally associated with securing increased real investment – which could lead to general increases in productivity, wages, and standards of living – in investment-banking during this period appears as monumental and crystallised class-parasitism.

6. Some concluding observations

A number of secular, policy- and technological developments have fundamentally changed banking and its relationship to accumulation. Particularly in the US, non-financial corporations have become less reliant on outside finance in general and bank-loans in particular for their operational investments. Their relationship with capital-markets has consequently changed, and, to a significant extent, consists of 'financial-engineering' operations aimed at capital-gains and involving the withdrawal of equity- and bond-borrowings. The privatisation of pensions-provision has facilitated this change by triggering unprecedented inflows of loanable money-capital into capital-markets in the form of retirement-savings. Banks have placed themselves at the heart of these processes, offering mutually beneficial, arms-length investment-banking services to corporations. They have also pursued the provision of various investment-fund instruments to ordinary savers, who systematically receive very unfavourable terms in those services.

More significantly, the steady privatisation of the provision of a growing number of social necessities has increasingly made access to money a precondition for the basic reproduction of ordinary wage-earners, including access to housing, education and health-care. Particularly in a setting of stagnant real wages and rising social inequality, this has forced wage-earners onto financial markets to secure mortgage-, education- and consumer-credit as well as private insurance-services. The relationships banks establish with them through those activities involve large and systematic appropriations of value drawing on individual income. As such, they are exploitative. While these changes are most clearly pronounced in the US and Britain, the micro-level evidence discussed in this chapter suggests the new banking practices are spreading, distinctively, to other advanced-capitalist economies.

The current financial crisis may be usefully understood as a crisis of this type of banking and attendant financial activities. Regulatory arbitrage and rising degrees of leveraging of financial intermediaries have played important roles in the crisis. Positivist hubris about the power of new, inference-based estimations of risk also played their part, as capital-market players came to believe that derivative-assets and their inference-based pricing formulae could actually describe and account for all market-eventualities. And competition among intermediaries ensured that even though many of them knew subprime mortgage-lending was going to lead to losses, they could hardly afford to miss out on the boom.[62] To borrow from former Citigroup boss Chuck Prince III, when the music stopped, most banks were caught dancing.

Yet, underpinning all of these factors was the drive by banks and broader financial system to increase the scope for financial expropriation. Unsurprisingly, problems arose as this expansion started to include historically oppressed layers of the US-population with very low and insecure wage-incomes. The unfolding economic depression is adding to the system's problems as increasing volumes of 'prime' mortgages and other consumer-debt go bad.

It was contemporary banking created the current financial crisis and is responsible for the consequent devastation of the lives of millions of people.

---

62. HSBC 2007, p. 8, noted in March 2007 that much of its US-subprime mortgage-portfolio had 'evidenced much higher delinquency than had been built into the pricing of these products'. Despite promises to shareholders of 'restructuring this business to avoid any repetition of the risk concentration that built up', the bank reported losses of US$1.8 billion in consumer-lending and US$1.2 billion in investment-banking for the US-operations one year later.

It is also central to contemporary capitalism. Whatever happens over the next period, it is unlikely that bank-appropriation of value at the expense of ordinary wage-earners will collapse by the power of its own contradictions. The revenues have been far too significant, and the beneficiaries far too central to the socio-political fabric of the different advanced-capitalist economies. The weakening of trade-union and of broader social organisations of ordinary people over the past thirty years facilitated the growing intrusion of the financial system into the everyday lives of ordinary wage-earners. It is the re-awakening of those organisations that can once again place on the agenda the social provision for housing, retirement, education, health and other necessities, as well as the broader desirability of conscious, democratic economic planning.

Appendix on Bank Corporate Reports

Unless otherwise noted, all information concerning individual banks was obtained from their respective Annual Reports for 2006 and 2007. The only exception is SMFC, for which the report for fiscal year 2006–7 was used. Given the significant accounting conventions across national regulators and individual institutions, it is necessary to specify the sources for particular data reported above. This is done by reported area of activity in the explanations below, which also include pertinent caveats and difficulties.

Credit-card and account-service charges

For all banks, these are fees from credit- and banking cards, and account-services. For RBS, total non-interest income from retail-operations is provided, which includes fund-management fees. For BNP Paribas, net commission-income not measured at fair value is given, which is a residual estimate of money-dealing commission and fees.

Financial-market mediation

The percentages are an understatement for SMFG and RBS, neither of which reported separate fund-management revenues. SMFG does not report narrow investment-banking revenues either. The figure given is exclusively for gains on own and trading account.

Fund-management and related commission-fees

The figures relate to net fees and or commissions on management of investment-, pension-, mutual and other funds. The exceptions are Citgroup, for which net income of Smith Barney and Private Banking divisions is given, and RBS for which fees earned at retail-level are given, which also include money-dealing fees.

Own and trading-account gains

For HSBC the figures are the sum of 'Net trading income and Net income from financial instruments'. For Citibank, they relate to 'Principal transactions' total revenue (the reported loss for credit-instrument tallied at US$21.8 billion). For Bank of America and SMFG, they correspond to 'Trading account profits' plus equity-investment income and gains on sales of debt-securities. The bank's trading-account loss for 2007 stood at US$5.13 bilion. The figures for RBS include net gains from trading plus gains from investments, asset-backed activities, and rental. The figures for Barclays are from 'Principal transactions' and include net trading and investment-incomes. Santander's 'resultados netos de operaciones financieras' are reported. Paribas reports prominently on its net gains on financial instruments at fair value and on available-for-sale financial assets. The figures for UBS and Goldman Sachs are, respectively, for net trading income and trading and principal-investments income.

Chapter Four

Central Banking in Contemporary Capitalism: Inflation-Targeting and Financial Crises

Demophanes Papadatos

1. Introduction

Financialisation is the result of the transformation of real accumulation in recent years, which has also led to the transformation of the financial system. Real accumulation witnessed a régime-shift in 1973–4, during the so-called first oil-shock that signalled the end of the long post-WWII boom. This régime-shift was accompanied by a profound institutional and political reaction as a response to the failure of official Keynesianism to deal with the stagflationary crises of the 1970s. The recent wave of financial globalisation started in the mid-1980s, with rising cross-border financial flows among industrial economies and between industrial and developing economies. This has, in turn, promoted financial innovation, such as the introduction of increasingly sophisticated financial assets and the growth of new financial players.

Against this background, the financial sector has been entirely transformed through rapid growth, deregulation, global expansion, introduction of new technology, institutional change and financial innovation. The weight of the financial sector has grown markedly in developed countries in terms of employment, profits, size of institutions and markets. Finance now penetrates every aspect of society in developed countries, and is becoming increasingly important in the developing world, as Lapavitsas notes in this volume.

However, with the surge in financial flows, came a spate of currency- and financial crises in the late 1980s and 1990s. The importance of the central bank has increased as bubbles and financial crises have become a regular feature of financialised capitalism, particularly since their nature has varied significantly from the turmoil of the mid-70s, due to the transformation of the financial system. Nevertheless, much ambiguity and confusion surrounds the operations of the central bank in the new environment, even as it aims to preserve the interests and social dominance of the capitalist class.

A first response to these trends by economic policymakers was to strengthen the monopoly of the central bank over legal tender. The financial system became even more dependent on using central-bank money as obligatory means of payment for the settlement of debts. At the same time, inflation-targeting and central-bank independence were also adopted.[1] Since the early 1990s, inflation-targeting has become the dominant ('best practice') monetary-policy paradigm in several high- and middle-income countries.[2] In addition to countries that follow fully-fledged inflation-targeting policies, several dozen countries have adopted it informally or implicitly, for example, by pursuing 'inflation-caps' (maximum desired inflation-rates) in the context of IMF-programmes. Such 'caps' are insufficient to define these policy-régimes as inflation-targeting, but they are evidence of a medium-term move towards inflation-targeting.

Moreover, the macroeconomic performance of most OECD-countries improved in terms of inflation, unemployment, output-volatility and interest-rates during the last ten to fifteen years. This is the so-called 'Great Moderation', which has been attributed by mainstream-theorists to neoliberal policies. In this context, monetary policy has become even more prominent, further strengthening the tendency towards adopting inflation-targeting.[3]

---

1. On how the central banks have strengthened their monopoly of legal tender in the era of financialisation, see Kneeshaw and Van den Bergh 1989.
2. The following countries are fully-fledged inflation-targeters: Australia, Brazil, Canada, Chile, Colombia, Czech Republic, Hungary, Iceland, Israel, Mexico, New Zealand, Norway, Peru, Philippines, Poland, South Africa, Republic of Korea, Sweden, Thailand and the United Kingdom (see Carare and Stone 2003 and Stone and Bhundia 2004).
3. Bernanke 2004.

This chapter discusses these developments by adopting a Marxist approach which stresses the social and political aspects of central banking and their relation to class-interests. It is shown that the current financial crisis has also become a crisis of the monetary-policy régime, while revealing the class-dimension of inflation-targeting. Essentially, inflation-targeting has been an attempt to preserve financial interests at the expense of the vast majority of society. The same underlying aims characterise recent mainstream-proposals to move central-bank policy beyond inflation-targeting. Devised partly in response to the current crisis, these proposals stress the central bank's function as lender of last resort and complement it by the novel function of 'market-maker of last resort'. Such policies aim at using the power of the central bank to socialise financial losses while defending private profits.

The chapter first analyses the inflation-targeting framework while advancing a political-economy critique of mainstream-views of inflationary phenomena. It then analyses the social relations characteristic of central banking by adopting a Marxist approach. Specifically, the theory of central banking as 'contested terrain' of class- and intra-class conflict is subjected to critical analysis. Further, capital/labour and finance/industry relations are examined in light of developments in the era of financialisation under the neo-liberal agenda. Finally, financialisation is analysed with regard to financial bubbles, establishing connections between bubble-bursting and sudden changes in monetary policy, while demonstrating the relation of monetary-policy changes to social and political interests.

2. The rise and fall of inflation-targeting

2.1. *The trajectory and effectiveness of inflation-targeting*

Inflation-targeting has been the dominant, 'best-practice' monetary-policy paradigm for nearly two decades and until the emergence of the subprime-mortgage crisis. Things have now changed and several policymakers and economists argue that central banks must move beyond inflation-targeting.

Early indications of the demise of inflation-targeting can also be detected in the previous period. Thus, until the Asian crisis of 1997–8, inflation-targeting was implemented in its original form, the primary focus of which was price-stability. However, after the financial crises of the 1990s, financial stability began to be considered as a goal for monetary policy of equal, if not greater, importance to price-stability. This contributed to a gradual weakening of the exclusive focus towards price-stability.[4] This gradual weakening of the primary focus on price-stability has encouraged a theoretical critique of inflation-targeting, which has supplemented older empirical critiques of its effectiveness.

Problems for inflation-targeting appeared already in the early period of its implementation, when conflicting conclusions came out of efforts empirically to measure its effectiveness. Several studies identified presumed gains regarding the rate, volatility and inertia of inflation, improved expectations, faster absorption of adverse shocks, lower sacrifice-ratio (the output-cost of reducing inflation), output-stabilisation, and convergence of poorly-performing towards well-performing countries.[5] However, other studies were more critical of the effectiveness of inflation-targeting. They claimed that there is no convincing evidence that inflation-targeting improves economic performance as measured by the behaviour of inflation, output or interest-rates, and it may even lead to a deterioration of some indicators, especially unemployment.[6]

These conflicting conclusions are partly due to the different approaches and econometric methodologies used in various studies. Yet, the divergence of assessment is also due to deeper reasons. There are strong indications that the performance of most OECD-countries has improved in terms of inflation, unemployment, output-volatility and interest-rates during the last ten to fifteen years. These improvements are evident in both inflation-targeting and non-inflation-targeting countries, which suggests that the underlying cause is something other than inflation-targeting.

In the words of Arestis and Sawyer:

> Both inflation-targeting and non-inflation-targeting countries performed over the inflation-targeting period equally well. The average rate of inflation and its variance have been reduced in both periods. This is true for both inflation-targeting and non-inflation-targeting countries.... We may conclude...by suggesting that on the basis of the average inflation and GDP growth rates performance, there is not much difference between inflation-targeting and

---

4. Siklos 2002, p. 8.
5. See, for example, Bernanke and Gertler 1999a, Debelle, Masson, Savastano, Sharma 1998, Mishkin and Schmitt-Hebbel 2001.
6. See, for example, Agenor 2001, Cecchetti and Ehrmann 1999, Chang and Grabel 2004, pp. 183–4, and Neuman and von Hagen 2002, pp. 149–53.

non-inflation-targeting countries....Consequently, inflation-targeting has been a great deal of fuss about really very little![7]

2.2. The framework of inflation-targeting

According to its advocates, 'fully-fledged' inflation-targeting consists of five components: absence of other nominal anchors for the economy, such as exchange-rates or nominal GDP; no fiscal dominance; policy-(instrument-) independence; policy-transparency and policy-accountability.[8] In practical terms, the central bank announces that it will strive to hold inflation within a specified target-range – rather than a plain number – typically established for horizons between one and four years. 'Price-stability' is usually defined as 2% inflation.[9]

The degree to which the central bank is formally accountable for meeting this target varies. In New Zealand, for example, the law links the tenure of the central-bank governor to the inflation-target, whereas, in other countries, there are no legal or explicit sanctions. At the institutional level, inflation-targeting is usually associated with changes in the law, which enhance the independence of the central bank from the elected government.[10] Some economists draw a distinction between goal-independence and instrument-independence.[11] This distinction may not mean very much in practice because the two kinds of independence are complementary – enhancing one kind of independence necessarily implies enhancing the other.[12]

Advocates of inflation-targeting insist that, at the level of the government, the policy institutionalises 'good' (i.e., orthodox) monetary policies, while increasing the transparency and accountability of the central bank and providing guidelines for other government-policies.[13] Apparently, inflation-targeting also helps to shape private-sector expectations, thereby reducing uncertainty and the costs associated with the necessary adjustment to the

---

7. Arestis and Sawyer 2006, p. 24.
8. See Mishkin and Schmidt-Hebbel 2001, p. 3; Bernanke, Laubach, Posen and Mishkin 1999.
9. Bernanke and Mishkin 1997, p. 99.
10. Bernanke and Mishkin 1997, p. 102; Mishkin and Schmidt-Hebbel 2001, p. 8.
11. Debelle and Fisher 1996.
12. Bernanke and Mishkin 1997, p. 102.
13. See however, Aybar and Harris 1998, pp. 20–38 for a critique from a radical political-economy perspective.

new, low-inflation régime. The implication is that other economic policy-objectives – such as employment-generation, economic growth and income-distribution – should be subordinated to inflation-targeting. Inflation-targeting, therefore, came to dominate all economic policymaking for nearly two decades. It reinforced the neoliberal view that government-intervention in the economy is either useless or counterproductive, and that inflation is largely due to fiscal deficits, adverse expectations and lack of policy-credibility.

It is worth examining a little more closely the economic model that under-pins inflation-targeting. The model is very simple and includes two key parameters: the inflation-target and expectations of inflation. The former is set by the government, while the latter arise from the private sector. The model also includes one discretionary policy-instrument: the nominal interest-rate. In this light, the main objective of the central bank is to eliminate the differ-ence between the rate of inflation and the inflation-target at some point in the future (the 'policy-horizon', usually set at between one and three years).

The model presumes that inflation is jointly determined by the inflation-expectations of the private (mainly financial) sector and the output-gap, explained below. The rate of unemployment presumably fluctuates around the 'Non-Accelerating Inflation-Rate of Unemployment' or NAIRU: when unemployment is below (above) the NAIRU, it leads to higher (lower) infla-tion.[14] The output-gap (expressed as the difference between the current rate of unemployment and the NAIRU) is determined by the level of real interest-rates. High real interest-rates raise the output-gap, while low interest-rates stimulate economic activity and reduce the gap. Finally, the real interest-rate is, by definition, equal to the nominal interest-rate minus inflation-expectations. The central bank attempts to hit the inflation-target by manipulating the nom-inal interest-rate in order to influence expectations and, at a further remove, fine-tune the level of aggregate demand.

It follows that inflation-control demands 'credible' macroeconomic policies, which, in essence, means adopting the 'orthodox' policy-view. It also follows

---

14. The NAIRU (non-accelerating inflation-rate of unemployment) derives from the monetarist concept of the 'natural rate of unemployment' (NRU). The NRU is the unemployment-rate at which all markets, including the labour-market, are in equilibrium. The NAIRU is defined as the unemployment-rate compatible with stable inflation in the long run (if the economy is operating below the NAIRU, inflation will presumably accelerate and vice versa).

that monetary-policy discretion should be used within a tight framework of rules. Furthermore, there should be liberalisation of the capital-account and elimination of residual inflationary pressures through import-liberalisation. It goes without saying that direct and indirect wage-restrictions should also be removed. Finally, when inflation-targeting is implemented by independent central banks, it is supposed to 'discipline the politicians' by removing the inflation-bias that they are supposed to generate due to elections.

Thus, the model and its policy-implications are based on two underlying claims. First, that persistent unemployment is essentially voluntary (natural), since involuntary (true) unemployment is a transitory phenomenon. Second, that attempts to lower unemployment below its 'natural' rate will trigger inflation, and perhaps even create accelerating inflation. In short, inflation-targeting is based on the notion that there is an empirical trade-off between inflation and unemployment. Yet, there is little evidence that this is true.

Drawing on empirical evidence, Shaikh has made three points to the contrary.[15] First, for much of the postwar-period, the rise in average unemployment-levels in OECD-countries was directly associated with a fall in average output growth-rates. Second, there is no general historical trade-off between unemployment and inflation in OECD-countries. Such a trade-off might have existed during 1975–91, but the very opposite pattern seems to hold for the period 1964–74. Third, inflation appears to be related to economic growth, namely lower growth is associated with higher inflation.

Shaikh's Marxist critique is consistent with the views of other authors within Marxist political economy.[16] Inflationary trends exhibit little homogeneity within capitalist economies, and are often associated with processes that the state cannot immediately and effectively control. A fuller understanding of both inflation and inflation-targeting from a Marxist perspective, therefore, requires placing these phenomena within a specific social and historical context.

---

15. Shaikh 1997.
16. See Saad-Filho 2000, Saad-Filho and Mollo 2002.

3. Central banking and class-interests

3.1. *The historical context of inflation-targeting*

The régime of inflation-targeting is a product of historical development. After the collapse of the Bretton Woods system in the early 1970s, the ability of the main central banks to exercise discretionary power over the rate of interest increased greatly. Monetary policy started to acquire its present historical significance because of the attenuation, or complete absence, of foreign-exchange-reserve discipline on the central banks. The rate of interest has acquired the character of an instrument of public policy, and a multitude of often contradictory demands has been placed on central banks regarding interest-rate manipulation. Typically, these demands have included price-stability, a satisfactory level of economic activity and a balance-of-payments outlook compatible with high growth and employment. However, the absence of gold-discipline, after the collapse of the Bretton Woods system, only served to emphasise the anarchic nature of the international capitalist system by encouraging exchange-rate instability, price-inflation and financial speculation.

The collapse of the Keynesian ideology of full employment and the emergence of rapid inflation in the 1970s gradually made price-stability the primary objective of monetary policy. Thus, Duménil[17] notes that the structural crisis of capitalism, beginning in the 1970s, created the conditions for the reassertion of the hegemony of finance. The rise of finance was combined with a broad set of other practices: deregulation, direct confrontation with the workers' movement and unions, a policy favourable to large mergers, and new methods of corporate governance favourable to the interests of shareholders. For Duménil, neoliberalism is a new phase of capitalism, also signalling the return of finance to hegemony.

The state has played an instrumental role during these transformations. Historically, there have been two primary and one secondary function of the state in relation to capital-accumulation. The primary functions are, first, securing the labour-system and, second, securing the money-system. The secondary function is mediating the contradictory interests of different parts of

---

17. Duménil 2007, p. 7.

capital. The primary functions are critical to accumulation but cannot be guaranteed by capital itself.[18] The necessity of the state to secure the labour and the money-system is due to the very nature of capitalism. On the other hand, the state's mediating role derives historically from the anarchy of market-based interactions.[19]

As a state- (or semi-state) institution, the central bank has varied greatly throughout history depending on the structure of the financial system, its connections with real accumulation, the social and political relations mediated by finance, and the past practice of interventions. The role of the central bank during the Bretton Woods era, for example, was the historical result of the great depression of the 1930s as well as the emergence of the Keynesian ideology of full employment. In the period of neoliberalism, which signalled the reassertion of the power of finance, the major event was the change of monetary policy in 1979, targeting monetary policy overwhelmingly toward price-stability. The Volcker coup in the USA took place primarily because of the experience of the stagflationary period of the 1970s,[20] and eventually led to the triumph of inflation-targeting.

3.2. *Central banking and the management of modern money*

Since the collapse of the Bretton Woods system, contemporary money has become overwhelmingly credit-money resting on central-bank money (banknotes and deposits) which is, in turn, backed primarily by state-instruments of debt. Central banks have been freed from the need to guard their gold-reserves. Consequently, they have acquired fuller discretion in making loans, in issuing their own money and, above all, in determining interest-rates. Under these conditions, stability of the value of central-bank money has come to depend on two factors: first, on the central bank's management of aggregate credit-flows and, second, on central-bank money being legal tender for the settlement of commercial and other debts.

---

18. De Brunhoff 1976.
19. Marx's first mention of the state in *Capital* is in relation to the production and distribution of coin, which is 'an attribute proper to the state'. The same point is made in relation to paper-currency (Marx 1976, p. 223, 227).
20. Mayer 2003.

The central bank's monopoly over legal tender is a fundamental component of contemporary finance. Modern central-bank money (banknotes and deposits) functions as obligatory means of payments, backed mostly by state-debt. Consequently, it has clear aspects of fiat-money, that is, money with arbitrary circulation backed by the power of the state. Nevertheless, modern central-bank money is still issued by a bank, in other words, it is fiat-money that has mutated out of credit-money. The management of modern fiat-money draws on the social power and trust invested in the central bank. In this light, central-bank management of modern credit-money – a continuous and evolving process – can be seen primarily as an effort to preserve the value of credit-money.

3.3. *Central banking as 'contested terrain' of class- and intra-class conflict*

The Marxist approach proposed here has common features with radical post-Keynesian treatments of central banking. Post-Keynesian economics pays particular attention to conflicting interests and especially to class- and intra-class struggles as determinants of central banking. Central banking is seen as 'contested terrain' in economy and society.[21] Four key factors determine monetary policy, namely the structure of the labour-market, connections between finance and industry, the position of the national economy in the world-economy, and the position of the central bank in the state-apparatus.

However, the interpretation of financialisation underpinning this article also differs significantly from the post-Keynesian analysis. Differences are pronounced with regard to the structure of the financialised labour-markets as well as the connections between finance and industry and their effect on monetary policy. Contrary to post-Keynesian analysis, the central bank is primarily a defender of financial interests rather than 'contested terrain'. This approach sheds necessary light on the various crises during the era of financialisation, including that of 2007–9.

To be more specific, with regard to relations between capital and labour, Epstein[22] distinguishes between what he calls the 'Kaleckian' and the 'neo-

---

21. See Epstein and Schor 1986, 1988, 1989, 1990, and Epstein 1992.
22. Epstein 1992.

Marxian' approach.[23] The latter posits a negative relationship between employment, capacity-utilisation and profit-shares. As the economy expands and unemployment falls, workers gain the power to raise real wages, or to improve working conditions, with the result of lowering productivity. Thus, as capacity-utilisation increases, unit labour-costs increase and industrial profit-share falls. In contrast, the 'Kaleckian' approach suggests that increased capacity-utilisation reduces competition and gives firms market-power, thus allowing firms to increase their mark-ups. Consequently, industrial profit-share rises as capacity-utilisation increases or, at worst, remains constant. Thus, the 'Kaleckian' labour-market postulates a non-negative relation between employment, capacity-utilisation and profit-share.

It is notable that neither of these approaches sheds much light on labour-markets in the current régime of financialisation. Ultimately this is because Epstein defines the structural characteristics of labour-markets by focusing on a very narrow aspect of the capital-labour relationship, namely the effect of changes in capacity-utilisation (and thus of the 'reserve-army' of the unemployed) on capital's profit-share.[24] But the structure of contemporary 'financialised' labour-markets has been determined partly by technological change, partly by regulatory change, and partly by bouts of unemployment at key junctures of the period of financialisation.

In the course of financialisation, as Lapavitsas notes in this volume, there has been a rebalancing of paid and unpaid labour, while information-technology has encouraged the contraction of private time as well as piece-work and putting-out practices. These changes have effectively led to an increase in the working day. Moreover, it is also likely that labour has been intensified. From the extensive literature on job-satisfaction, for instance, it transpires that work-intensification associated with new technology is a key reason for dissatisfaction with work in developed countries, together with loss of discretion over work-choices counting for a deterioration of their living standards. Finally, the process of work has also been critically affected by institutional changes in the labour-market. This includes casualisation of labour and entry of women in the labour-force which effectively increased the

---

23. Neo-Marxism includes authors such as, Boddy & Crotty 1975; Schor 1985; Goldstein 1986; Schor and Bowles 1987; Weisskopf 1988; Bowles and Boyer 1989; Bowles, Gordon, and Weisskopf 1989.

24. Epstein 1992, p. 7.

working population. Thus, the fluidity of labour has increased at the cost of greater insecurity of workers.

In this environment, it is hard to advocate either a 'neo-Marxian' or a 'Kaleckian' relationship between employment and capacity-utilisation. Rather, new technology has intensified competition even among firms which previously possessed significant market-power. In 'financialised' labour-markets, employment is positively associated with profit-rates, while being institutionally dissociated from the wage-level.

Furthermore, post-Keynesian analysis of the relationship between finance and industry under current conditions suggests that finance holds a dominant position relative to industry.[25] The reason is, presumably, that financial institutions have the ability to continue making profits even when real accumulation meets difficulties. As a result, in the current régime of capitalist accumulation, finance plays a pivotal role in promoting capital-accumulation as a whole. However, this is a problematic view. In spite of its rising relative autonomy, finance continues to comply broadly with the essential motion of capitalist accumulation because its objective foundations continue to be found in idle money generated by capitalist enterprises.

The importance of this point can also be seen in connection with the 'contested-terrain' approach. According to this perspective, the primary concern of the central bank is to keep monetary policy out of the hands of labour. But it is also argued that, when industrial and financial capitalists are strongly divided, central-bank independence often serves to keep monetary policy out of the hands of industrial capital. In this case, the central bank tends disproportionately to favour financial, or 'rentier'-interests.[26] This means that there is space for political alliances between labour and the industrial fraction of the capitalist class to defeat the financial fraction.

It is important to note that Epstein has recently argued that:

> There seems to be further evolution in these class interests. Increasingly, in the United States and, probably Europe, rentier and industrial interests may be merging, but not as in the case of old German and Japanese financial structures (Zysman, 1984; Pollin, 1995; Grabel, 1997) where industrial interests dominate finance. Rather, it may increasingly be the case that

---

25. Very selectively, see Stockhammer 2002, 2007, Orhangazi 2007.
26. See Epstein and Ferguson 1984, pp. 957–83; Epstein 1992, pp. 1–30.

with the deregulation of financial markets – that is, with financialisation – industrial enterprises themselves are beginning to be increasingly guided by rentier motives. In short, 'financialisation' may have changed the structure of class relations between industry and finance, making their interests much more similar.[27]

In this connection, Marxist work shows that the foundations of the 'contested terrain' are flawed and the analysis has to be reconsidered.[28] First, it implies the existence of pure 'functioning' capitalists who possess investment-projects but no money. This is an ideally abstract assumption: in practice, borrowing capitalists typically possess some of their own capital plus some that they borrow. Second, revenue in the form of interest tends also to accrue to industrial and commercial capitalists, and it is not the exclusive foundation of a separate social group, such as financial capitalists. The separate and often opposing interests of lending and borrowing capitalists cannot be fully analysed in terms of the functioning-industrial section of the capitalist class confronting the financial-monied section.

Lapavitsas, in this volume, makes further relevant observations regarding the characteristics of contemporary *rentiers* in financialised capitalism. These confirm the view that revenue in the form of interest tends to accrue to industrial and commercial capitalists and cannot be the exclusive foundation of a social group. *Rentiers* in the era of financialisation are able to draw extraordinary incomes because of their position relative to the financial system, and not through ownership of financial capital. It follows that financialisation ought to be approached by treating the financial system as a structured whole that is connected organically to real accumulation. The recent ascendancy of finance has systemic origins. Its social outcomes are far more complex than *rentiers* squeezing industrialists. By the same token, there is no reason for labour to support industry against finance.

To recap, financial institutions have continued to make profits despite the problems faced by real accumulation during the period of financialisation. Consequently, the significance of the financial system has increased enormously, since, under such conditions, finance has become a source of profits for the capitalist class as a whole. Meanwhile, capital-labour relations have

---

27. Epstein 2002, p. 17.
28. Lapavitsas 1997a, pp. 85–106.

been rebalanced with an eye to keeping central bank 'immune' from the influence of class-struggles. The implication is that, in the era of financialisation, the central bank is not 'contested terrain' but the primary defender of financial interests. This is clear in the context of financial crises, considered below.

4. Central banks and financial crises

4.1. *The false belief that low inflation guarantees financial stability*

The policy of inflation-targeting has been eventually rendered redundant by the emergence of major financial instability in the course of financialisation. It has taken some time for this development to become clear, including several episodes of financial instability in the 1990s and the gigantic crisis of 2007–9.

The period of rapid inflation in the 1970s and 1980s was followed by nearly two decades of stability in terms of prices, output-volatility and interest-rates. The mainstream attributed these outcomes to monetary policy that focused on inflation-targeting.[29] It did not take long for the false view to emerge that price-stability also guaranteed general financial stability. On this basis, the central bank only had to concern itself with keeping inflation low, and the financial sector could look after itself.

Schwartz[30] has been the main advocate of the view that price-stability guarantees financial stability, also shared by Bernanke and Gertler.[31] Relying on earlier work with Friedman,[32] Schwartz argued that the major threat to financial stability, especially for the banking sector, comes from unexpected changes in the rate of inflation. Therefore, by promoting price-stability, the central bank 'will do more for financial stability than reforming deposit insurance or reregulating'.[33] If the central bank focused on low inflation, it would apparently reduce the chances of lending booms (induced by high inflation) and recessions (induced by unexpected deflation or disinflation). The 'Schwartz

---

29. Bernanke 2004.
30. Schwartz 1988, pp. 33–62; 1998, pp. 34–41.
31. Bernanke and Gertler 1999a, pp. 18–51.
32. Friedman and Schwartz 1963.
33. Schwartz 1998, p. 38.

Hypothesis' has been tested by mainstream-economists, who found a positive 'association', not causation, between price-instability and financial instability (meaning bank-panics).[34]

These views are transparently fallacious, but they rest on ideological and political considerations. The inflationary crises of the 1970s and 1980s represented failure to defend the value of credit-money. That failure had social and political implications, at the very least because rapid inflation meant losses for creditors and because wage-bargaining was disrupted as workers attempted to obtain compensating increases in money-wages. The adoption of inflation-targeting and central-bank independence was a sign of the ability of the capitalist class to learn from this experience.

Thus, the convenient legal fiction of independent-central banking was created, separating the electoral process from monetary policy. The latter was apparently to be determined by disinterested and class-neutral experts on 'objective technical grounds'. Financial interests were assured that inflation – which is deeply damaging to them – would not be tolerated. Financial bubbles, on the other hand, were seen as irrelevant to central banking, and even declared unlikely if inflation was kept low. In effect, financial interests were told that the central bank was not going to intervene in their speculations, while protecting them from high inflation.

4.2. *The significance of bubbles and financial crises*

The emergence and burst of financial bubbles in the 1990s has undermined inflation-targeting, while showing the limits of contemporary central banking. Bubbles are unsustainable, continuous increases in financial-asset prices. They result from a climate of optimism, which is fostered by rises in financial prices and leads to further price-rises, thus creating the phenomenon of asset-price inflation. In an asset-price bubble, consumers and enterprises tend to over-borrow. Rises in asset-prices may also lead to a misallocation of resources through time. There might be excessive capital-accumulation in the short term, for example, followed by an extended period of over-capacity. In this context, it becomes very difficult for the central bank to set

---

34. See Bordo, Dueker and Wheelock 2000 and Bordo and Wheelock 1998, pp. 41–62.

monetary conditions in a way that deals with changing expectations regarding to the future pace of capital-accumulation. As a result, there is greater risk of policy-error.

Moreover, according to Shaikh's aforementioned Marxist critique of inflation-targeting, there is no homogeneity to inflationary phenomena in the context of the capitalist market-process. Contrary to mainstream-beliefs, inflation does not result simply, or mostly, from government-policy but also from the activities of the private sector, which are sometimes revealed as changes in asset-prices. These activities could undermine the ability of monetary authorities to meet inflation objectives. Consequently, it is mistaken to think that asset-prices can be ignored, allowing monetary policy to focus exclusively on inflation.

It is important to note that in all countries that suffered financial bubbles during the last fifteen years, inflation was either low in absolute terms, or low relative to its earlier history.[35] In each case, the emergence of an asset-price bubble was closely correlated with apparent success in lowering inflation, an achievement much prized by the advocates of the so-called 'Great Moderation'. This is not to exclude the fact that sometimes low inflation was only a temporary phenomenon associated with a beneficial external shock, for instance, in the UK in the late 1980s.[36] Still, bubbles tend to emerge in conditions in which inflation remains under control (see Figures 1 and 2).

It is clear from Figure 1, for instance, that Japan's inflation-rate in the 1980s remained at very low levels. Even when it rose toward the end of the decade, it remained lower than that of Japan's competitors. Put another way, for much of the late 1980s, Japan would have easily met most of the inflation-targets currently in use. Very low interest-rates in Japan in the second half of the 1980s went together with low and stable inflation as well as rapid rises in equity- and land-prices.

Moreover, when asset-prices started to fall, Japanese monetary authorities failed to recognise the dangers this posed for the economy. Expectations of future growth collapsed, and industrial enterprises were left with excessive debt-levels that prompted a slow move toward deflation. Yet, the rela-

---

35. King 1999.
36. King 1999, pp. 10–18.

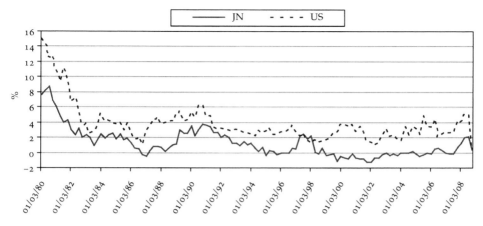

Figure 1   Japan, US. Inflation-Rates 1980q1–2008q4

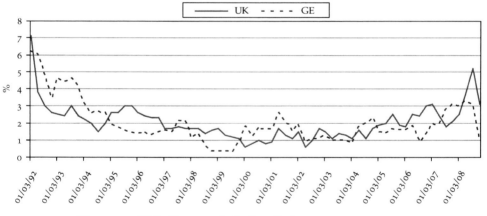

Figure 2   UK, German Inflation-Rates, 1992q1–2008q4

tive stability of inflation at the time gave policymakers an unjustified level of confidence in the underlying health of Japanese capitalism. The Japanese experience shows that catastrophic asset-price bubbles can be consistent with pursuing low inflation. The US-experience in the late 1990s and more recently is a similarly good example of this phenomenon. On this basis, it is probable that financial bubbles tend to develop when inflationary pressures are low and, as a result, central banks feel comfortable with levels of interest-rates that eventually prove too low.

Furthermore, bubbles tend to develop when periods of low inflation are accompanied by strong expansion of the domestic money-supply (see Figures 3, 4, and 5). A temporary absence of price-pressures allows central banks to tolerate excess money-growth for an extended period of time. A common rationalisation is that monetary expansion is not problematic, if it reflects financial innovation. Thus, strong growth of money could in practice lead to rapidly rising asset-prices which, in turn, enable borrowers to offer increasing collateral on loans, apparently lowering risk for lenders.

Finally, it is common for traditional risk-assessment and valuation-models used by financial institutions to break down in the course of a bubble. This phenomenon has been particular pronounced during the US-bubble of 2001–7. Technological progress and financial innovations made it possible for banks to manage their liabilities more efficiently and therefore more profitably. Instruments such as derivatives, transactions of securities, money-trust, insurance, as well as a variety of other services related to open markets encouraged banks to turn toward financial-market mediation. Also other activities, such as lending for mortgages, consumer-loans, credit-cards and so on, which turn banks toward the personal revenue of workers, became very prominent. A climate of optimism fostered a huge asset-bubble, contributed to lack of proper risk-assessment, and eventually led to burst. Low inflation offered no protection against the ensuing disaster.

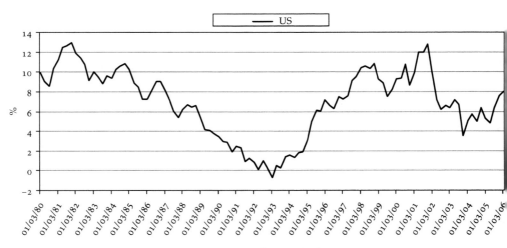

Figure 3   US Money-Supply M3 YoY 1980q1–2006q1

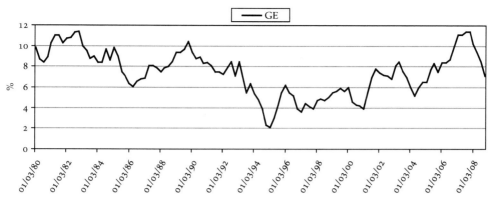

Figure 4   German Money-Supply M3 YoY 1980q1–2008q4

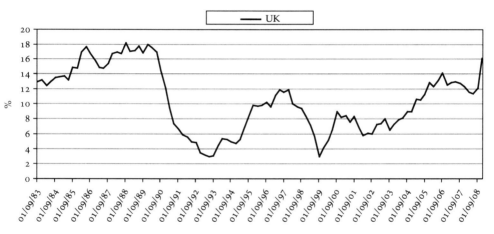

Figure 5   UK Money-Supply M3 YoY 1983q1–2008q4

To mitigate the consequences of bubbles bursting, central banks have tended
to shift their focus pragmatically, effecting emergency-changes in monetary
policy. This practical response has been prepared by analytical work, such
as that by McGee and Bean,[37] arguing that price-stability offers no guarantee
of financial stability. Along similar lines, Borio and Lowe have claimed that,
if financial imbalances in the economy are pronounced, there is a strong

---

37. McGee 2000 and Bean 2003, pp. 787–807.

possibility of financial instability triggered by price-stability.[38] Therefore they proposed the so-called 'flexible approach to inflation-targeting'. This has found some support from Mervyn King, the Governor of the Bank of England, arguing that monetary policy may need to be tightened in response to rising asset-prices, even if inflation is not rising significantly.

The problem is that, in a capitalist economy, it is very hard to distinguish at an early stage between a bubble and a period of lasting improvements in productivity-performance. Moreover, technological revolutions are often used to justify extended gains in asset-prices. It is historically documented that technological revolutions often give rise to bubbles.[39] This means that an initial expansion in economic activity based on productivity-growth can give way to unsustainable bubbles as the money-supply begins to increase and asset-prices rise to exceptionally high levels.

A case in point is the response of the Federal Reserve under Alan Greenspan to the so-called 'New Economy' stock-market bubble and the subsequent housing bubble in the USA. Greenspan chose to restrain neither the former nor the latter. He declared himself right not prick the equity-bubble of the 1990s, allowing it to burst by itself and then 'mopping up' the mess through lower interest-rates. Greenspan justified his action on the grounds that one can never be sure that what looks like a bubble really is a bubble. Apparently, he could not use interest-rates to 'prick' the bubble, because interest-rates affect the economy more like a sledgehammer than a scalpel. A modest rise in interest-rates would be unlikely to halt rising prices, but an increase sufficient to pop the bubble would slow the whole economy and could even cause a recession. On this basis, Greenspan concluded that it was safer to wait for a bubble to burst by itself and then to ease monetary policy to soften the downturn.

In practice, Greenspan allowed financial interests to make enormous profits during the bubble in the hope that the costs of the burst would not be unmanageable. It was taken for granted, of course, that these costs would be passed on to society as a whole. Thus, inflation-targeting has gradually come to acquire the aspect of protecting private profits in a bubble, while socialising losses during the burst. This approach led to disaster in 2007–9.

---

38. Borio and Lowe 2002.
39. See Kindleberger 1989.

4.3. *Socialising losses to protect private profits*

The crisis of 2007–9 has thrown inflation-targeting in turmoil. As was previously explained, the policy can be characterised as the epitome of sophisticated monetarism, which emerged primarily because of the experience of the stagflation of the 1970s.[40] The policy limits the central bank to pursuing a low inflation-target subject to broad rules, while downplaying the traditional function of lender of last resort.

Imposing the rule of targeting inflation can be quite restraining on the central bank.[41] Since the capitalist economy develops dynamically, any rule which limits discretion by the central bank is necessarily static. The recent crisis has shown that the dynamic evolution of finance in the era of financialisation has undermined what was considered the greatest achievement of inflation-targeting régimes, namely central-bank credibility. Thus, mainstream-economists are at present advocating renewed emphasis on the function of lender of last resort.[42] Others have proposed complementing that with market-making of last resort.[43]

The crisis of 2007–9 has manifested itself primarily as turmoil in financial markets. Uncertainty and fear, which easily extended to panic, meant that little or no trade occurred in certain classes of financial instruments. Subprime-backed Collateralised Debt-Obligations, for instance, were often impossible to trade as there was no market-maker capable of valuing the necessary funds credibly to establish buying and selling prices. Such market-failures occurred in different ways across financial assets, including exchange-traded and over-the-counter instruments. But a common solution has been suggested: the central bank should be the market-maker of last resort. The function of market-maker of last resort, could involve, first, outright purchases and sales of a wide range of private-sector securities and, second, acceptance of a wide range of private-sector securities as collateral.[44]

---

40. Mayer 2003.

41. Even when it is perceived as 'constrained discretion', as in the USA, which allows for stabilisation of output and employment subject to a declared target-range for inflation. See Bernanke 2003.

42. De Grauwe 2007, pp. 159–61.

43. Buiter and Siebert 2007.

44. Buiter and Siebert 2007, pp. 171–2.

But extending the function of the lender of last resort and complementing it with the function of the market-maker of last resort would be far from easy. First, severe moral-hazard problems could arise as central banks substituted public credit for bankrupt private credit. On this basis, Vives has even argued that the outbreak of crises might be desirable to maintain investment-discipline.[45] It is even postulated that some barely solvent institutions should not be rescued.[46] Second, it is possible that, as central banks acquire problematic private securities, their own solvency might become problematic.[47] Thus, it is proposed that the state (as national fiscal authority) should provide ultimate support for the central bank acting as lender and market-maker of last resort. One way of doing this would be for the state explicitly to underwrite the balance-sheet of the central bank.

From the Marxist perspective adopted in this chapter, the proposals are evidence of the central bank being used to socialise losses in order to protect private profits. Central-bank independence and inflation-targeting have allowed repeated bubbles to emerge, partly because of low inflation-rates. The ensuing disaster has led to renewed emphasis on lender of last resort supplemented with the novel function of market-maker of last resort. Financialisation has turned central banks into the main agent protecting financial interests at the expense of society as a whole.

5. Conclusion

The current period of capitalist development is characterised by an apparent paradox: the political power of central banks continues to rise, while their economic power is in serious doubt. This paradox is related to the role currently played by financial interests in promoting capitalist accumulation as a whole. Thus, in the era of financialisation, the central bank has emerged as the primary protector of financial interests. The basis of the power of the central bank is provided by its monopoly over legal tender, and this has been

---

45. Vives 2008, p. 99.
46. From a different perspective Dickens (1990, pp. 1–23, 1999, pp. 379–98) argued that financial instability is a problem created by the dynamics of the capitalist market reflecting the contradictions of capitalist accumulation. Financial crises are primarily due to political decisions and are political in nature.
47. Buiter 2008.

greatly enhanced in the course of financialisation. But the inherent instability of the capitalist economy, to which monetary and financial factors contribute strongly, sets limits on what central banks can do. The relative autonomy of the credit-system is an important factor in explaining financial instability in mature capitalism. In the era of financialisation, during which financial fragility has increased, the triggering of financial crises also has political aspects. It is similarly subject to considerable inter-class struggle between financially fragile (and thus less competitive) capitals and financially strong (and more competitive) capitals.

Inflation-targeting and central-bank independence have aimed at promoting capitalist accumulation at the expense of working people by 'immunising' central banks from the effects of class-struggle. Inflation-targeting and central-bank independence have facilitated extraction of private profits at the cost of increased financial instability with enormous ensuing losses for society. Capitalist states now recognise that central banking must go beyond inflation-targeting to protect the capitalist system from itself, without however abandoning the neoliberal agenda. This has meant renewed emphasis on the function of lender of last resort supplemented with the newly-fangled function of market-maker of last resort. In practice, this amounts to socialising financial losses in an effort to preserve private financial profits. Nonetheless, the crisis of 2007–9 has shown that there are limits to what central banks can do to stabilise finance.

As the burden of financial instability has become greater for the vast majority of society, the need for central banks to be subject to democratic control has become clearer. Through social control, central banks should be made to reflect the broader interests of workers and others, rather than primarily those of banks and finance. Central banking is often called an art, but it should certainly not be an art for the benefit of the few.

Part Two

International Financialisation and the Global Impact of the Crisis

Chapter Five

The Historical Significance and the Social Costs of the Subprime Crisis: Drawing on the Japanese Experience

Makoto Itoh

The financial turmoil that started in the USA in the summer of 2007 has become a global financial crisis, battering the real economy of developed countries, and fast becoming a world-economic crisis. The term 'subprime crisis' is used in this chapter to capture this entire process. Its historical significance is examined below in three separate but related ways.[1] Section 1 considers the specific features of the subprime crisis particularly in comparison with the Japanese bubble of the 1980s and the ensuing crisis of the 1990s. Section 2 pursues the comparison further by discussing briefly the great depression that followed after 1929, and suggests reasons why the current crisis might not be equally drastic. Finally, Section 3 probes into the social costs of the crisis.

---

1. The author is grateful to Costas Lapavitsas for editing the early draft of this chapter and offering insightful advice on how to revise it.

1. The specific features of the subprime financial crisis and a comparison with the Japanese bubble

The historical significance and specific features of any economic crisis are always determined by the character of the preceding economic boom. Thus, the subprime financial crisis originated in the US housing bubble and the associated boom. To understand why this financial crisis has become so destructive for the US and the world-economy, it is first necessary to examine the magnitude and character of the preceding US housing boom.

The US housing boom started in 1996, along with the 'New-Economy' boom, and lasted for about ten years. After the burst of the 'New-Economy' (or information-technology) bubble in 2001, the housing boom became the main source of US-economic recovery and growth, particularly from 2002 onwards. It is estimated that about 40% of the US-economic growth in this period depended on the housing sector.[2]

The housing boom would have been impossible without the expansion of housing finance. In the USA, housing loans are divided mostly into prime and subprime, the latter being typically loans to people of lower income and with low creditworthiness. More concretely, subprime loans are made to people with a record of delayed repayment on past loans, or an estimated FICO credit-score of under 660 (this is a credit-scoring system initiated by Fair Issac Co. with a maximum score of 900), or even debt-repayments comprising more than 50% of their income.

In the past, people classed as subprime were typically excluded from housing loans. But, after 2001, there was rapid growth of housing loans in the USA, and especially subprime loans. The result of growth in lending was to push house-prices steadily up, until by 2006 their level was double that of 1996. Total outstanding US housing loans reached $13tr (almost equal to GDP) at the end of 2006. Within that volume of debt, the proportion of subprime loans increased rapidly, especially after 2001. By 2006, subprime loans represented 20% of the flow of new housing loans. At the end of that year, the stock of subprime loans amounted to $1.7tr, or 13% of the entire stock of housing loans.[3]

Some simple calculations can further convey the relative magnitude of the subprime loan-expansion. The typical size of subprime loans is around

---

2. Kaneko and DeWit 2008, p. 9.
3. Mizuho Research Institute 2007, pp. 69, 77.

$200,000,[4] and thus they have been obtained in the USA by roughly 8.5mn households (or more than 25mn people). Further, assuming that the average size of a housing loan is about $300,000 dollars, the total volume of housing credit in the USA at the end of 2006 ($13tr) was taken up by roughly 43.3mn households, or about 43% of the US-population. In contrast, total outstanding housing loans in Japan in 1993 (soon after the burst of the bubble) were estimated at ¥141tr (about 29% of GDP). Given that the average housing loan stood at ¥27.4mn in 1992, the total housing debt in Japan referred to roughly 5.1mn households, or 12.3% of the population.[5] It is clear that US housing loans in general, and subprime loans in particular, far exceeded Japanese housing loans in the course of the bubble of the late 1980s.

Nonetheless, the Japanese bubble was big enough to cause major capital-losses, rising to more than ¥1400tr during the 1990s (including falls in prices of shares and real estate). But it is important to bear in mind that the housing market was only a part of the bubble. There was also a speculative boom in the stock-market as well as in whole real estate. In contrast, the US-economic boom that preceded the current crisis occurred in two relatively distinct waves. The first was the swell and burst of the information-technology (IT) bubble, mainly in New York stock-exchange during 1996–2001. The second was the housing boom and its burst, which followed in the 2000s.

Pursuing the comparison with Japan further, there was obviously a common factor to both Japanese and US-bubbles, which eventually led to their burst. Namely, there was abundant availability of money-funds that could be easily mobilised for speculative trading. In the course of the long downturn that began in the late 1970s, big businesses have become increasingly reliant on self-finance. Consequently, banks and other financial institutions in advanced countries have found themselves in possession of funds that could be used flexibly in fields other than industrial activity. For banks and other financial institutions, this has meant necessity of advancing funds for consumer-credit, housing loans, and speculative trading in real estate and various securities. Against this background, monetary policy that lowered interest-rates also tended to ignite speculative trading in real estate and securities, as happened in Japan following the Plaza accord of 1985 and in the USA after 2001.

---

4. Japan Cabinet Office, Policy Planning Room 2007, p. 7.
5. Itoh 2006, Chapter 6, which is also in Dymski and Isenberg (eds.) 2002.

A further common factor to both bubbles was the use of IT for specula-tive financial trading, including housing loans. The development of IT has facilitated rapid estimation of the schedule of return-payments with variable interest-rates, as well as swift financial transactions and flexible expansion of banking credit. In US-finance, in particular, IT was applied to deriving credit-scores for individuals as well as to designing and maintaining hybrid housing loans that had 'teaser'-rates of interest during the initial years thus attract-ing workers with lower income. Information-technology also made possible structured securitisation in case of US-housing loans and the subsequent spread of securities across the world.

There were, however, two political (and institutional) factors that facilitated the swelling of the US housing boom. First, the neoliberal policies that lifted regulations on financial transactions also made possible the introduction of housing loans with flexible 'teaser'-rates of interest. Second, the Community Reinvestment Act (1977) (encouraging banks to recycle a certain part of house-hold-savings in local-community areas) and the Alternative Mortgage Trans-action Parity Act (1982) (preventing discrimination against lower-income persons' living areas in housing finance) facilitated the advance of subprime loans. Such loans appeared as an innovative policy to promote urban renewal through the mobilisation of private-financial funds. Thus, financial busi-nesses took advantage of the democratisation of financial services, which was thought to be an achievement of the civil-rights movement since the 1960s. This unfortunate and paradoxical development led to aggressive expansion of housing loans to people on lower incomes, eventually resulting in disaster.

To place this development in a broader context, note that, in the long his-torical process of capitalist development, the financial system has functioned mainly as a set of social mechanisms that mobilise idle money to serve pur-poses of accumulation by capitalist enterprises. However, in the twentieth century, saving by working people, including pension-funds and insurance-payments, has been increasingly incorporated into the social mechanisms of the financial system. Similar considerations apply to consumer-credit.

Credit for consumption has been traditionally provided by pawn-shops and loan-sharks (a carry over from the precapitalist era) as well as by consumer-credit companies. These mechanisms of consumer-credit have been relatively small and marginal to the modern banking and financial systems. However, as large enterprises became increasingly reliant on self-finance, formal financial institutions have had fewer opportunities to lend to non-financial enterprises. Thus, major banks and other financial institutions began to expand consumer-credit and especially housing loans to working people, gradually advancing toward lower-income layers. In this sense, the commodity of labour-power has become increasingly financialised.[6] This tendency can be called finan-cialisation of labour-power, and was clearly present already in the course of the Japanese bubble, but has been enormously exacerbated during the recent US housing boom. Banks and related real-estate agencies have aggressively tempted workers to borrow by dangling the prospect of capital-gains in the course of the US housing boom.

Note, though, that the Japanese bubble was financed mostly by funds drawn domestically from high household-savings that stood around 15% of GNP. The US housing boom, in contrast, had no comparable domestic source of funds as the savings of US-households were extremely low. Thus, it was financed through global fund-raising via securitisation of mortgages. Con-sequently, financial practices in the US housing market were quite different from the earlier practices of Japanese banks, and even of the US Saving and Loan Associations (S&L) until the 1980s.

During the 1980s, the lending model for US-financial enterprises that under-took mortgage-business (typically S&L) was 'originate-to-hold'. But, during the recent boom, the main originators of mortgages were mortgage-compa-nies that did not accept deposits and proceeded to sell their loan. The buy-ers were typically 'Special-Purpose Vehicles (SPV)' owned by big commercial and investment-banks. After acquiring these mortgages, SPVs combined large numbers of them into mortgage-backed securities (MBS) that were then sold to other financial institutions. Banks also originated mortgages that were then taken off the balance-sheet through sale to SPVs established for the purpose. This is the substance of the 'originate-to-distribute' model.

Through these techniques, the US housing-loan market was structurally doubled: the first layer comprised original lenders (typically, mortgage-companies) and household-borrowers, while the second included financial institutions that distributed mortgage-backed securities across the world.

---

6. This notion is essentially similar to Lapavitsas in this volume, for whom finan-cial expropriation of wage-workers is central to the financialisation of contemporary capitalism.

These new practices freed the original lenders, such as the mortgage-companies, from the limits imposed by deposits as a lending resource, and encouraged banks to seek non-deposit funds, thus leading them to wholesale borrowing in the money-market. It also appeared to free banks from credit-risk (individual default) and interest-rate risk (fixed interest-rates on housing loans but fluctuating rates on deposits).

This mode of operation characterised the US housing-loan market since the middle of 1990s. There were no mechanisms of this type in Japan when the speculative bubble in housing emerged in the late 1980s. This explains why the collapse of the US housing market – subprime and other – became the source of a global-financial crisis, whereas the burst of the huge Japanese bubble had essentially localised effects. By the same token, Japanese banks as holders of mortgages suffered mainly due to the deterioration in the quality of their loans following the burst of bubble. But, after the US-bubble burst, the effects spread far and wide as falls in the prices of mortgage-backed and asset-backed securities damaged the balance-sheets of a broad array of financial institutions. These include, in addition to investment-banks and commercial banks, hedge-funds, insurance-funds, pension-funds, and securities-companies.

This difference is an important reason why US-authorities initially committed public funds to purchasing or guaranteeing mortgage-backed and other securities from various financial institutions. In contrast, Japanese authorities injected public funds mainly into the equity-capital of major banks. It was only after the crisis became deeper that the US-government redirected its rescue-operations of banks to include direct injection of public money into bank-equity.

The Japanese (and German) financial system is often contrasted to the US (and UK) financial system. The former depends more on indirect finance (or 'originate-to-hold' banking credit) while the latter depends on direct finance (or 'originate-to-distribute' credit operating through the securities-market). In recent years, the view prevailed that US-UK are superior to Japanese-German methods. One apparent reason is that competitive securities-markets are more transparent, rational and efficient in allocating money-funds compared to indirect banking credit that relies on personal relationships (even resulting in crony-capitalism) and private information. Such views gained credibility during the housing boom, as the US-system of securitising loans successfully mobilised global funds to feed credit-demand and house-prices continued to rise.

Unfortunately, there was no real basis for the theory (or belief) that the risks contained in housing loans – including subprime loans – could be dispersed and objectively reduced through mortgage-backed securities. In reality, the risks contained in mortgage-backed securities were not at all transparent, and became even more obscure due to misleading grading by credit-rating agencies, such as Standard and Poor's or Moody's. Thus, in June 2007, two hedge-funds attached to the giant investment-bank Bear Stearns failed due to losses in subprime mortgage-backed securities. This set in train a rapid process of downgrading more than a thousand mortgage-backed securities by Standard and Poor's and Moody's. About six months after the end of the housing boom, the real risks contained by mortgage-backed securities issued in the USA and held across the world were suddenly revealed.

In 2007, there were roughly $700bn of subprime mortgage-backed securities, $600bn of (slightly better quality) 'Alt-A' bonds, and $390bn of Collateralised Debt-Obligations (CDOs)[7] circulating in the global-financial markets. In the summer of 2008, Fannie Mae (Federal National Mortgage Association, FNMA) and Freddie Mac (Federal Home Loan Mortgage Corporation, FHLMC) went into serious crisis, and were virtually nationalised in September. These enterprises guarantee almost half of prime US housing loans. It then became clear that the quality of loans across the whole of the US housing market had seriously deteriorated. Thus, the securities generated by that market began to deliver destructive blows to global-financial institutions in entirely unpredictable ways. The world-financial markets entered a minefield, regularly reporting huge losses and running the risk of bankruptcy.

The subprime financial crisis has shown that the neoliberal belief in market-efficiency is without foundation, especially regarding financial markets. At the same time, it has forced a rethink of the supposed superiority of the US (and UK) over the Japanese (and German) financial system. Once the speculative bubble in the housing market had burst, the US-financial system spread disaster across the world, causing major instability domestically and globally. In contrast, the Japanese crisis remained largely local, affecting mainly, and most severely, the banking sector. By the same token, the injection of public funds in the financial institutions of the US and Europe may have different results from Japanese policy in the 1990s and 2000s. The current financial

---

7. CDOs are securities that are backed by mortgage-backed securities and other consumer-credit, such as automobile-loans.

crisis is likely to prove more difficult to confront. The Japanese economy went through a decade and more of stagnation (with almost zero growth after 1991), but the current crisis might cause severe falls and longer depression in major economies.

2. Once in a hundred years?

In May 2007, at a time when the subprime problem was clearly in the offing, the OECD predicted a slowdown of the US-economy. It thought that this would not herald a period of worldwide economic weakness but, rather, a 'smooth' rebalancing of the global economy, with Europe taking over the baton of growth from the United States. This was called the 'decoupling scenario'. This expectation was obviously built on the experience of previous speculative bubbles – for instance, the burst of the Japanese bubble after 1990s, the Asian crisis in 1997–8, and the burst of the US 'New-Economy' bubble in 2001. These had relatively limited and localised effects, and were even followed by bubbles elsewhere in the world.

Unfortunately, this scenario failed because of the specific features of the subprime financial crisis, which meant that it could not remain local. The subprime crisis is now turning into a vicious world-economic crisis in a 're-coupling scenario'. The merry-go-round of bubble-crisis-bubble in successive parts of the world has broken down. As the destructive force of the subprime financial crisis became apparent, Alan Greenspan, the former Chairman of the Federal Reserve Board, called it a once-in-a-century 'tsunami'. The Japanese prime minister, Taro Aso, followed Greenspan's lead and stated that the world finds itself in a financial crisis that happens once every hundred years. These statements seem to reflect the real threat posed by the current world-economic crisis.

The question inevitably is: will the destructive force of this crisis prove greater than that of 1929? In brief, the crisis of 1929 occurred at the end of a US-economic boom, became progressively deeper over the next three and a half years in the USA, entailed a fall of share-prices of almost 90%, caused nine thousand bank-failures in three waves, led to a rise in the unemployment-rate to 25%, and resulted in a decline of GDP of about 46%.[8] In its wake came a

---

8. Takumi 1994, 1998 presents a detailed analysis of the Great Crisis following 1929.

severe deflation-spiral, a world-agricultural crisis, the breakdown of the gold-standard that had been restored in the 1920s, a contraction of international trade because of formation of trading blocs, and general devastation in economic life across the world. Are we approaching a similar, or even greater, economic breakdown through the current financial crisis? This fear began to spread among international financial and business-circles as sharp falls in share-prices took place following the Lehman shock, which was caused by the failure of Lehman Brothers in September 2008.

The possibility that such devastation would occur again can be no longer ignored. In itself this is a contemporary manifestation of the inner contradictions of the capitalist economy. But the issue has to be approached cautiously. There have been several financial crises during the last two decades, most prominently the burst of the giant Japanese bubble of the 1980s, the Asian crisis of 1997–8, and the burst of the 'New-Economy' bubble. They have involved the meltdown of financial assets, the value of which relative to GDP was comparable, or even larger, to the great crisis of 1929. Yet, none – and this also holds for subprime financial crisis at the time of writing – brought a comparable acute collapse of the economy through mutual destruction between finance and the real economy. Conditions are different from 1929, and the current financial crisis has to be seen in appropriate perspective. Consider the following four factors that could lessen the impact of the current crisis relative to 1929.

First, following the initial shock of 1929, the gold-standard restricted the flexibility of both fiscal and monetary policy by fixing exchange-rates and forcing countries to hoard gold-reserves. The formation of trading blocs subsequently accelerated the decline in world-trade. In contrast, the system of floating exchange-rates currently frees major countries from the need to keep reserves of international means of payment. This provides room for flexible operation of fiscal and monetary policy. Thus, it has become possible to inject enormous amounts of public funds to rescue banks and other financial institutions, following the Japanese methods of the late 1990s.

There is no doubt that injecting public funds into financial institutions mitigates the danger of acute collapse of the world-economy, particularly when combined with emergency fiscal and monetary policies in the USA. At the same time, these policies tend to increase budget-deficits and raise the burden of public debt for several years, thus contributing to persistent economic stagnation, as experienced in Japan. Furthermore, large US budget-deficits can be financed only through a huge expansion of international debt, thus raising the spectre of a fall in the value of the dollar. This makes it necessary for the US-government to seek international-political co-operation to avoid a collapse of the dollar as well as creating a new international-monetary order.

Second, in the course of the great crisis of 1929, monopoly-capitals in major countries rapidly reduced production and employment in order to maintain monopoly-prices and profits. This behaviour is characteristic of monopolies, and generally exacerbated the macroeconomic performance of major economies at that time. But, under current conditions, the monopolistic malady is not nearly so evident. Even the largest enterprises are operating under global-competitive pressure, and are finding it difficult to sustain monopoly-prices and profits in their domestic markets. This lies at the root of the difficulties that the Big Three in the US automobile-industry have faced. Thus the collapse of output and employment by big enterprises would probably be less severe than 1929, and mostly the result – rather than the cause – of the decline in consumer-demand. Moreover, and as was mentioned above, large multinational enterprises have become increasingly self-financed. Consequently, their business-activities might not suffer a heavy direct effect from the constriction of credit due to the financial crisis. On the other hand, smaller and medium-enterprises that depend heavily on banking credit have suffered badly in the course of the crisis.

Third, and related to the first two, the destructive impact of the financial crisis on employment and real wages in the industrial sector remains milder than in 1929, though it is becoming increasingly severe. Workers' savings, insurance, pensions, and social security, including unemployment-benefits, have supported workers' consumption to some extent, though with rising anxiety for the future. At the same time, the rise in unemployment, the cuts in working hours, and the reductions of wages among workers will probably allow capitalist enterprises flexibly to reduce their costs in the face of crisis.

Fourth, in the age of globalisation, the economic vitality of developing countries, for instance, China and other Asian economies, has been greatly enhanced. Their success has depended on continuous mobilisation of cheap labour, supported by direct investment by multinational enterprises from abroad. Transfer of economic surplus from developing countries through trade, investment, and finance serves directly or indirectly as a cushion to mitigate the economic crisis in the major developed countries. Imports of cheap consumer-goods, for example, help to lessen the difficulties brought by economic crisis for working people, though they also press wages in a downward direction.[9] This logic also means an increased business-opportunity for China and other Asian developing countries. Finally, the accumulation of oil-revenues during the period of high oil-prices, subsequently recycled through the international-financial markets, has also worked to mitigate the financial crisis, though it also promoted the speculative bubble in the previous period.

These factors taken together have, for the time being, mitigated the subprime financial crisis and made it less severe than the 1929 crisis. However, this effect cannot be regarded as absolute and everlasting. It is not clear to what extent these factors can resist the intrinsic self-destructive tendency of contemporary finance. Much will depend on the interaction between the real economy and finance, and the mutual damage inflicted. The danger would be that the severe pressure on enterprises and the state would then be transferred to working people. At the very least, the gap between rich and poor would probably increase across the world, as would the numbers of the working poor.

3. The social costs

Neoliberalism was the dominant policy-framework in advanced-capitalist countries since the 1980s until recently. It draws on neoclassical microeconomics and believes in the efficiency of competitive and unregulated markets. Consequently, it has promoted privatisation of public enterprises as well as deregulation in various areas, including the financial sector. In particular, global emphasis has been placed on the presumed efficiency of US-type finance, based on securities-markets. Therefore, it should be noted emphatically that the current subprime financial crisis has occurred not due to an external shock, such as an earthquake or war, but largely due to the internal motion of the US-financial system itself.

The consequent economic losses are clear evidence that neoliberal beliefs in market-efficiency as well as in the apparent advantages of US-type finance are false. The economic losses have several aspects and may be defined as the social costs of the subprime financial crisis. The notion of social cost generally

---

9. The theory of unequal exchange by the dependency-school, including Emmanuel 1972, is worth re-reading from this point of view.

comprises a variety of phenomena, such as externalities imposed on a third party or society as a whole, macroeconomic losses from failure to attain optimal allocation as well as costs due to public policy. Although the total social costs of the current financial crisis are far from definite, the following four aspects can already be identified, particularly when the earlier experience of the Japanese bubble is borne in mind.

First, there are economic losses on the part of mortgage-debtors. More than 2mn foreclosures had taken place in the USA already by 2008. For these debtors thrown out of their houses, past payments on loans as well as expenditure on house-durables have been totally wasted. These losses have hit mostly low-income borrowers in the subprime category. But even prime mortgage-borrowers have suffered in terms of declines in both asset-prices and incomes. As housing prices fall, the market-value of a house could easily become less than the mortgage-debt and yet, repayment is demanded even for the capital-losses.

Following the burst of the bubble in Japan, house-prices in the 1990s fell by more than a half in some metropolitan areas. From the point of view of the debtors, continuous repayment of the corresponding housing loans had no equivalent – it was in vain. In the USA, the pace of house-price decline is already faster than that of the 1929 crisis, and the fall could finally exceed the drop of 26% reached at that period.[10] Given that the total volume of US housing loans is roughly equal to GDP, the payments made in vain by debtors over a period of years could reach one third of current GDP. This would make an enormous social loss, without even considering the costs of foreclosures.

Second, there are vast capital-losses due to price-falls of a broad range of securities – mortgage-backed securities, asset-backed securities, shares, and so on – across the world. Following the burst of the Japanese bubble, total capital-losses from share-prices were estimated at about ¥500tr, roughly equal to Japan's GDP at the middle of the 1990s, and this is without including similar capital-losses in real estate.[11] It remains to be seen whether the total capital-losses in securities in the USA and elsewhere will currently reach similar proportions relative to GDP. But there is no doubt that their absolute size will be several times bigger than the Japanese losses of the 1990s.

---

10. Kaneko and DeWit 2008, p. 22.
11. Itoh 2006, Chapter 6, which is also in Dymski and Isenberg (eds.) 2002.

What can be said about the implications of capital-losses in securities, shares and real estate, particularly from the standpoint of the labour-theory of value? To a certain extent, such losses might be offset by gains made during the preceding boom, but there is no guarantee that they would exactly balance out. On the other hand, the price falls that occur during the burst of a bubble operate as a pure loss for individual workers, enterprises, and society as a whole. It is true that a part of these capital-losses remains latent as long as assets are not actually sold, and this is an aspect of the fictitious estimation of asset-values. Moreover, when capital-losses are actually realised through the sale of securities, the possibility exists that others might gain through such transactions. Even so, the net result is most probably negative, making this a non-zero-sum game. Understanding the social dimension of the (negative) value of such capital-losses remains a thorny theoretical problem.

For the Marxist theory of value, the living labour that is embodied in the social total products per annum forms the substance of value that is newly created. This is distributed between the capitalist class (including landowners and *rentiers*) and wage-workers. It is possible that some part of the value produced is lost due to the difficulty of realising it in the markets (being unable to sell or selling commodities below normal prices). However, capital-losses for society would not necessarily be related to, or correspond to an unrealised part of the value produced by annual living labour. Rather, the volume of capital-losses is likely to be much larger.

It is probable that such capital-losses signify, first, the destruction of part of the stock of claims on accumulated past labour and, second, the redistribution of the flow of income arising out of annual living labour. This is theoretically different from, but reminiscent of the 'moral' depreciation of machinery, that is, the social destruction of accumulated labour-time in machinery when more efficient technology in one industry becomes the social standard. In an economic crisis, it is possible that such a destructive blow can take the form of capital-losses in securities, shares, and real-estate prices (as a devaluation of fictitious capital, to use Marx's term). This would impose (directly or indirectly) changes in the distribution of the annual flow of income as well as probably reducing the aggregate flow.

Irrespective of its impact on the size and distribution of income, a drop in securities-prices certainly imposes losses on banks and other financial institutions. Under Basle II regulations on capital-adequacy (introduced in 2004 by the Bank of International Settlements, BIS), the Current (or Fair) Value Accounting System has become the global standard for banks. This fits with the practices of securitised financial markets since it facilitates current estimates of the value of shares of financial corporations and other business-companies. It is also another example of imposing US-type financial practices across the world in an attempt to provide a more transparent environment within which to undertake risk-management in securities- and stock-markets. The impact of these regulations has been damaging to banks because rising (but latent) capital-losses have made it difficult to maintain capital-adequacy ratios. The regulations have worsened the impact of the subprime financial crisis.

Japanese banks suffered greatly in the 1990s from the earlier Basle I regulations on capital-adequacy, imposed by BIS in 1987. These regulations required that banks should maintain a capital-adequacy ratio of at least 8%. They prolonged the crisis in Japan by worsening banks' ability to advance credit to small and medium-enterprises. In short, BIS-regulations, both I and II, have been ineffective in preventing the burst of bubbles and rather worsened the ensuing banking crises.

At the same time, it has to be noted that banks and other financial institutions, including institutional investors, currently manage not only the money-funds of capitalist enterprises and the wealthy, but also savings and pension- and insurance-contributions by the mass of working people. Since large proportions of these funds are invested in shares and other securities, it is probable that capital-losses and associate failures by financial institutions would also greatly affect working people. The potential costs are an important reason why the injection of public funds to rescue the financial system has not elicited stronger opposition by working people.

Third, public money used to rescue banks and other financial institutions is a type of social cost. In the USA, for example, the Bush administration eventually succeeded in passing the Financial Stability Law at the beginning of October 2008, allowing it inject up to $700bn into the financial system. This is about equal to the total volume of Japanese public funds (¥70tr) injected into the banks in the 1990s. This took place mainly in the form of equity to allow banks to meet the regulations of Basle I. In some cases, the funds functioned as a kind of subsidy aimed at restructuring failed banks by effectively nationalising them, only to re-privatise them subsequently. This was the case, for instance, for the Long-Term Credit Bank of Japan, which became Shinsei Bank, and for Nippon Credit Bank, which turned into Aozora Bank. In other cases, however, the bulk of the injected public funds were returned to the state as the economy recovered after 2002, and following rationalisation and mergers among banks. Nevertheless, roughly ¥10tr remains uncollected, and that is a pure social cost. As public funds in the USA are largely used to buy problematic securities from banks, it is possible that a proportionately larger social cost would result as these securities become progressively worthless.

Funds committed under the Financial Stability Law, however, do not cover the whole of the public funds expended by the US-government and the Federal Reserve Board in the course of the current crisis. According to one report, the USA has pledged up to $7.7tr to ease frozen credit-markets.[12] This includes $3.2tr already tapped by financial institutions as well as $2.4tr committed by the Fed to intervening in the commercial-paper market. The total of committed funds runs to about half the size of the US GDP, and is nine times what the USA has spent so far on wars in Iraq and Afghanistan. It is probable that a significant part of those funds would also be lost through default or deterioration in the prices of securities, thus being shifted onto the shoulders of tax-payers. (Here is a reason why Obama administration is demanding a new charge to banks and other financial institutions operating in the USA.)

More broadly, the UK and several other EU-countries have been committing public funds to rescuing financial institutions. This passes under the name of international co-operation with the aim of preventing a worsening of the current global-financial impasse. Through injection of public funds, several banks and other financial institutions have effectively been nationalised, or are close to submitting their management to public control. This development is completely contrary to the theoretical precepts of neoliberalism, and actually runs closer to socialist arguments about managing the capitalist economy than even to traditional Keynesianism.

Fourth, there are also social costs caused by the destructive effects of the subprime financial crisis on the real economy. These are hard to estimate but are plainly vast. They include, for instance, a fall in profits and revenue of capitalist enterprises, a fall in production, and a rise in idle capacity and idle

---

12. Pittman and Ivery 2008.

resources more generally. Actually, growth-rates in the major economies had to fall in 2009, and became generally negative. For the OECD as a whole, the growth rate fell from 1.4% in 2008 to −3.5% in 2009; for the USA, from 1.4% to −2.5%; for Japan from 0.5% to −5.3%; and for the euro-area, from 1.1% to −4.0%.[13] A significant part of the costs imposed by these developments – both for the individuals involved and for society as a whole – includes the ensuing rise in unemployment. It is likely that this will become greater as the real economy is progressively hit harder. The International Labour Organisation, for instance, announced in January 2010 that unemployment across the world increased from 197 million in 2007 to 212 million in 2009, its highest level, and is likely to remain continuously high also in 2010.[14]

In conclusion, the subprime financial crisis has clearly signified the historical limits of neoliberalism and showed the need to bring three decades of neoliberalism to an end. At the same time, the crisis has also revealed the fundamental instability and contradictoriness of the capitalist economy, and cannot be attributed to mere mismanagement, or wrong economic policies. Neither the Japanese type of indirect finance, nor the US-type of direct finance was able to prevent the disastrous swell and burst of huge bubbles. Under the dominance of neoliberalism, the capitalist economy has been largely freed from social control and regulations, especially in the field of finance. Financialisation of labour-power advanced headlong. The subprime financial crisis is nothing but the disastrous result of such unleashed financialised capitalism being promoted by neoliberalism.

The current crisis has shown that neoliberal theories and policies are deeply problematic. However, it is not yet clear what theoretical approaches can offer well-founded alternatives. Keynesianism should not be the only other approach contesting the field. Radical-political economy, based on Marxist theory of money, credit and finance, finds in the current crisis an opportunity to test and develop its ideas and proposals.[15] It could also propose alternatives to neoliberalism that serve the interests of working people more successfully than alternative ideas emanating from the mainstream.

---

13. OECD 2009, No. 86.
14. ILO bureau-report, in *The Financial Express*, 2 February 2010.
15. Some of these ideas were put forth in Itoh and Lapavitsas 1999.

Chapter Six

The Globalisation of Financial Capital, 1997–2008 [1]

Carlos Morera Camacho
José Antonio Rojas Nieto

1. The transformation of the world-economy

The world-economy has experienced thirty years of
dramatic changes, deriving from the profound economic turmoil that followed the oil-crises of 1973–4
and 1980–1, the collapse of 'actually existing socialism', and the transformation of China. Global and
generalised restructuring took place as a result of
these developments. Gradually, new characteristics
emerged in a world-economy including, first, predominance of financial capital subject to dollar-hegemony;
second, strong dynamism and new characteristics
of the world-financial sector; and third, intensified
articulation between national-financial markets
and monetary systems. To a large extent, these
characteristics flowed from the deregulation- and

1. This chapter is part of a bigger study currently under way on the 'The World
Financial and Oil Markets, 1997–2007'. It has benefited from critical observations by
Costas Lapavitsas, particularly with regard to credit. The development of the data-
base and the diagrams received support from Lidia Salinas Islas, Isaac Torres and
Iván Mendieta.

liberalisation-measures implemented initially by the United States and the United Kingdom between 1979 and 1982. But the majority of industrialised and developing countries have followed suit.

What has emerged is the consolidation of an international-financial space through which practically all national-financial processes are obliged to pass in an articulated manner. This imperative also applies to national productive and commercial activities. Without a doubt, major technological changes have sustained these transformations. Modern microelectronics and the internet have enormous capacity to maximise volume and minimise costs of transmiting information. Technical changes have made structural transformations possible and gave them momentum.

The transformation of world-capitalism has further been sustained by numerous and substantial changes in the processes of work, which have typically meant generalised attacks on workers' conditions. Without a doubt, some of the most important changes experienced by capital in the last three decades correspond to both waged and unwaged labour.[2] These have included, first, substantial changes in production-technologies, particularly control and automation of processes; second, the extension of so-called temporary layoffs; and third, proliferation of flexible forms of hiring. Workers' conditions have been adversely affected through prices rising faster than wages, falls in money-wages, worsening conditions of social security, layoffs, old-age provision and retirement, and finally, business-insolvencies and bankruptcies.[3]

Nevertheless – as demonstrated by the extremely critical conditions of 2008–9 – global capital has not succeeded in re-establishing the rhythms of growth and profitability that characterised the early post-World-War II era. On the contrary, the effects of continuous restructuring during the last thirty years have been asymmetrical on production and circulation. This asymmetry has intensified since 1998 – in favour of circulation. The current crisis comes at end of a boom in the US-economy that lasted for nearly ten years, and which – as is now apparent – was prolonged far beyond what was justified by its true foundations. The (relatively artificial) boom actually rested on an unprecedented expansion of credit to government, to businesses and to US-

---

2. Munck 2002, pp. 19–27. Anderson 2006, p. 28.
3. Moseley 2007, pp. 2–3. Gill 2002, pp. 643–4.

households. To establish this point, consider the following aspects of the US economy.

2. The restoration of profitability and the performance of the US-economy

Marxist theory identifies profit as the engine of capitalism, and asserts that the rate of profit tends to fall as a result of intensified capital-accumulation relative to the generation and appropriation of surplus-value. However, the process is complex since, on the one hand, there is a tendency for the rate of profit to fall but, on the other, there are substantial increases in the mass of profit. These two different movements make disputes among all the factions of capital more controversial and violent.[4]

The performance of the US-economy can be analysed in line with the evolution of the rate of profit. The crisis and stagnation phase of the US-economy in the 1970s were based on a fall in the rate of profit by approximately 50% from 1950 to 1970.[5] There was further fall of 30% in the following decade (see Figure 2 below).

The recovery of the rate of profit began in 1981, based on intensified exploitation of labour. Nevertheless, the circumstances of exploitation have also changed. The changes in the labour-process were expressed in what is known as *deterritorialisation* – the relocation of the production-process to other areas of the world-economy where wages, raw materials, fuels and energy are lower – which was promoted in the 1990s. However, the major strategy for restoring the rate of profit in the United States was *financialisation*, based on an increase in international debt and over-expansion of credit. Three moments stand out in the evolution of international debt: first, the United States becoming a net debtor, beginning in 1986; second, the arrival of crisis in Southeast Asia; and third, the impact of financial crisis of 2001 and 2008–9 on the markets.

In the second half of the 1990s, the prices of raw materials, fuel, energy and labour costs were relatively low. Interest-rates were at their lowest since World-War II. Substantial increases in productivity took place in the USA

---

4. Marx 1976 [1894], 57–82.
5. Moseley 2007, p. 6.

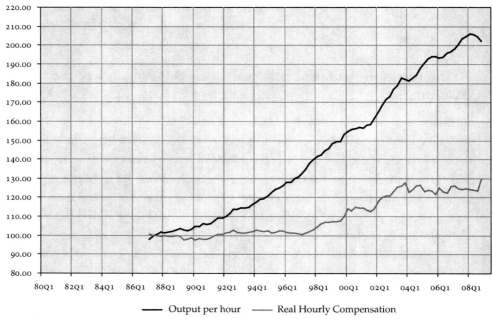

Source: Developed by authors, with data from the Federal Reserve Bank of St. Louis.

Figure 1   USA: Productivity and Real Wages in Manufacturing 1980–2009
1987=100

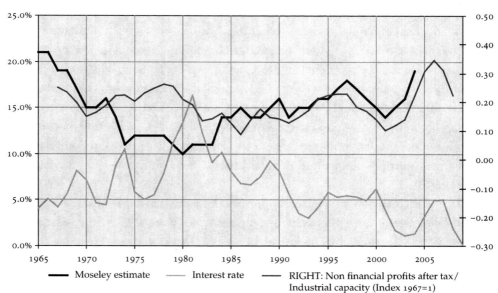

Source: Developed by authors, with data from the Federal Reserve Bank of St. Louis.

Figure 2   USA: Rate of Profit and Interest-Rate 1965–2009 Annual
Percentage-Level

(see Figure 1 above). Consequently, there was an impressive recovery of the profit rate in the United States, thus expressing improvements in the overall profitability of the world-economy. However, dramatic and violent increases in the prices of the raw materials, fuels and energy followed soon after. On the other hand, and in contrast to past experience, interest-rates not only remained low but tended to fall.

As a result, many mainstream-economists concluded that the boom at the end of the 1990s was a landmark. Apparently, the US-economy had left behind the long stagnation that began in the 1970s, and opened a new period of high economic growth, increased employment, inflation-reduction and moderate increases in wages. Yet, the crisis of 2001 showed that things were different, and recession established itself once again. Recovery, beginning in 2002, was slow, and growth in jobs lagged behind output. The dynamic of job-losses and insufficient employment-opportunities to absorb new labour-supplies has been extraordinarily severe. Profound transformations have ensued across the spheres of the world-economy (real sector), as well as in the financial and commercial system (virtual sector) and in technological development.[6]

The international credit-crisis that began in August 2007 has revealed the magnitude of the transformations that have taken place not only in banking but in all forms of capital and the state. The crisis itself was the result of an enormous expansion of mortgage-loans and consumer-credit, some of which were granted to the poorest and most oppressed sections of the working class.[7] Borrowers were heavily black and Latino, giving to the crisis a racial dimension.[8] US- and European banks were heavily affected by the collapse in the value of the mortgage-backed securities that they had created, and which turned out to be a significant portion of their assets. The resulting insolvency provoked a credit-crisis, and the initial reaction of financial institutions was to hoard funds, thereby intensifying the crisis.

---

6. Lapavitsas 2009.
7. Lapavitsas 2009.
8. Dymski 2009.

3. The Mexican and Asian financial crises of the 1990s, and the subsequent evolution of finance

The roots of the actual crisis and of the evolution of finance in the 2000s are to be found in the Mexican crisis of 1995 and the Southeast Asian (Thailand, Indonesia, Malaysia, and Philippines) crisis of 1997–8. Both crises evolved in similar fashion. They began with a devaluation of the local currency as a result of high trade-deficits, which had reached serious levels because of the link of the currencies to the dollar in the first place. This was followed by short-term capital-flight and collapse of weak financial markets.

As a result, there was strong contraction of credit and a severe drop in production, to say nothing of the brutal increase in the cost of public foreign debt. There was also a sharp rise in private-sector debt (banks and enterprises), which, in the case of Mexico, was transferred to captive taxpayers and to fiscal revenue from oil-profits. Simultaneously, there was withdrawal of short-term foreign and domestic investments and insolvency of local banking systems, which, in some cases, led to the collapse of both banks and national companies.

The Mexican crisis and the so-called 'tequila-effect' were contained. This can be attributed to several factors including, first, support from the United States, which was at the time experiencing considerable economic strength; second, the US-origin of the bulk of private capital-flows to Mexico, which prompted immediate support by the Clinton administration;[9] third, the trade-links of Mexico with the United States, in contrast to the intense trade-interdependence among the affected Asian economies; and fourth, the deepening of the privatisation-process in telecommunications and transportation, and even in areas forbidden by the country's constitution, specifically oil and electricity.

In the case of Southeast Asia, the private and fragmentary character of the economies tremendously hindered negotiations on how to deal with the crisis. In addition, the mechanisms of contagion in the Asian region were heavily located in the productive and commercial spheres, given that the development strategy of these economies since the 1960s was to orient themselves toward foreign markets. For Thailand, Indonesia, Malaysia, and the Philippines, as well as China in 1997, approximately 50% of their trade was regional, and a

---

9. Morera 1998, pp. 218–20, 2002, pp. 430–32.

similar proportion of this regional trade was with Japan. South Korea was also strongly affected and entered a recession.[10] In addition, Russia's external bankruptcy occurred in mid-1998, and subsequently Brazil.[11]

Following the Asian crisis, the international banking system became more closely articulated with both the private and public sectors of these countries. The new relationships included easy terms of refinancing agreed with the national banking systems in these countries. Debts did not disappear but rather increased as the crisis was expressed as a drop in production, trade, and employment. Asia accounts for a third of world-trade and, during the 1990s, it represented the only region that experienced sustained industrial growth, together with the United States. It is precisely in this region where most US-industrial exports are sold. In 1998, contraction in production and trade affected the US-economy and spilled over to countries that export raw materials, including oil.

However, in 1999 oil-prices began to rise, partly due to the tremendous dynamism of China and India, and partly due to the low margin of production capacity in relation to the levels of world-demand for crude. Consequently, capital-flows deriving from oil-profits and rent as well as from savings in emerging economies began to flow toward developed countries and particularly the United States. This allowed the US-economic cycle to go beyond what the internal savings rate would have permitted. And it also provided finance for the enormous US-deficit.[12]

Against this background, global-financial liberalisation and the ongoing technological revolution fostered an unprecedented financial boom after 1998. At the same time, it became impossible for monetary authorities to carry out monitoring and evaluation of financial conditions.[13] This boom reflects the powerful development of banking and non-banking financial institutions across the world. The close articulation of these institutions with the world-financial centre (the United States) is the reason why the 'momentary' crash of key debtors in the late 1990s actually translated into further increases in international banking assets. There was further global-financial expansion after 1998, and conditions were created for an even greater crisis.

---

10. Chesnais 1999, pp. 9–10.
11. UNCTAD 1999, pp. 59, 71–2.
12. BIS 2003, pp. 9–12, 50–3 and 2005, pp. 41–9.
13. *New York Times* 2002.

Underlying the phenomenal expansion of finance during the last ten years has been the relentless liberalisation of interest-rates, financial activities and international capital-flows. But note that the share of commercial banks (and savings institutions) in the total volume of loans has been declining. During this period, as was mentioned above, technological innovation became more intense in the areas of telecommunications and information, as well as in the new systems, processes and instruments used by financial institutions. The financial sector in the USA made the most intensive use of technological information, as measured by relative spending on computer-equipment and software.

Consequently, the activities of major US- (and British) banks during the last two decades have shifted away from meeting traditional demand for loans on the part of industrial and commercial corporations. Banks have developed profitable lines of lending to individuals as well as drawing income from a wide variety of fees charged (see Figure No. 3).

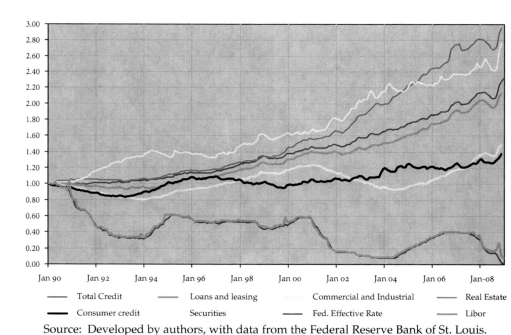

Source: Developed by authors, with data from the Federal Reserve Bank of St. Louis.

Figure 3   US Banking-Credit Index 1990–2008 (1990=1)

These developments have had a strong impact on credit-distribution and the socialisation of credit-risk, thereby introducing new elements of fragility in financial markets, which emerged sharply in 2008.[14]

4. The role of stock-markets

Stock-markets played a decisive role in the crises of 1997–8 as well as in the subsequent recovery of finance, and now, in the severe financial crisis, and it is important to examine them more closely. The stock-market is at the heart of fictitious capital, which takes the form of financial assets, both stocks and bonds.[15] In this market, the speed of transmission is almost instantaneous, making it even more difficult to foresee crises. As a rule, falls occur after phases of calm and recovery, and they can be local or regional, as in Asia in 1997–8, or worldwide, as in the USA after 2008. The collapse of Wall Street in 1997 was avoided by massive share-buybacks by large conglomerates.

But the crisis of 1997–8 also revealed the consequences, limits, and contradictions of financial liberalisation, dominated by large investment-funds (pension-funds and mutual funds), major transnational corporations, international banks and state-debt. A key pillar of this international economy of capital-money valorisation is the secondary capital-market, which generates increasing volatility and instability.[16] The origin and formation of fictitious capital is to be found in this market, through the issuing of securities, the formation of large companies via equity, and the immense accumulation of financial assets.

During the 1990s, the US-economy exhibited considerable dynamism and was able to promote innovative companies, particularly in the 'new' fields that encompass information-technologies and biotechnologies. This was also expressed in the stock-market sector, taking the NASDAQ-index from 400 points at the beginning of the decade, to a peak of 5000 points. The speculative bubble was particularly acute in 1999–2000. When it burst, the NASDAQ was brought down to slightly more than 1,000 points. To date, the index has not recovered the levels reached in 2000. (See Figure 4)

---

14. Lapavitsas 2009.
15. Marx 1976 [1894], pp. 511–31.
16. Bannock and Manser 2003, p. 238.

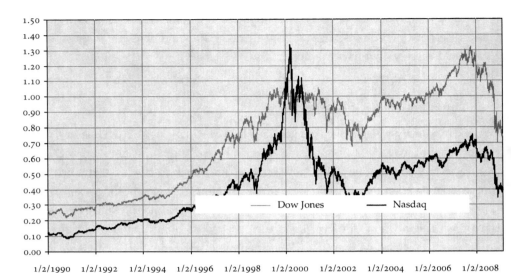

Note: Last data at February fifth

Figure 4   Evolution of US Stock-Market (Dow Jones and NASDAQ, 1990–2009) Index (2000=1)

Speculation, as a phenomenon characteristic of contemporary capitalism, tends to be interpreted as an aspect of the 'casino-economy'. But the crises discussed above are not only the result of the inherent instability of financial markets. Rather, they can be attributed to slow growth and endemic over-production throughout the 1990s, which spilled over into the crisis of the US-economy in 2001 (see Figure 5).

Moreover, fictitious capital is a property-title and, in the course of the development of capitalism, property-rights are continually reallocated. Mergers and acquisitions were pronounced in the 1980s, up to the crash of 1987. They recovered in the 1990s and evolved to their historic peak in 2000. Following the collapse of Wall Street and NASDAQ in 2000, mergers and acquisitions again recovered their dynamism, particularly after 2004. It appears that the process of capital-concentration (mergers and acquisitions) is cyclical, and historically occurs in periods of calm, following crisis and the recovery of the economy. As concentration takes place, it brings changes in the control of capital and rearranges financial powers, thus affecting world-economic conditions on all levels.

5. Foreign-direct investment, mergers and acquisitions, and the rising power of transnational companies

The new financial structure that has emerged encompasses complex processes formed by actors and instruments of a very diverse nature, both in terms of their origin and their operations. They include large companies and investment-banks specialising in the issuing and placement of securities; mutual funds (small and medium-investors); hedge-funds (companies specialising in speculative short-term operations); pension-funds (workers' retirement-savings); insurance-companies and treasuries of the transnational companies. The new structures developed in a contradictory manner. On the one hand, they cheapened credit but, on the other, they created new elements of instability, such as greater dispersion, volatility, and capital-speculation. In the emerging Latin-American markets, for instance, they initially cheapened credit, but later made it more expensive. But there is no doubt that the so-called globalisation of financial markets has led to an extraordinary transnationalisation of the holdings of debt-securities.

The result of this process was that foreign investment emerged as the predominant form of capital-transactions on an international scale. The relationship between foreign-direct investment and portfolio-investment has varied in the past 25 years. In 1981, fully 19% of the annual flows of private investment were portfolio-investment. However, the 1990s were characterised by growth of capital-flows toward developing economies mostly through institutional investors engaging in speculative investment and intensifying the volatility of these economies. Simultaneously, foreign-direct investment by transnational companies grew. In the second half of the decade, foreign-direct investment became the predominant form of capital-transactions, undertaken by transnational companies and international financial groups in the form of mergers, strategic alliances and privatisations.

From 1993 to 1998, developing economies received 35.3% of total foreign-direct investment, the highest percentage in the past two decades. This figure is even more significant if we consider that the total flow of foreign-direct investment throughout 1990–5 remained at an annual average level of slightly more than $225bn. However, in 1996, the figure rose to $386bn and in 1997 to $478bn. During 1995–8, developed countries channeled an annual average of 50% of these flows toward mergers and acquisitions, while the corresponding figure for the developing countries was 31%. During this period, the figure became double what it had been during the first half of the decade.[17]

Latin America was the most important recipient of foreign-direct investment aimed at mergers and acquisitions throughout the entire decade. Its annual average during the entire period was approximately 57.5%. A total of more than $196bn was earmarked for mergers and acquisitions, and most of these resources ($125bn) were invested during 1996–8 in Brazil, Argentina, and Mexico. During this period, South Asia (India) and East Asia (China, Hong Kong, Taiwan), as well as Southeast Asia (Indonesia, Republic of Korea, Philippines, Singapore, Thailand, and Malaysia) also witnessed significant mergers and acquisitions ($44bn). The largest volume of such resources was directed toward China, Hong Kong, and South Korea. Nevertheless, the greatest volume of mergers and acquisitions was registered in 1999–2001, when investment almost doubled ($82bn).[18]

The coming together of productive, financial, technological and organisational factors altered the profile of transnational corporations and gave them the greatest power they have ever had in the world-economy. Their percentage share of the world-GDP rose from 17% in the mid-1960s, to 24% in 1982, and to more than 30% in 1995. In that year, there were 39,000 transnational companies (including more than 4,000 in developing countries) that already dictated the course of the world-economy, with 270,000 subsidiaries abroad (of which 119,000 operated in developing countries). At present, there are 60,000 transnational companies with 800,000 subsidiaries. But the degree of concentration and centralisation of capital is even greater if we consider that the 100 largest transnational companies (not including banks and financial companies) controlled a third of foreign-direct investment. During 1988–95, 72% of these flows went to mergers and acquisitions of all types which, together with strategic alliances, were the international transactions that grew the most rapidly.

---

17. UNCTAD 2002, pp. 7, 33, 303, 306, 337.
18. Figures were calculated based on statistical information from UNCTAD, 2002.

6. Extreme weakness of US-industry in the late 2000s

During the past two decades, the behaviour of US-industry (representing almost a third of the world-total) has been very uneven. From 1991 to mid-2000, industrial production rose continuously at an annual average real rate of approximately 4.6%. Nonetheless, beginning in 1998, industrial production grew at increasingly lower rates, and, during the first few months of 2001, at negative rates. Only in mid-2002 (almost 18 months later) did rates of change become positive again. And it was not until the beginning of 2004 that the level of industrial production reached again the levels of the half of 2000. In all, US-industrial growth stagnated for three and a half years. The retreat and stagnation of industry during a period of almost forty months was reflected in two indicators: first, in the stagnation of industrial capacity for almost thirty months (see Figure 5); and second, in the severe fall of capacity-utilisation.[19]

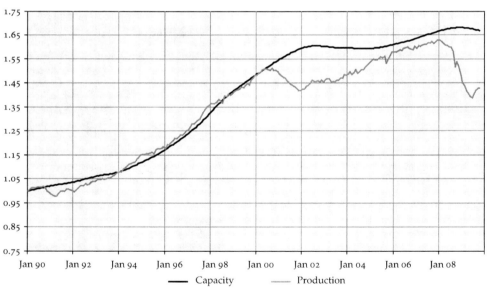

Source: Developed by authors, with data from the Bureau of Economic Analysis, Department of Commerce.

Figure 5   US-Industrial Production and Capacity 1990–2009.
January (1990=1)

---

19. Morera and Rojas 2008, pp. 112–13.

In December 2008, the level of industrial production in the USA was equivalent to that in the summer of 2004. Compared to December 2007, the drop was nearly 8%. This was the biggest fall in US-industrial production since the spring of 1975. US-industry currently stands at the level of five years ago and presents the dynamism of thirty-five years ago – a difficult predicament. Meanwhile, capacity-utilisation dropped to 73.6%. At its highest, between 1968 and 1973, years of unrestrained growth, capacity-utilisation in the USA stood at nearly 90%. In the 1980s, the average level of utilisation was above 80%, and at times it was almost 5% higher.

In the autumn of 1982, US-industry experienced one of the worst falls in its history but still managed to recover. Nevertheless, capacity-utilisation dropped to a mere 72% at the end of that decade, while in the 1990s – in the winters of 1995 and 1997 – it achieved maximum-levels of 85% during certain months. From 1998 to the present, US-industry was never able to return to those utilisation-levels, even with the dramatic expansion of credit in the 2000s, which stretched production beyond its real potential.

During the boom of the 2000s, the maximum-level of capacity-utilisation level was registered at the end of 2006 and the beginning of 2007. From that time to 2009, there was not merely a deceleration but a clear decline. The level in December 2008, as was already mentioned, stood at 73.6%, which is worse than the drop at the end of 2001, but similar to the level registered in December 1982. That was the lowest level in recent US-economic history, and furthermore, the most drastic decline since 1975. Actually – February 2009 – the industrial capacity-utilisation level is similar to December 82, the month of the history' lowest: 70.8%. In short, the fall has been tremendous.[20] (see Figure 6).

7. Savings and investment on a world-scale

The import of foreign-direct investment, however, becomes clear only in the context of global savings and investment (see Figure 6). Relative to world-GDP, international savings and investment have progressively declined over the past thirty years. The share of industrialised countries in both savings and investment has remained dominant, but their share relative to world value-added has declined steadily, falling from 26% in the 1970s to 20% in

---

20. Morera and Rojas 2008, p. 114.

the new millennium. At the same time, the emerging economies and oil-producing countries have boosted their share from negative or very small numbers to nearly 7%.[21]

Historically, money-capital has flown toward developing countries as a result of savings in industrialised countries. This trend was reinforced by the activities of pension-funds in industrialised countries coupled with international-monetary flows. But this international circulation of money-capital has been recently transformed by the rapid industrialisation of some developing countries as well as the growth of oil-revenue in petroleum-producing countries. Indeed, emerging economies and oil-producing countries have played a strong role in generating world-savings during three periods in recent years. First, at the time of the second oil-shock, 1978–82; second, at the time of the industrial boom in Southeast Asia, 1994–8; and third, after the recovery of oil prices in 2000–7, and the industrial boom in China and India.

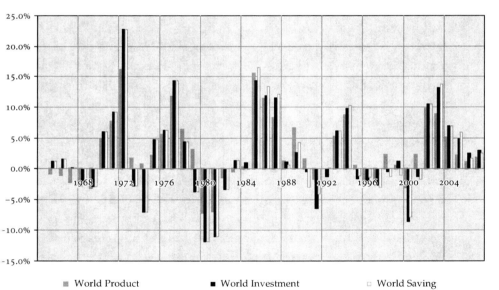

■ World Product　　　　　■ World Investment　　　　　□ World Saving

Source: Developed by authors, with data from the Bureau of Economic Analysis, Department of Commerce.

Figure 6　World-Product, Saving and Investment 1965–2008.

Annual Growth in %

---

21. Morera and Rojas 2008, pp. 101–2.

Nonetheless, savings and investment relative to world-output remained on a downward trend since the beginning of the 1970s. They reached their lowest historical growth-rates in 2002, and, since then, they have gradually recovered (see Figure 6). At the same time, in emerging markets and oil-producing countries a tendency toward increasing savings and investment began two decades ago, except for the years of the Asian crisis. After 2000, the participation of emerging economies and oil-producing countries in world-savings took an ever greater importance, in view of booming oil-prices and industrial development of China and India.[22]

Total savings and investment have doubled in the past twenty years. Specifically, during the past five years, savings rose by 50% and the savings rate reached 22.9% of world-output. In broader historical perspective, world savings in 1965 amounted to nearly $4.43tr (in constant 2007 US-dollars, as for the rest of the figures in this section). They then fell but rose again during the oil-boom of the 1970s, reaching almost $7.35tr in 1979, a rate of 24.7%. With the drop in oil-prices and the debt-crisis in 1982, world-savings experienced a strong decline, falling to $5.36tr in 1983, a rate of 21.4%. In the course of the 1980s and 1990s, savings began slowly to rise again, reaching $8.95tr in 1997, corresponding to 23.1% of world-GDP. This fell subsequently and savings reached their lowest historical level in 2002, at $7.68tr and 20.5% of world-output.[23]

Since 2002, savings have slowly recovered, reaching 22.9% of world-GDP in 2007, standing at approximately $11.09tr. The recovery of savings in the 2000s was due to the emerging economies and oil-producing countries, something unprecedented in the history of capitalism. It was also a result of the activities of pension-funds in the USA, Great Britain and Japan.[24] Pension-funds have played an important role in savings and investment, partly due to regulatory changes that allowed entry of foreign capital in areas and countries previously closed. This led to proliferation of high-risk securities and financial assets.[25]

The circulation of money-capital toward emerging markets is an expression of the international dynamics of savings, but also reflects the conditions of valorisation in emerging markets, namely dynamic industrialisation and oil-

---

22. Morera and Rojas 2008, p. 125. IMF-GFSR 2007, pp. 20–4. UNCTAD 2006, pp. 2–3.
23. Morera and Rojas 2008, pp. 101–3.
24. IFSL 2007, p. 1
25. Morera and Rojas 2008, p. 107.

production. How did the world-economy arrive at this position? It is possible that this outcome has a connection with the phenomenon of overproduction. However, for most economists, the catalyst of this development is the qualitative transformation of Asia, where savings have increased but investment has fallen abruptly since the end of the 1990s. This, in turn, has served to finance the enormous deficit in the US current account. Other economists also stress monetary and fiscal policies deployed by Asian countries. However, this does not explain why investment-flows have been directed to the United States even though other emerging markets offer higher interest-rates.

The important point is that the world-financial system is structured under the hegemonic power of the dollar.[26] This was established in the 1980s, when the United States reached agreements with representatives of other capitalist states, including the Plaza Accord and the Louvre Accord. It was strengthened in the 1990s when complex economic and political mechanisms were applied for the purpose of facilitating the handling of world money-capital. This includes regulations and prudential interventions in the practices of the international-banking system and financial markets. The Bank of International Settlements has played a vital role in this regard, centralising information and making international banks comply with accepted practices in financial markets. The role of the International Monetary Fund has been even more important, since it has influenced and designed the capital-accumulation of entire countries through regulating access to liquid-funds.

These policies account for the decrease in world interest-rates that facilitated the recovery of international-financial flows and the end of the crisis. This is also the context in which the behaviour of world-savings has changed. Three major trends emerged in the past decade, as indicated by Jaime Caruana, director of the Monetary and Capital Markets Department of the IMF: first, increases in foreign capital-flows, primarily toward emerging markets, second, the globalisation of financial institutions, and third, the globalisation of financial markets.[27] That is the background of the dramatic increase in foreign capital-flows (accumulation of financial assets with international investment-banks, public and private debt-portfolios, stocks and debt-portfolios,

26. Morera and Rojas 2007, p. 5.
27. Caruana 2007.

loan-portfolios, deposits and foreign-direct investment). By April 2007, these flows had risen to $9tr, almost a fifth of world-output.[28]

8. The accumulation of US foreign debt and its impact on developing countries

The USA remained an international creditor until 1985, a position it had maintained since World-War I. However, its strength as world-creditor had been deteriorating for some time. From 1986, US foreign debt increased, and its liabilities continued to rise throughout the 1990s, as is shown in Figure 7. At the end of 1996, US net debt had reached $456bn (including market-securities). A year later, the debt had risen to $776.5bn, equivalent to 13% of its GDP, and before the end of 2000 it had become $1.3tr, equivalent to 18% of its GDP.

After 1998 the volume of capital-flows to and from the USA increased signif-icantly. In 2004, debt stood at $2.2tr, though, as a result of the dollar's devalu-ation in 2004, the net value of US-liabilities decreased from 20.5% to 20.1% of GDP.[29] Nevertheless, the dollar-value of assets held by foreigners rose as proportion of US-GDP. At the end of 2003, foreigners held assets worth 97% of US-GDP, while, in 2005, the proportion had gone up to 107.4%. The net inflow of foreign investment in 2004 and 2005 was much greater than the necessary sum to finance the deficit in the US current accounts, and the excess flowed back to the world-economy.

There are significant asymmetries in the composition of foreign property in the hands of US-residents compared to US-property in the hands of foreign-ers. In 2005, for instance, 27% of US total assets abroad was direct investment (facilities and equipment), in contrast to only 19% of US-liabilities in the hands of foreigners. Foreign investors in the USA tended to purchase negotiable financial assets (stocks, bonds, public securities and banking liabilities) that could be liquidated more easily than direct investments.[30] A further major difference is that the Federal Reserve and other entities in the US-government invested insignificant amounts in other countries. In contrast, foreign public

---

28. Caruana 2007.
29. Morera and Rojas 2008, p. 116.
30. D'Arista 2007, pp. 14–15.

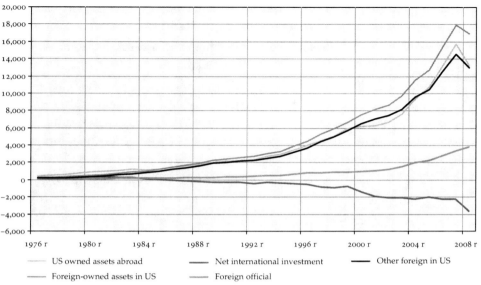

Source: Developed by authors, with data from the Office of the Comptroller of the Currency and Bank for International Settlements

Figure 7   US-International Investment-Position 1986–2007, Derivatives Not Included. Billions dollars

sectors had invested approximately $2.3tr in the USA in 2005, around 16% of total foreign investment. By the middle of the decade, foreign-public institutions had become important sources of capital-flows to the United States.

Large flows of private-foreign investment and rapid expansion in world-liquidity were the result of monetary policies in industrialised countries in response to the recession of 2001.[31] Abundant liquidity and low interest-rates propelled a global search for greater returns. With a view to protecting profitability, the Federal Reserve increased interest-rates after 2004 and reduced the rate on sovereign-bonds, a process that lasted until September 2007. At the same time, securities-markets in emerging economies were stimulated. Moreover, the Federal Reserve encouraged commercial loans in dollars in place of loans in yen, thereby renewing speculative interest in US-financial securities. All these developments took place while the international system

---

31. BIS 2004, pp. 3–9.

of bank-payments continued to be dominated by a few currencies, above all, the dollar, the euro, the yen and the pound.

As a consequence of these trends, foreign portfolio-investment in emerging economies reached high levels in the third quarter of 2005.[32] The increase in liquidity in the United States, Japan and many emerging economies intensified in 2005. The plethora of capital spilled over into other national markets, and, in some cases, even returned to the markets where it had originated. Still, excess-liquidity was spread throughout the world-economy, encouraging growth of domestic credit in the USA and elsewhere.

The link between domestic and foreign debt was fundamental, since both have an effect on US- and global demand. Rapid financial liberation in the 1980s and the relaxation of prudential norms for granting loans exacerbated domestic debt-accumulation. US-households went increasingly into debt during 1995–2005, associated with a decrease in the rate of saving and increases in consumption.[33] Aware of easy credit-availability, consumers considered access to credit as a substitute for savings, especially after 2002, when debt was used both to acquire appreciating residential property and to extract liquidity for consumption. Enterprise also took advantage of low rates in bonds-markets to apply for loans in order to repurchase bonds or stocks in the secondary market, thus strengthening their profitability.

In short, private capital was the driving force behind international capital-flows and an important source of the expansion of credit in the USA. At the same time, excessive volumes of foreign private capital appeared, exacerbating investment-flows out of the USA, and increasing liquidity both in the USA and the world-market. Moreover, massive amounts of foreign-government investments took place in the USA. For emerging economies, these trends had considerable repercussions, driving monetary authorities in those countries to intensify the level of intervention. The aim was to stop appreciation of domestic currency and contain domestic growth of money and credit. Consequently, the accumulation of reserves played a fundamental role in the process of expansion and contraction, creating further scope for generation of international liquidity (see Figure 7).

---

32. BIS 2005c, pp. 1–3.
33. Family-debt increased from 65.7% of the GDP in 1995 to 92.1% at the end of 2005. Federal-government debt, on the other hand, diminished during that same period from 49.2% to 37.2% of the GDP. Federal Reserve Bank, Flow of Funds, various.

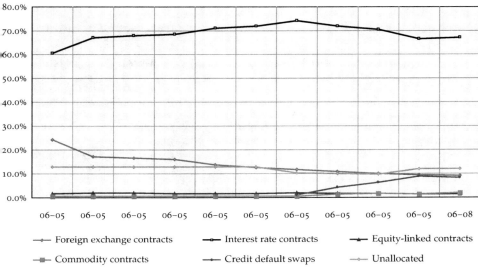

- ◆— Foreign exchange contracts   —□— Interest rate contracts   —▲— Equity-linked contracts
- ■— Commodity contracts   —✦— Credit default swaps   —◇— Unallocated

Source: Developed by authors, with data from the Office of the Comptroller of the Currency and Bank for International Settlements

Figure 8   Non-Stock-Market Credit by Instrument, June 1998–June 2008, Total Contracts

To put it differently, the strategies used by the large private-financial institutions dominating the international payments-system to increase their profits also intensified the vulnerability of emerging economies. As more developed and developing countries freed their capital-accounts in the 1990s, the value of their currencies came increasingly to depend on the operations conducted by financial among various financial instruments and markets, rather than depending on trade.[34] Changes in the differentials among interest rates denominated in different currencies became the driving force behind capital- and foreign-currency flows. Thus, the problems in monetary control world-wide were exacerbated (see Figure 8).

The extraordinary increase in the reserves of emerging economies during the last decade points to the pressure to use surpluses from trade to create a buffer to diminish vulnerability to external forces.[35] In order to undertake this policy, emerging countries were obliged to lend their savings to developed

---

34. Conford 2005, pp. 3–6.
35. Painceira 2009. BIS 2007, pp. 44–52.

countries, instead of investing in their own economies. In effect, countries with high rates of savings were obliged to accumulate idle money to cover imports and to service foreign debt in case of future financial crises.[36]

Consequently, emerging economies lost some capacity to invest productively. They were obliged to concentrate massive reserves as a mechanism of compensating for the inflow of foreign capital. The enormous accumulation of reserves strengthened their reliance on the dominant currencies, and particularly on the dollar, the main international currency.[37]

Finally, global losses in derivatives are also likely to affect developing countries. At the end of 1995, US-commercial banks possessed derivatives – (mostly futures, swaps and options) of nearly $15tr, while holding assets of about US $4tr. In June 2008, derivatives amounted to $182tr, while assets had risen to just $11tr (see Figure 9). Derivatives across the world amounted to $684tr, according to the Bank for International Settlements.[38]

These derivatives have a gross market-value of no more than $20tr, and are controlled by investment-funds, pension-funds, commercial banks, and other financial institutions. By September 2008, the value of derivatives held by US-commercial banks had dropped to $176tr, while assets stood at $12tr. About $6tr was lost, equivalent to nearly seven times Mexico's GDP. After the sustained fall of the Dow Jones from June to December, the notional amount of derivative-value lost was at least 35%, or more than $60tr. This is a terrible loss, from any point of view. Similar losses took place across the world. On this basis, the question naturally arises: who lost more than $60tr in the USA, and possibly $235tr across the world – equivalent to five times the value of the world-output? And who will recover this value?

---

36. 'Although foreign-exchange reserves held on the books of central banks provide support for expansions of money and credit in the domestic economy, monetary authorities in these countries must sterilize some or all of the buildup in reserves by selling holdings of domestic assets or issuing central bank liabilities to prevent over-expansion. Both of these sterilization techniques inhibit the growth and stability of domestic capital markets by constraining the central banks' ability to support those markets.' (D'Arista 2007, p. 32).

37. Lapavitsas 2009.

38. BIS 2008.

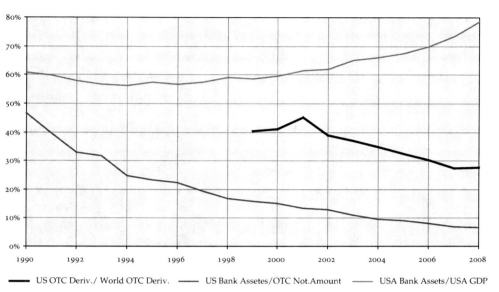

—— US OTC Deriv./ World OTC Deriv.   —— US Bank Assetes/OTC Not.Amount   —— USA Bank Assets/USA GDP

Source: Developed by authors, with data from the Office of the Comptroller of the Currency and Bank for International Settlements

Figure 9   Non-Stock-Market Credit in US, 1990–2008 (OTC-Derivatives) (%)

9. Conclusion

Restoring the rate of profit has been the focus of efforts by both state and by capital, since the crisis of the 1970s. Profound changes have taken place in the social relations of production between capital and labour for more than three decades. The scope of capitalist operations has been considerably broadened by the collapse of the so-called socialist régimes and the profound transformation of China. But a most striking development is that, under the predominance of banking capital and the hegemony of the US-dollar, the strategy of 'financialisation' was imposed on all forms of capital.

Vital to 'financialisation' were changes in the labour-force as well as a trans-formation of the state. The nature of work has altered and many of the social advances achieved in earlier periods were reversed, particularly in educa-tion, health-services, and pension-systems. New financial institutions, operat-ing under the logic of private profitability, transformed the wage-income of both productive and unproductive labour into financial assets. Workers were thus subjected to even greater exploitation. In addition, the state privatised strategic enterprises under its control, and allowed central banks to play a strategic role in determining interest-rates and operating monetary policy. These transformations generated favourable conditions for placing great masses of savings in the hands of capital as never before, thus making it possible to expand credit to the limit. Large parts of this wealth came from developing countries.

The world-economy has become integrated in different ways, also as a result of the immense social, political and cultural transformations that have taken place. But, at present, the world-economy is once again in crisis, perhaps one of the worst crises in the history of capitalism. This is the first fully-fledged crisis of globalisation, or 'financialisation', with the United States at the epicentre. Despite the triumph of neoliberalism in recent years, the crisis presents an opportunity to put alternatives in place and prevent a mere reorganisation of neoliberal policies and methods.

Chapter Seven

Developing Countries in the Era of Financialisation: From Deficit-Accumulation to Reserve-Accumulation

Juan Pablo Painceira

1. Introduction

Financialisation represents a profound transformation of capitalist economies based on changes in real accumulation since the early 1970s.[1] Financial activities have spread into several new economic sectors and areas of daily life – housing, pensions, consumption, and so on. Growth of finance has provided fresh scope for the form of value to expand, mainly in developed-capitalist countries. Important elements of this process have been the privatisation of activities and capital-assets that were previously under state-control, as well as the deregulation of financial markets and institutions. Moreover, deregulation of labour-markets has contributed to fostering 'financial discipline' among workers.

This chapter takes the analysis of financialisation further by addressing its impact on developing countries. The focus of the chapter lies on the international-financial transactions of developing countries since 2000, particularly in relation to the US-economy. It is shown that international capital-flows have grown,

---

1. Lapavitsas 2009.

but developing countries have also accumulated enormous international reserves. The outcome has been net flows of capital from developing to developed countries. The social costs of this aspect of financialisation for developing countries have been very large, while developed countries, and especially the USA, have drawn considerable benefits. Financialisation in the 2000s has brought net gains to the USA as issuer of quasi-world-money at the expense of developing countries. This is an aspect of financial exploitation characteristic of the period.

In a little more detail, the chapter addresses the inter-relationship between international capital-flows, reserve-accumulation and US-financial conditions, analysing the consequences for developing countries and the benefits for key developed countries. The chapter also examines the spread of financialisation in the domestic economies of developing countries, showing that financial institutions have become steadily more important. It is further established that developing countries have gone through two distinct periods since their financialisation effectively commenced in the early 1990s. The first period was characterised by substantial private capital-flows and large current-account deficits; the second period has been marked by reserve-accumulation and net capital flows to developed countries.

The chapter is organised as follows. Section 2 examines theoretical arguments in favour of financial liberalisation in developing countries as well as political-economy critiques of the process. It shows that financial liberalisation is an integral aspect of the financialisation of capitalism more generally. Section 3 recapitulates arguments of Marxist political economy in connection with finance and development, paying particular attention to international finance and its crises, focusing on the role of world-money. The objective is to obtain a fuller theoretical understanding of the swing of developing countries from deficit-accumulation in the 1990s, to reserve-accumulation in the 2000s. Section 4 is the core of the chapter and considers the strategy of international reserve-accumulation which developing countries adopted (or had forced on them) after the financial crises of the late 1990s. The strategy was a reaction to speculative and unstable capital-flows, revealing the problematic nature of contemporary world-money. Section 5 discusses the substantial social costs imposed on developing countries by reserve-accumulation. Reserves have facilitated net transfers of capital from developing to developed countries, and have acted as a mechanism of exploitation of developing by developed countries, above all, the USA. Section 6 concludes.

2. Emergence of financial liberalisation in developing countries and the crises of 1997–8[2]

Financial liberalisation is part of the structural reforms typical of the neoliberal approach to development in the last three decades. It is also a vital aspect of financialisation since it has increased the exposure of national economies to the activities of the global-financial system since the 1990s. This section considers mainstream-theoretical claims in favour of financial liberalisation in developing countries. The objective is to establish the background on financial liberalisation by analysing its key characteristics as well some of its empirical consequences. This provides necessary historical and analytical perspective on what has happened since the beginning of 2000s.

The flow of capital from poor to rich and the huge costs imposed on developing countries by reserve-accumulation in the 2000s (discussed in Sections 4 and 5) are evidence of the pernicious effect that financial liberalisation has had on developing countries. The beneficiaries have been developed countries, primarily the USA. Further theoretical analysis is undertaken in the next section through discussion of Marxist political economy of international finance.

The initial aim of financial liberalisation in the 1970s was to lift constraints on financial activities in order to facilitate the flow of domestic savings to investment. Opening the capital-account of the balance of payments was not a concern of the liberalisers. But financial liberalisation was gradually extended to the capital-account, thus promoting the growth of international capital-flows. In the 1990s and 2000s, opening national economies to the international-financial markets became a fundamental element of financial liberalisation.

Liberalisation of the international movement of capital denotes greater ease and flexibility for domestic residents to take positions in assets and liabilities denominated in foreign currency, as well for non-domestic residents to operate in domestic financial markets. According to Akyuz,[3] the financial opening

---

2. It is important to clarify that the term 'developing countries' is used heuristically in this chapter. The author is fully aware of the class-implications and imperialist dimension of 'development'. From a Marxist, and particularly Leninist, perspective the relationship between 'developed' and 'developing' countries contains exploitative and imperialist aspects. This relationship is also shaped by the overall tempo of the international accumulation of capital. In essence, this chapter demonstrates some new aspects of international exploitation that have emerged through financialisation, free capital-flows, reserve-accumulation and use of the dollar as quasi-world-money.

3. Akyuz 1992.

of developing countries includes liberalising the inflow and outflow of capital as well as allowing easy convertibility of currency.[4]

Pressure on developing countries to implement these changes has come from multilateral-international organisations, such as the IMF and World Bank. However, private international-financial institutions were also in favour for two reasons. First, the changes allowed developing countries to refinance existing external debt in terms determined in open markets, and thus more favourable to private capital. Second, liberalisation of the capital-account opened domestic economies to international-financial operations.

Liberalising the capital-account was one of the main conditions of the Brady Plan that restructured the external debt of several developing countries in the early 1990s (mostly in Latin America). The Brady Plan played a crucial role in creating sovereign-debt markets among developing countries, the so-called emerging-market bonds. From the point of view of developing countries, the Brady Plan can be considered the beginning of their financialisation. By adopting it, developing countries were opened to huge capital-inflows as well as becoming effectively committed to further financial-liberalisation reforms.

It is notable that mainstream-economics does not provide very strong theoretical justification for capital-account liberalisation. The original theoretical advocates of financial liberalisation, McKinnon and Shaw, treated financial 'repression' as any government constraint that limits the efficient functioning of domestic financial markets.[5] But, gradually, the concept of financial 'repression' was also applied to legal restrictions on the mobility of domestic- and international-financial capital. According to neoclassical-economic theory, savings should flow from capital-abundant (developed) countries to capital-scarce (developing) countries because of differentials in expected capital-returns. It could be argued, therefore, that international restrictions on the

---

4. The inflow of capital refers to residents borrowing from foreign markets for reasons not connected to international trade, as well as non-residents offering credit in the domestic-financial markets. The outflow of capital refers to residents transferring capital and acquiring financial assets abroad, as well as non-residents issuing liabilities in domestic market. Currency-convertibility refers to legal permission to undertake credit-relations among residents in a foreign currency, including bank-deposits and lending.

5. McKinnon 1973 and Shaw 1973. Such constraints typically refer to regulating the activities of banking and non-banking financial institutions, setting compulsory reserves for many types of banking deposits, and fixing the level of market interest-rates.

movement of capital and controls on the convertibility of domestic currency (i.e. external financial 'repression') presumably hinder such beneficial flows.

According to this approach, financial opening would improve the flow of foreign savings in countries facing capital-scarcity. It would also reduce risks for investors, domestics and foreign, due to the possibility of asset-diversification. Financial opening would also help countries deal with balance-of-payments problems, thus allowing for flexible adjustment of domestic demand. Finally, the efficiency of domestic-financial systems would rise due to competition between foreign- and domestic-financial institutions, and possibly due to exposure to the international-financial market.[6]

A further important argument by the mainstream in pushing for financial opening was that free mobility of capital would lessen the autonomy of developing countries in forming economic policy. Apparently, this would reduce the damage caused by inappropriate economic policies in the context of financial globalisation.[7] Greater homogenisation of 'good' economic policies would thus occur in the global economy.

It is also important to note that advocacy of financial liberalisation has passed from a period of favouring 'shock-treatment' to another favouring sequential implementation of reform.[8] The original 'shock-treatment' was not concerned with the sequencing of liberalisation-measures, focusing only on its putative benefits.[9] In contrast, sequential reformers claim that the first step should be domestic 'de-repression' of interest-rates and financial activities.[10] Deregulating the foreign-exchange market should take place next to avoid discrimination against exporters and/or importers.[11] Following this, foreign trade should become freer and, finally, there should be liberalisation of the

---

6. Levine 1996, p. 225 and Poret 2001, p. 3.

7. See Mathieson and Rojas-Suárez 1992, p. 3 and Eichengreen et al. 1998, p. 14, and 1999.

8. See McKinnon 1973, Chapters 1–6, and 1991.

9. See McKinnon 1973.

10. Fiscal reform should also take place to control public deficits, thus allowing for improved refinancing of the public debt and, supposedly, reducing short-term interest rates.

11. The main objective is to eliminate exchange-rate controls that supported import-substitution and export-promotion as part of the industrialisation-strategy of developing countries.

capital-account.[12] The sequential approach has come to dominate actual liberalisation-policy.

However, the reality of the first major wave of liberalising the capital-account and opening up to international trade in the 1990s proved very different for a broad range of developing countries. The result was huge increases in capital-inflows, on the one hand, and accumulation of current-account deficits, on the other.[13] This combination led to severe financial and foreign-exchange crises in developing countries in the late 1990s and early 2000s, above all, South Korea and other Asian countries (1997–8), Russia (1998) and Brazil (1999). Further currency-crises also took place in Argentina (2001) and Turkey (2001). The effects of these crises were severe, causing increases in unemployment, falls of GDP, and collapse in consumption and investment. The costs were enormous, in societies that were already relatively poor.

There is no doubt that these crises had complex corporate, banking, foreign-currency and sovereign-payments aspects, which varied according to the structural and institutional characteristics of each economy. In East Asia, for instance, the currency-crisis of 1997–8 found most economies already facing serious problems in their corporate and financial sectors. A feature that many developing countries had in common, however, was that they had typically adopted a pegged exchange-rate régime. For these countries, the interruption of external finance – coupled with problems specific to each – caused major exchange-rate crises. The salient features of these crises were sudden reversal of capital-flows and collapse of pegged exchange-rates régimes. For our purposes, then, financial liberalisation in the 1990s acted as catalyst for currency- and financial crises in general, while also encouraging rapid contagion among developing countries.

There have been several attempts to account for developing-country crises of the late 1990s and early 2000s. One approach, drawing on the mainstream-theory of asymmetric information, emphasised the imbalances existing within the private sector of developing countries, including financial-market failures

---

12. There is consensus that the last element to be liberalised should be the capital-account, see Williamson and Molly 1998.

13. Average net lending to developing and emerging countries between 1994 and 2001 was 0.7% of the aggregated GDP. However, during 1993–9, the average stood at 1.5%. (IMF 2008a and 2008b).

and interventionist government-policies.[14] These are sometimes called 'third-generation' crisis-models.[15]

Perhaps the most prominent exponent is Krugman,[16] who presented the Asian currency-crisis as result of crony-capitalism. The crisis apparently emerged due to moral hazard created by implicit government-guarantees on the liabilities of financial intermediaries, which were moreover unregulated. This encouraged excessively risky lending by financial intermediaries, temporarily boosting the business-sector and capital-assets, and thus reacting positively back on the intermediaries. This circular process generated a situation of overinvestment and overpricing in some capital-assets, such as land. Along similar lines, Corseti et al. offered a further explanation of the crisis based on the existence of implicit government-guarantees also for the corporate sector.[17]

Mainstream-accounts were opposed by influential non-Marxist political-economy explanations of the crises.[18] For Chang et al., the South-Korean crisis occurred because of dismantling the government-mechanisms of coordination of industrial policy and financial regulation. In the same spirit, Taylor stresses that the main reason for the East-Asian financial crises was government-withdrawal from regulating the real economy, the financial market, and mainly the capital-account.[19] For Wade, finally, financial liberalisation seriously affected seriously the capacity of state to coordinate foreign-private borrowing.[20] Since controlling the flow of funds for investment became more complex and difficult, the Asian model of development became less sustainable.

Other prominent non-Marxist political-economy explanations drew on financial-instability theory, mostly associated with Minsky's work. According to this line of argument, the cause of the Asian crises lies in Ponzi-type indebtedness, where short-term over-leveraged positions were financing investment

---

14. This interpretation came out to explain the East-Asian financial crisis and is also denominated of 'third-generation' crisis-model. In simple words, the first crisis-model is associated with an unsustainable fiscal policy. In the second-generation model, the crisis is a self-fulfilling process where the financial institutions in order to protect themselves against the currency-depreciation precipitate the foreign-exchange crisis.
15. See Krugman 1998 and also Chang and Velasco 1998 and 1999, Mishkin 1996, Calvo and Reinhart 2000 and Corseti et al. 1998.
16. Krugman 1998.
17. Corseti et al. 1998.
18. See Chang, Park and Yoo 1998, Taylor 1998 and Wade 1998.
19. Taylor 1998.
20. Wade 1998.

projects with long gestation-lags in sectors that already faced overcapacity. Financial instability is an endogenous process in which there is convergence of perspectives between corporate sector and financial institutions regarding returns and performance during the business-cycle. At the start of the cycle, the need to refinance capital-assets through financial institutions is very low or null. However, once the upswing of cycle is apparent and well established, the economy moves gradually toward speculative positions in which the need to refinance increases and the maturity of lending and borrowing operations becomes shorter and shorter.

Applying this approach, the increase in external liabilities in East Asia could be seen as due to the confidence of economic agents in the stability (or appreciation) of the exchange-rate and continuing low cost of external borrowing. Financial liberalisation exacerbated indebtedness by facilitating financial operations between domestic and foreign investors. For Kregel, this brought a decrease in the margins of safety (liquid-assets) as exchange rates appreciated.[21] The reversal of capital-flows exposed the fragility of the low margins. Along similar lines, Arestis and Glickman have also claimed that financial liberalisation was fundamental to financial instability in South-East Asian countries.[22]

These non-Marxist political-economy analyses share a common emphasis on the fundamental role of financial liberalisation in causing the crises. The main difference between them is that the former current focuses on loss of capacity by the state to coordinate the economy, while the Minskian current focuses on the speculative outcomes of liberalising the domestic-financial system and opening the capital-account. Still, they all stress the systemic aspect of the crises. This makes them far more insightful than mainstream-explanations, for which moral hazard or information-problems were presumably at the root of the trouble.

Nevertheless, the relationship between real accumulation and financial development is not fully analysed by the non-Marxist political-economy approaches. In particular, they have little to say on the endogenous way in which development of the capitalist economy induces development of the financial system, which then fosters further capitalist development. It seems

---

21. Kregel 1998.
22. Arestis and Glickman 1998.

intuitive that financial crises are generally associated with such a process.[23] Moreover, the non-Marxist accounts offer even less regarding the role of international money in the flows of global finance, and the resultant relations of power, hierarchy and exploitation. Yet these are vital aspects of relations between developed and developing countries.

For these reasons, non-Marxist political economy gives little theoretical insight into the gigantic swing of developing countries toward reserve-accumulation in the 2000s. It also offers little insight into the ensuing, systematic transfers of value from developing to developed countries. International reserves of the dollar as quasi-world-money played a pivotal role in both the crises of the 1990s and the reverse capital-flows of the 2000s. The next section puts forth elements of a Marxist explanation of international financial crises. Following this theoretical analysis, the empirical dimensions of these phenomena are analysed in Sections 4 and 5.

3. A Marxist analysis of international finance and its crises

3.1. *Credit, accumulation and crisis*

The analysis of financial liberalisation and the international-financial system from a Marxist perspective requires the establishment of some principles regarding the development and role of the financial system in the capitalist economy. A key point here is that capitalist finance relies on the continuous generation of idle, or stagnant, sums of money-capital in the normal course of the turnover of capital. These resources of idle money provide the foundation of the capitalist credit-system. For Itoh and Lapavitsas 'the credit system mobilises the stagnant money generated in the course of capitalist reproduction, transforms it into interest-bearing (loanable) capital and redirects it toward accumulation'.[24] Thus, finance and economic development are integrally related with real accumulation, providing the underpinnings of finance.

The fundamental relationship between finance and the real economy can be usefully analysed in terms of the functioning of money as money and as

---

23. The following section analyses the general aspects of this process.
24. Itoh and Lapavitsas 1999, p. 61.

capital.[25] Finance is a set of institutions, markets and assets that necessarily emerges in a capitalist economy and facilitates the transformation of money into money-capital across society. More specifically, finance involves transactions in loanable (or interest-bearing) capital. This is capital existing always in the money-form, available for lending to those engaged in real accumulation, earning interest rather than profit. It also predates the capitalist mode of production.[26] The banking system plays a pivotal role in the movement of loanable capital, thus being linked to real accumulation, and earning returns out of the self-expansion of value in production.

The banking system is the backbone of the capitalist-financial system, and regulates the impact of loanable capital on the capitalist economy. Historically, the process of emergence of banks was connected to the development of commercial and industrial capital. Thus, banking activities are related to trade-credit and money-dealing. Analysing the economic foundations for the emergence of the banking system, Lapavitsas proposes that '[a]t the core of advanced capitalist banking lie activities that relate to both trade credit and money-dealing. This approach offers two analytical advantages. First, it postulates a specific link between banking lending and money-dealing, the latter covering foreign exchange, account management, clearing, money transmission and safe-keeping of assets...Second, the approach fits well with banks' tendency to concentrate in commercial centres where trade credit transactions and instruments proliferate.'[27] In this light, banks are specialists in the monetary and financial aspects of capitalist circulation. In so doing, they reduce the turnover-time of the industrial capitals and lessen the circulation-costs.

The financial system is also fundamental to crises, which are an integral aspect of the capitalist economy. Marx in *Capital*, Volume I) showed that capital incorporates the inherent contradiction between money as general form and commodities as particular forms of value. Capitalist crises are extreme forms of this contradiction since, in a crisis, commodities cannot be turned into money. The fundamental reasons for crises lie within real accumulation and are summed up in falling profit-rates. Typically, constant capital becomes too large relative to variable capital, or the proportions between different sectors of the economy are disturbed. But since the financial system mediates

---

25. As will be seen below, this relationship is contradictory and provides the basis for two different types of financial crises analysed by Marxist political economy.
26. Marx 1972, p. 376.
27. Lapavitsas 2007, p. 424.

the flows of loanable capital and thus the expansion of output (which become impossible to sell in a crisis), capitalist crises inevitably have financial and monetary aspects. These frequently involve the difficulty of obtaining fresh money to repay debts.

In this light, Marxist political economy distinguishes between financial crises that are integrally related to the process of production, and those that occur due to overstretching of finance caused by the internal operations of the financial system.[28] The latter reflect the inherent autonomy of finance from real accumulation. Crises that are integrally related to the process of production are called Type I, and those that are due to the financial system alone are called Type II.[29]

In Marx's own words: 'the monetary crisis, defined in the text as a particular phase of every general industrial and commercial crisis, must be clearly distinguished from the special sort of crisis, also called a monetary crisis, which may appear independently of the rest, and only affects industry and commerce by its backwash. The centre of movement of these crises is to be found in money capital, and their immediate sphere is therefore banking, the stock exchanges and finance.'[30] So this distinction is very important for analysis of contemporary crises of financialisation, which owe much to the internal operations of finance, and reflect the growing autonomy of the financial system in the last three decades. The present financial crisis can be considered as Type II crisis as so far has its roots lying on the operations of financial institutions in the US housing market.[31] But it also has roots in the process of real accumulation, given that financialisation has permeated the economy. In other words, the trigger and proximate causes of the current financial crisis lie within the financial system, but its deeper roots are to be found in the transformation of real accumulation.

3.2. World-money and international crises

The recent crisis became a global-financial crisis due to the connection between financial operations undertaken within the US-financial system and the

---

28. The analysis of money's contradictions and the way further development of the credit and monetary relations creates other contradictions can be seen in Rosdolsky 1977, Part Two.
29. This typology can be seen in Itoh and Lapavitsas 1999, Chapter 6.
30. Marx 1976, p. 236.
31. See Lapavitsas 2009 for full analysis.

global-financial system. These operations are denominated in the dollar which has the property of being quasi-world-money.[32] Moreover, they are typically monetary and credit-transactions which include also operations of securitisation. This role of the dollar as world-money creates a direct link between the issuer's country domestic sphere and the international-financial sphere. Thus, serious problems in the US-financial market in 2007–8, characterised by liquidity- and solvency-problems among banks have damaged the global-financial system as these problems happened in the issuer of quasi-world-money.

Broadly speaking, the financial crises of the 1990s in emerging countries manifested themselves as problems of liquidity or solvency in world-money. Given their inability to issue world-money, emerging countries assume a subordinated role in relation to international finance.[33]

Therefore, having in mind the central role of world-money in the international-financial system and to capital-flows, further analytical requirements are necessary to understand developing-country crises in the late 1990s and the shift toward reserve-accumulation. Financial crises are global events, occurring in the world-market, which is structurally different from the domestic market. The world-market has fewer homogenising mechanisms of law, institutional practice, custom and regulation compared to the domestic market. Moreover, there is no globally integrated credit-system with a central bank at its heart, which could support the world-market. International finance is fundamental to the world-market but, unlike domestic finance, it does not comprise a structured and layered set of institutions. Finally, the world-market contains relations of states as well as private capitals, thus incorporating relations of power and national exploitation.[34] Consequently, the role of money in the world-market has very particular weight, significance, and meaning.

---

32. The term quasi-world-money (instead of world-money) is used to describe the US-dollar because there is no formal agreement as there was in the gold-era. Moreover, the issuer of world-money is a country, not an international-multilateral organisation. Furthermore, there is no clear mechanism of international adjustment as we had in the gold-era. However to keep things simple, world-money and quasi-world-money are sometimes used indistinguishably.

33. In the crisis-moment, where the sudden movement for protection against wealth-loss rise the money-demand, the contradiction between monetary and credit-systems becomes clear. In the financialisation-era, that demand rise has been mainly in world-money and not in domestic currencies.

34. Lapavitsas 2006.

For Marxist political economy, money is the universal equivalent and performs certain functions linked directly or indirectly to the process of commodity-exchange. Those directly related to commodity-exchange are measure of value and means of exchange; those indirectly related are hoarding, means of payments and world-money, which Marx called 'money as money'.[35] According to Marx, world-money 'serves as the universal means of payment, as the universal means of purchase, and as the absolute social materialisation of wealth as such. Its predominant function is as means of payment in the settling of international balances.'[36] World-money supports the world-market, and provides the organising impetus that it lacks compared to domestic markets. For the same reason, world-money crystallises the tensions present in the world-market, and is the focus of global crises.

Historically, world-money has taken the form of commodity-money, primarily gold. The operations of the global-monetary and financial system, consequently, used to depend on the accumulation and transfer of gold-hoards kept by capitalist countries. Global-capitalist crises were characterised by sharp swings in gold hoards, while market-participants had difficulty obtaining money, or selling their commodities in the world-market. For Marx, 'whenever these hoards are strikingly above their average level, this is, with some exceptions, an indication of stagnation in the circulation of commodities'.[37]

However, in the contemporary international-monetary and financial system, holdings of world-money play a more complex role. Commodity-money has been reduced to a hoard of last resort, and the US-dollar functions as quasi-world-money. One of the main challenges for political economy today is to fully explain the role of the dollar as quasi-world-money. Among other important points, according to Itoh,[38] it is vital to note that the dollar has become universal money without any formal international agreement, while its exchange-value has been relatively stable despite the constant danger of a collapse in its value.

The role of the dollar as quasi-gold-money becomes apparent comparing US-dollar flow-movements during developing countries' crisis-period and

---

35. Itoh and Lapavitsas 1999, pp. 45–52.
36. Marx 1976, p. 242.
37. Marx 1976, p. 244.
38. Itoh 2006, p. 110.

gold-flows in the previous international-monetary arrangement (the gold-standard period). In both instances, the demand for protection against wealth-loss lead to a sudden rise in the demand for dollar or dollar-denominated assets and gold respectively.[39]

Consequently, in the time of crisis, the contradiction between the monetary and the credit-system is revealed as the demand for money as money increase as 'in times of squeeze, when credit contracts or ceases entirely, money suddenly stands as the only means of payment and true existence of value in absolute opposition to all other commodities'.[40] In the present monetary-international arrangement, however there is a rise in the demand for dollar-denominated assets (credit-money), mainly to US debt-securities which are backed by the issuer of quasi-world-money. Therefore, differently from the golden era, where there was no clear group of beneficiaries in the international-monetary system as the reserve-asset was a commodity, the present arrangement has a country as the issuer of world-money.

Thus, the world-money being issued by a sovereign-state has important implications for the working of the international economy. Some of those implications related to international capital-flows, developing countries and financial crises are analysed in the next sections. As the US-dollar is world-money, developing countries have to hold dollar-reserves to protect themselves against financial crisis, which, in turn, had a dampening effect on the yield-curve in the USA which in turn helped the US-financial conditions.

3.3. *World-money and financialisation*

From our point of view, the relation between world-money and financialisation taking place in the US-economy during the 2000s can be grasped through the effect of foreign capital-flow on the US yield-curve and, consequently, its domestic financial conditions. As we are going to show in Section 4, foreign capital-flows into US debt-securities helped keeping favorable financial

---

39. In the present crisis, it is possible to see the same movement when the crisis became global in September of 2008. However, the full analysis of those movements is not objective of this section, which is concentrated on international finance and its crisis, focusing on the role of world-money.

40. Marx 1976, p. 516.

conditions as it reduced the long-term interest-rates[41] despite a continuous increase in its policy-rate by the Federal Reserve.[42] This chapter argues that these foreign capital-flows and its lowering effect on the US interest-rate contributed to the increase in household-debt mainly through mortgages. It could also explain the fact that companies raised more funds in open markets through issuance of corporate bonds and other debt-instruments instead of borrowing from banks. Finally, it is conjectured that these flows allowed the US-banks to increase their lending operations, raise the size and importance of securitisation-operations in financial markets, and redirect their business-focus towards individuals (households) and trading activities rather than corporate lending.[43] More generally, in the recent boom-cycle in the USA, one can observe a rise in the dominance and profitability of financial operations, including households when they refinance their mortgages with equity-gains. However, these developments would not have been possible without the role of the US-dollar as world-money once the US-economy would not have got those domestic advantages of international capital-flows. Moreover these dynamics and changes in the working of the US-economy have influenced other countries, including developing ones, towards a more financialised capitalism, or in other words, they have reinforced the financialisation-era around the world.

In relation to real accumulation, the functional and dysfunctional character of finance (flows of loanable capital) can be analysed through the dynamic of the US-dollar during the cycle. Despite its depreciation, the dollar has maintained its role of global reserve-currency in the boom-phase as there has been a huge flow to dollar-denominated assets analysed Section 4.[44] When the crisis burst, in turn, finance reveals its dysfunctional character as there is a return to the US-dollar and US dollar-denominated assets, interrupting the credit-flow

---

41. The US Treasury's yield-curve is the benchmark to the majority of financial assets as the US debt-securities are considered free-risk assets. Therefore, a drop in the yield-curve mainly in the long-term part, normally improves the financial conditions of the economy.

42. Between 2004 and 2006, the federal funds' target-rate increased to 5.25% from 1%.

43. On the rise of banking profitability in those operations among major global banks, see Dos Santos 2009.

44. For example, capital-flows from East-Asian countries are also connected to the dynamic of global capital-accumulation, as these countries have to keep their currencies value at a competitive level in order to sustain their domestic accumulation.

to real accumulation. In other words, one can observe a return to money as form of value in order to preserve wealth but in contradiction with the expansion of value in production.[45]

With reference to the dynamics of currencies and world-money, the recent boom-phase during the 2000s has been characterised by a depreciation of the US-dollar against the major developed currencies around the global market and by an appreciation of major emerging-countries' currencies after their financial crises of the end of 1990s. As we are going to analyse in the subsequent sections, focusing on the circulation-sphere, the recent dynamic of world-market and capital-accumulation characterised by the role of the US dollar as quasi-world-money has allowed the US-economy to finance its current-account deficit and expansion of public debt through foreign capital-inflows with hardly any constrains. On the developing countries' side, the main consequences have been a huge foreign exchange-reserve accumulation and the rise of domestic public debt, which will be analysed in the next section. In this sense, it is important to highlight the institutional processes related to the circulation-sphere as financial liberalisation, mainly the rise of capital-account convertibility, and other reforms to raise capital-flow mobility which have facilitated the process of value-transfer to the issuer of world-money over the last two decades.

For our purposes, this transformation in the international-monetary system has meant that hoards of reserve-currency have become a matter of monetary policy as well as management of the national currency of the leading country in the world-market. This is a vital privilege for the USA in the world-market allowing it to extract exclusive benefits. It is also an exploitative relationship with other countries, particularly developing ones. The next sections of this article will show the expropriating aspect of quasi-world-money in the current configuration of the world-market. Issuing quasi-world-money has become an international mechanism for the rich to extract value from the poor in the context of financialisation and free capital-flows. In this sense, reserve-accumulation is an exploitative process, a form of tribute accruing passively to the issuer of quasi-world-money.

---

45. This dysfunctional movement happened in September of 2008 when the global credit and monetary relations backed by quasi-world-money damaged capital-accumulation. However, in despite its importance, this analysis is not part of this chapter.

To sum up, it is the international aspect of financialisation – rise of finance domestically (banks, markets, enterprises, individuals) which is accompanied by export of loanable capital backed by the US-dollar as quasi-world-money, where the main beneficiary has been the leading imperialist country as we are going to point out in the next sections. Moreover, crises have been a regular outcome of these arrangements.

4. Advanced financialisation of developing countries

4.1. Global growth of financial assets and rise of domestic indebtedness in developing countries

The global crisis of 2007–9 was caused primarily by financial speculation in the US subprime mortgage-market, against the general transformation of the financial system of developed countries.[46] In this sense, the causes of the global-financial crisis can be found in the internal behaviour of developed countries' financial systems. However, speculative activities in the US-financial system have mattered internationally because they took place in the economy that generates the main reserve-currency, or quasi-world-money. The impact of the US housing-market collapse on developing countries was further magnified by the growth of global finance during the last three decades, which has been a key feature of financialisation.

Table 1 shows the growth of global financial assets since 1980. Note that the ratio of financial assets to global GDP rose from 109% in 1980, to 201% in 1990, to 294% in 2000, and to 346% in 2006. In short, there has been pronounced 'financial deepening' since 1980, which has accelerated after 1990.[47] The growth of financial assets of developing and emerging economies has also been very pronounced: from $3.9 trillion in 1995 to $23.6 trillion in 2006.[48] The share of emerging markets in total financial assets has increased from 6% in 1995 to 14% in 2006.

Table 1 also shows that government-debt has been vital to growth of finance, never dropping below 15% of the total since 1980. Even more important for

---

46. See Lapavitsas 2009 and dos Santos 2009. For a explanation based on lack of regulation and mispricing of risk see Goodhart and Persaud 2008.
47. McKinsey 2008, p. 10.
48. McKinsey 2008, p. 11.

Table 1   Global Financial Assets[1] ($ trillion)

	Government Debt-Securities	Total Financial Assets	Government-debt as % of total
1980	2	12	17%
1990	8	43	19%
1995	13	66	20%
2005	24	142	17%
2006	26	167	16%

Source: McKinsey 2008
[1] Financial assets include equity-securities, private debt-securities, government debt-securities and bank-deposits

our purposes is Table 2, which shows that, in 1995, domestic public-sector debt of developing countries was 8.8% that of developed countries. By 2005, the proportion had risen enormously and stood at 34.5%.[49] From 1995 to 2005, for instance, domestic-public debt relative to GDP in Brazil, Mexico, Korea and China increased from, respectively, 21%, 6%, 9% and 0% to 53%, 20%, 66% and 28%. BIS (2007) further confirms that, since 2002, developing countries have witnessed huge increases in domestic-public debt and a shift in the denomination of debt from foreign exchange to local currency. In short, in the 2000s, developing countries became hugely indebted internally.

Financialisation in developing countries in the 2000s was based on the growth of public debt.[50] The most striking aspect of this phenomenon, however, is that public debt grew in order to support flows of capital *from developing to developed countries*.[51] Financialisation has meant that developing countries became more heavily indebted internally precisely in order to send capital to developed countries, primarily the USA. This has been the most striking development in global finance since 1997–8.

---

49. In the next section, it is shown that the increase of domestic-public debt in developing countries is an outcome of international reserve-accumulation.

50. The role of government-securities has been broader that fostering domestic financialisation. They have are been vital to the global OTC (over the counter) derivatives-markets, in which the most heavily traded contracts are based on interest- and exchange-rates that are largely influenced by macroeconomic policies. Thus, in the foreign-exchange (FX) market in April 2007, the US-dollar stood as the leading currency with 89% of all contracts having, at least, one 'leg' denominated in that currency, see BIS 2007a, p. 15. This is also an expression of the role of the US-dollar as world-money, discussed in the previous sections.

51. It is shown in the section that this is the opposite of what is expected by supporters of financial liberalisation.

Table 2 Total Emerging Markets Debt Outstanding¹ ($ billions)

Regions	1995				2000				2005			
	Total	Internat.²	Domestic-public sector³	Domestic-private sector⁴	Total	Internat.²	Domestic-public sector³	Domestic-private sector⁴	Total	Internat.²	Domestic-public sector³	Domestic-private sector⁴
Latin America	430	186	221	24	806	299	432	74	1,282	272	797	212
Asian, larger economies⁵	198	45	94	59	962	70	505	387	2,426	122	1,532	772
Total EM	1,002	294	593	114	2,463	504	1,430	530	4,927	621	3,196	1,110
Industrial countries⁶	15,471	985	6,743	7,743	22,059	3,461	6,344	12,255	35,851	8,267	9,270	18,314

Source: BIS 2007

¹ Includes bonds, notes and money-market instruments

² International bonds, notes and money-market instruments from the BIS-database

³ Sum of: Central Government, Other Government, Central Bank, Quasi-government and Non-resident offcial issuers

⁴ Sum of: Banking sector, Non-bank financial institutions, Non-financial corporate sector other than quasi-government and other non-resident issuers

⁵ China, India, Korea and Taiwan (China)

⁶ Australia, Belgium, Canada, Germany, Spain, the UK and the USA.

The main holders of the enormously expanded public securities in developing countries have been financial institutions (banks and other). In 2000, financial institutions held 57% of total domestic debt while, by 2005, this percentage had reached 80%. In particular, the holding of public securities by banks increased across developing countries.[52] The implication is that the economic power of financial institutions has increased substantially within developing countries' economies. This has also reshaped the class-structure and the distribution of income and wealth in developing countries.[53] The social and economic implications for developing countries have been severe, as is shown below.

4.2. Reserve-accumulation after 1997–8 and capital-flows from developing to developed countries

For most of the 2000s, capital has flowed from developing to developed countries. Table 3 below shows that net lending by developing to developed countries has been positive and rising after 2002. The figure for net lending derives from balancing out sources and uses of the available resources of each national economy. Negative net lending means that the national economy needs funds (from external sources) to cover its domestic expenditures; positive net lending means that the domestic economy is exporting national resources to the rest of world. This directly contradicts mainstream-arguments regarding the desirability of international-financial liberalisation.

Table 3   Net Lending – Sources and Uses of World-Savings (% of GDP)

	Average 1994–2001	2002	2003	2004	2005	2006	2007
Advanced Economies	−0.2	−0.7	−0.8	−0.7	−1.2	−1.4	−1.1
USA	−2.6	−4.2	−5.1	−5.5	−6	−5.9	−5.1
Japan	2.3	2.9	3.2	3.7	3.6	3.9	4.8
UK	−1.3	−1.6	−1.3	−1.6	−2.5	−3.9	−4.9
Euro Area	0.3	0.7	0.6	1.1	0.2	−0.2	−0.4
NI Asian economies	3.1	5	6.8	6.3	5.3	5.3	6.3
Emerging and developing economies	−0.7	1.2	1.9	2.4	4.1	4.8	4.2

Source: IMF 2008a

---

52. See BIS 2007, pp. 68–9.
53. Full analysis of domestic financialisation in developing countries lies beyond the scope of this chapter.

Figures 1 and 2 provide further detail on international capital-flows to developing countries in the last decade. Figure 1 shows that, after the crises of the late 1990s and early 2000s, private capital returned to developing countries in the form of direct investment and other capital-flows. In particular, foreign-direct investment kept constant even during the crises, and has increased substantially since 2002.[54] In 2008, as consequence of the current financial crisis, total capital-flows dropped as a result of decline in their more volatile components.

As Figure 2 shows, however, the most important aspect of international capital-flows has been the huge increase in international reserves. Reserve-assets are typically held by monetary authorities and comprise various types of deposits and securities, gold, repurchase-agreements and derivatives. The sources of reserves are found in funds streaming in as current-account surpluses as well as private capital-flows.

Thus, instead of using incoming funds productively, developing countries have deployed them to accumulate huge foreign-exchange reserves. There are two reasons for adopting this strategy: first, to defend the stability of exchange-rates and, second, as defence against sudden reversals of capital-flows.[55] Both of these problems were characteristic of the crises of the late 1990s. Developing countries have gone down this path partly under pressure from international organisations, such as the IMF, and partly due to the painful experience of the earlier crises. Table 4 shows how widespread reserve-accumulation has been among developing countries, even in impoverished Africa.

Massive reserve-accumulation led to a negative net capital-flow, as is shown on Graph 2.[56] Foreign reserves are necessarily invested in the safest assets in global-financial markets, and these are issued by developed countries. The mainstay of reserves is US-Treasury securities, since they provide the safest access to dollars. In short, despite huge private capital-flows to developing

---

54. It shows that the process of "shift" in the capitalist production from West to East was not so damaged with the developing countries' crises. The foreign-direct investment-flow therefore shows that the global-productive capacity has been partly transferred for developing countries. The huge current-account surplus, as can be seen in the Graph 2, is also an important aspect of that 'shift'. However, the analysis of that dimension of global accumulation of capital is not the addressed in this chapter.

55. For developing countries, especially some East-Asian countries, stability of exchange-rates is related to maintaining competitiveness in foreign trade.

56. The net capital-flow includes private-capital and official flows as well as the change in reserves.

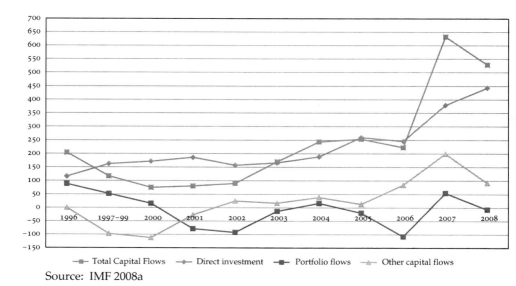

Source: IMF 2008a

**Figure 1   Net Private Capital-Flows – Emerging and
Developing Countries**

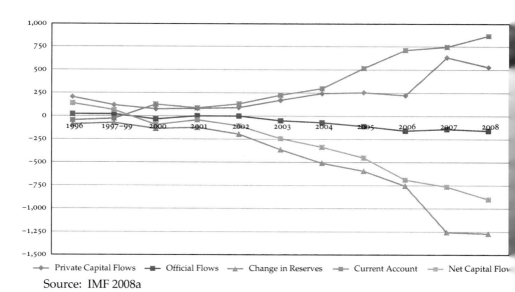

Source: IMF 2008a

**Figure 2   Net Global Capital-Flows – Emerging and
Developing Countries**

Table 4   International Reserves – Selected Countries ($ billions)

	2000	2003	2006	2007
Developing Asia	320.7	669.7	1,489.1	2,108.4
China	168.9	409.2	1,069.5	1,531.4
India	38.4	99.5	171.3	256.8
Excluding China and India	113.4	161.1	248.2	320.2
Russia	24.8	73.8	296.2	445.3
Brazil	31.5	49.1	85.6	180.1
Mexico	35.5	59.0	76.3	86.6
Africa	54.0	90.2	221.3	282.7

Source: IMF 2008a

countries since the early 2000s, net capital-flows have been negative. The primary reason is that the international reserve-currency is generated mainly by the USA.[57]

Reserve-accumulation has been accompanied by a large increase in domestic debt in developing countries, as is shown in Table 5. The main reason is that developing countries had to engage in monetary sterilisation to offset the inflationary impact of foreign capital-inflows. Sterilisation is the practice of issuing public debt by the Treasury or the central bank with the aim of absorbing increases in domestic liquidity (the money-supply) due to surpluses of foreign exchange. Developing countries were forced to sterilise in order to comply with the inflation-targeting régime characteristic of macroeconomic orthodoxy in recent years.[58] In other words, developing countries increased their domestic borrowing not in order to engage in investment but to avoid increases in the money-supply that might have made them miss tight inflation-targets.

To recap, the strategy of reserve-accumulation has had two major implications for developing countries. First, it has led to capital-transfers (positive net lending) from developing countries to developed countries. Second, it has contributed to large increases in domestic public debt because of monetary sterilisation rather than to support national development.

---

57. In the end of 2006, 65.3% of international reserves were denominated in US-dollars (IMF, International Financial Statistics).
58. See Papadatos 2009.

**Table 5   Changes in Stocks of Domestic Bonds and Notes.
Annualised, in $ billions**

	1995–99	2000–04	2005	2006
Latin America	42.0	36.2	83.2	88.4
Asia, larger economies	90.1	161.4	202.6	218.4
Other Asia	20.8	22.2	23.6	26.3
Central Europe	7.3	14.1	24.0	23.1
Other countries	24.5	35.4	38.8	25.2
Total	184.7	269.3	372.2	381.4

Source: BIS 2007

**Table 6   Foreign Holdings of US Long-Term Securities
(in Percent of the Total Securities)**

	Mar-00	Jun-06
Equity	6.9	10.2
US Treasury debt	35.2	52
US Government Agency	7.3	16.8
Corporate and other debt	12.3	20.4
Total	9.7	16.7

Source: US Treasury 2007

4.3. *The impact of reserve-accumulation on the USA*

Since the US-dollar is the main form of contemporary reserve-currency (or quasi-world-money), international reserve-accumulation has had significant implications for the US economy.[59] Evidence of its impact comes from the monthly survey conducted by the US Treasury International Capital (TIC) system. This has notorious limitations and distortions but nonetheless provides a reasonable picture of the role of foreign investors in the US securities-markets.[60] In March 2000, foreign holdings of long-term US-public securities

---

59. The huge current-account deficits generated by the US-economy in the last years are also important to explaining the direction of global capital-flows. However, the focus of this section is on the impact of global flows on the USA.

60. TIC-weaknesses are due to the methods of data-collection, relying on surveys among US-financial institutions about holdings and transactions of US state-securities by foreign investors. Surveys suffer from disclosure-problems among financial institutions as well as absence of law-enforcement on financial institutions. Hence the foreign holdings of US state-securities – mainly by central banks – are probably underestimated (Frey and Moec 2005).

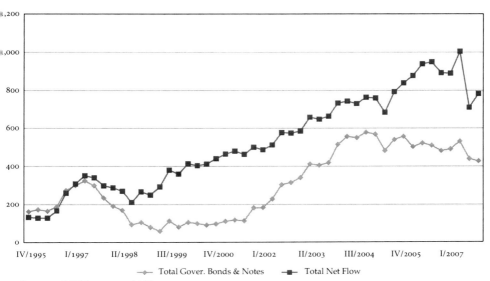

Source: US Treasury 2008

Figure 3   Net Foreign Capital-Flow – USA

stood at $3.6 trillion, while in June 2007 they had risen to $9.1 trillion.[61] Table 6 shows that foreign holdings as proportion of total US long-term securities (public and private) rose from 9.7% in March 2000 to 16.7% in June 2006. The proportion stood at 18.8% in June 2007.

Figure 3 shows the relationship between the flow of foreign capital and US-public debt from the middle of the 1990s to 2007. The correlation is particularly close at the end of the 1990s and during 2002–5.

The main foreign holders of US-public debt in recent years have been official institutions, that is, mostly central banks. During 2000–7, the share of central banks in total foreign holdings of US-debt rose from 18.3% to 28.1%. Figure 4 shows the huge increases in US-liabilities (mostly public debt) held by foreign-central banks after 2001.

In a little more detail, the total of outstanding US-Treasury securities in March 2000 stood at $2.5 trillion, rising to $3.5 trillion in June 2007. During

---

61. These securities originate in the US Treasury as well as government agencies, such as Federal National Mortgage Association (Fannie Mae) and Federal Home Loan Mortgage Corporation (Freddie Mac), which are the main Government Sponsored Enterprises (GSEs).

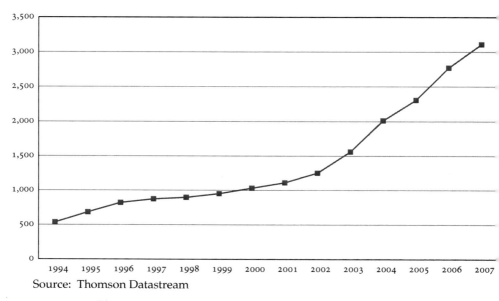

Source: Thomson Datastream

Figure 4   US Foreign-Owned Assets – Central Banks

the same period, the holdings of foreign investors rose from $0.9 trillion to $2 trillion. The main buyers were central banks, whose holdings went from $0.5 trillion to $1.45 trillion.[62] Central banks also increased their holdings of US agency-debt during the same period. While the total of agency-debt increased from $3.6 trillion to $6.1 trillion, holdings by foreign investors rose from $300 billion to $1.3 trillion, while those by central banks jumped from $90 billion to $750 billion. Since the debt of US government-agencies is directly related to the US-housing market, purchases by foreign-central banks were important to the housing bubble of 2001–6.[63]

The importance of international capital-flows for the US-economy has not escaped the attention of mainstream-economics. According to Frey and Moec,

---

62. The data are based on US Treasury 2008, pp. 8–14.

63. As consequence of the 2007–8 financial crisis, the short-term funding practices of the two major government-agencies (Fannie Mae and Freddie Mac) have been seriously affected. In July 2008, the US-government put together a rescue-plan using public money. Justified criticism has been levelled against the plan on the grounds that it commits taxpayers' money to rescuing speculators. But the alternative would have been to let the bondholders of these agencies take losses. As these include foreign investors and central banks from developing countries, this would have directly affected the role of the US-dollar as world-money. It is not surprising that this option has not been adopted by the US-authorities.

since 2002: 'the increase in net purchases by foreigners has resumed, driven this time by the official sector. This trend can mainly be ascribed to the fact that Asian central banks have built up their foreign reserves with a view to curbing the appreciation of their currencies against the dollar.'[64] The increased supply of loanable funds in the US-markets is estimated to have reduced the yield on long-term financial assets by as much as 1% in the summer of 2004.

Warnock and Warnock also estimate that funds supplied by foreign investors to the USA have reduced long-term yields, perhaps by up to 1.5% in 2004 and 2005.[65] Roubini and Setser put the impact at 2%, caused mainly by central-bank flows.[66] Note that the holdings of central banks continued to rise until June 2007. The dampening effect on interest-rates, therefore, continued throughout the period of the housing bubble, and has had a major impact on general conditions in US-financial markets.[67]

To summarise, since the early 2000s, foreign-central banks (mainly from Asia) have invested their international reserves heavily in US-public debt. By doing so, they have helped to lower long-term yields on US-debt. Therefore, there is a direct connection between boom-conditions prevailing in US-financial markets during 2001–7 and the international reserves of developing countries. By the same token, there is a direct connection between the US housing bubble and the huge savings generated in developing countries since the early 2000s (mainly in East Asia).

The trade-surpluses that many developing countries have generated in recent years are partly due to the structural shift in the allocation of productive capacity across the world in recent years. This shift has resulted in huge increases in the exploitation of labour in East Asia and elsewhere in the developing world. The result has been a net flow of capital from poor to rich countries in the world-economy, primarily to the USA. The US-financial markets have been among the main beneficiaries of these flows, eventually leading to the emergence of a gigantic bubble in 2001–7.

The flows of capital to the USA are due to the role of the dollar as international reserve-currency (quasi-world-money). Moreover, the ability to create

---

64. Frey and Moec 2005, p. 21.
65. Warnock and Warnock 2005.
66. Roubini and Setser 2005.
67. Japanese international reserves have also had a significant impact on the holdings of US-debt abroad (Frey and Moec 2005). However, since early 2004, the central banks of developing countries have clearly surpassed the Bank of Japan as sources of capital for US-financial markets, see BOJ 2008.

dollars has allowed the USA to run very large trade-deficits throughout this period. Essentially, the USA has been paying for its growing imports through issuing public debt-securities that rest on government-promises to pay dollars. At the same time, US-deficits have provided a source of demand for the world-economy and sustained global growth. Truman estimates that they contributed at least 0.3% to annual global growth during 2000–4.[68]

Financialisation has thus resulted in the absurd situation of the poor financing the rich in the world-economy, while allowing the USA to run vast trade-deficits. This bizarre configuration of trends cannot last forever. According to King: '[t]he rise in the US current account deficit to more than 6% of national income has raised fears of how the inevitable correction will eventually be achieved. [F]or much of the past twenty years, as evidenced by the Asian crisis of the late 1990s, we have worried about emerging market countries accumulating excessive dollar liabilities. Now we seem to be worried about their accumulating excessive dollar assets. Capital has flowed "uphill" from poor to rich countries. The invisible hand of international capital markets has not successfully coordinated monetary and exchange rate policies.' It is likely that there will be a readjustment of consumption and capital-flows globally. This has probably started already due to the crisis of 2007–9.[69]

5. The costs of reserve-accumulation for developing countries

The social and economic costs to developing countries from the strategy of reserve-accumulation have been enormous. To fully appreciate the significance of these costs, it is necessary to refer briefly to mainstream-debates on the optimal level of international reserves. Three indicators are employed: first, the ratio of reserves to imports, second, the ratio of reserves to short-term external debt and, third, the ratio of reserves to the money-supply (typically M2).[70]

The first indicator focuses on reserves in connection with unexpected deteriorations of the balance of trade. Thus, it typically expects countries to keep reserves that could cover at least three months of imports. The second indicator, known as the Greenspan-Guidotti rule, emerged in the early 2000s as

68. Truman 2005.
69. King 2006.
70. On short-term debt as target, see Bussiere and Mulder 1999 and Garcia and Souto 2004. For the effects on exchange-rates see Hviding et al. 2005.

a response to the crises of the late 1990s, and focuses on short-term external debt. It expects that countries should have enough reserves to cover all of their short-term external debt. The third indicator is also a response to the crises of the late 1990s, but is broader than the second. It focuses on sudden capital-outflows and expects that countries will keep reserves at least equal to 20% of their money-supply (M2).

The third indicator is normally higher than the second, which is higher than the first. This is because increases in financial activities (assets and liabilities) in recent years have far exceeded increases in trade. Since the third indicator necessitates the highest level of foreign reserves, it has been the favourite of the international-financial system. The indicator acts as a form of insurance for international capital entering developing countries. It is notable that, in recent years, the actual levels of international reserves have been even higher than the third indicator.

Against this background, Rodrik pioneered the measurement of the social cost of reserve-accumulation.[71] Rodrik suggests that the cost should be measured by the difference between interest on short-term borrowing abroad (since countries hold reserves equivalent at least to their short-term borrowing) and the yield on international reserves (since these are invested in assets abroad). The former is obviously higher than the latter. On this basis, Rodrik estimates the annual loss to developing countries at close to 1% of GDP – a very large sum. Akyuz also offers a measure of the cost of reserves, but considers reserves to impose costs only if they are due to borrowing rather than trade.[72] Even so, Akyuz's estimate of the annual cost is around $100bn.

Rodrik has also raised the issue of why developing countries have not tried to reduce their short-term foreign liabilities since the early 2000s.[73] Had they done so, they could have reduced the cost of holding foreign reserves, without necessarily losing liquidity. This is an important puzzle and it is not clear where the answer lies. It is likely that the rise of short-term external debt is associated with the tendency of the developing-country exchange-rates to appreciate in recent years. This tendency has affected the behaviour of international capital-flows, and prevented developing countries from reducing their short-term borrowing.

---

71. Rodrik 2006.
72. Akyuz 2008.
73. Rodrik 2006.

To be specific, once the tendency toward exchange-rate appreciation became established for particular developing countries, investors began to borrow in the international-financial markets in order to invest in domestic capital-assets, such as domestic-public and private bonds, stocks, real estate and others securities. It is important to note that such investors could also be domestic, originating in both the financial and the non-financial sector. Assuming that the domestic currency appreciated, they could repay their external financing under better terms, or simply roll it over. Put differently, investors would sell assets in a weak currency with relatively low interest-rates, and then use the funds to buy assets in a strong currency, yielding higher interest-rates. Such operations have been called the 'carry trade', and have generated huge profits for international financial investors.[74]

As financialisation progressed, the financial assets of developing countries have become susceptible to the 'carry trade'. Interest-rates in developing economies have been generally higher than in developed economies in recent years, while fixed investment as proportion of GDP has declined. Since 1990, there has also been an increase in financial assets relative to GDP in developing countries, as was shown in Section 5. Thus, while developing-country international reserves have increased enormously, their short-term external debt has also risen substantially. The result has been intensification of the financial exploitation of developing countries, partly captured by the measurement of the social costs of international reserves.

6. Conclusion

In the era of financialisation, of which financial liberalisation is a fundamental aspect, there have been two distinct periods of international capital-flows relating to developing countries. The first took place in the 1990s and was characterised by the eventual reversal of the turn of flows, current-account deficits and the spread of financial and foreign-exchange crises. In contrast, the second period commenced in the early 2000s and has been characterised by the accumulation of international reserves. These aim at protecting developing countries from sudden reversal of international capital-flows, while allowing them more actively to participate in the global-financial markets.

---

74. IMF 2008a.

This article has established that, for different reasons, both periods have entailed enormous social and economic costs for developing countries. For the former, costs arose due to the devastating effect of financial and currency-crises, while, for the latter, costs have resulted primarily from the low yield of foreign-exchange reserves relative to borrowed funds. Financialisation since the early 2000s has meant that developing countries have held huge reserves of quasi-world-money thus facilitating their financial exploitation by developed countries, primarily the USA. As the crisis of 2007–9 unfolds, it is possible that further losses will accumulate as US-financial assets lose value.

It is clear that developing countries need stronger social controls over the policy of reserve-accumulation, whose results have been extremely costly. Moreover, participating in free capital-flows has fostered domestic financial-isation, thus exacerbating the power and influence of financial institutions in developing countries. The development-implications of these trends are deeply problematic. It is a tragedy that such policies have been forced on developing countries, given their poverty and huge social needs.

Chapter Eight

Global Integration of Middle-Income Developing Countries in the Era of Financialisation: The Case of Turkey

Nuray Ergüneş

1. Introduction: financialisation has several aspects

During the last three decades, the world-economy has been marked by financialisation, typified by the dominant position of finance and the extraordinary growth of financial activities.[1] Financial systems have grown in terms of employment, profits, size of institutions and markets all of which have been promoted by technological revolution. However, financialisation has been associated with a number of further developments. One of these has been the transformation of the relationship between state and economy.

An indication of the changing relationship between state and economy is given by the role of the central bank. Throughout the process of financialisation, central banks have become ostensibly independent from political decision-making mechanisms. Moreover, the importance of central banks has increased

---

1. For his support and comments, I am indebted to Costas Lapavitsas. Thanks are also due to members of Research Money and Finance (RMF) at SOAS for helpful comments on earlier draft of this chapter.

and their main goal has been reduced to price-stability. Inflation-targeting policy has become the main monetary-policy agenda across the world.

Financialisation has also changed the relationship between developed and developing countries. Huge international capital-flows to developing countries forced the latter to accumulate international reserves which, in turn, served to finance the US current-account deficit. The main beneficiary of this process has been the US as issuer of the main form of the international means of payment. The result has been net lending by the poor to the rich in the world-economy thus positing the issue of imperialism afresh.[2] Following Harvey's definition, echoing Ranajit Guha, this can be referred to as 'domination without hegemony'.[3]

Further phenomena of financialisation include deregulation of the financial sector, proliferation of new financial instruments, liberalisation of international capital-flows and increasing instability on foreign-exchange markets. There has also been a shift toward market-based financial systems, emergence of institutional investors as major players in financial markets, and domination of corporate governance (of financial and non-financial business) by shareholder-value.[4]

The literature on financialisation has also expanded, and the phenomenon has been differently described by scholars. According to Epstein, financialisation refers to 'increasing role of financial motives, financial markets, financial actors and financial institutions in the operation of the domestic and international economies'.[5] Aglietta and Bretton focused on equity-markets as the dominant force of 'new financial system' which shapes the growth-régime.[6] For the regulationists, financial liberalisation has been the most important institutional driver of changes in the growth-régime.

Stockhammer, Crotty, Skott and Ryoo[7] mostly focused on macroeconomic results of financialisation and used the term to describe the transformation between non-financial and financial market-relations. Other authors, such as Froud, Haslam, Johal and Williams,[8] have analysed financialisation at the

---

2. See Lapavitsas in this volume.
3. Harvey 2007, p. 69.
4. Stockhammer 2007, p. 2.
5. Epstein 2005, p. 3.
6. Aglietta and Bretton 2001.
7. Stockhammer 2004; Crotty 2005; Skott and Ryoo 2008.
8. Froud, Haslam, Johal and Williams 2001.

micro-level. They have sought financial-market influences on corporations and individual behaviour, organising their analysis around the concept of coupon-pool capitalism.

However, Arrighi, Harvey and Lapavitsas[9] seek roots of financialisation in the capital-accumulation process, and highlight the crisis of overaccumulation in their critical works. From a still different perspective, Lapavitsas emphasises the newly exploitative aspects of finance and stresses the transformation of financial system. Particular attention is paid to banks as a key mediating institution with a decisive presence in contemporary capitalism.[10]

Financialisation emerged mostly as an internal process in developed countries but has also become a global process involving developing countries. Developing countries, following capital-account liberalisation, have had intense experience of the impact of financialisation. This has taken the form primarily of extraordinary capital-inflows in the form of foreign direct investment (FDI) and portfolio-equity investment. Huge international capital-flows stemmed from developed countries in search of profitable markets and were directed toward developing countries. Private capital-flows to developing countries stood at 74.8bn in 2000 but rose to $605bn in 2007.[11] These flows have caused unpredictability and instability, inevitably resulting in financial crisis. The last two decades have brought massive crises to developing countries, the most remarkable being Mexico 1994–5, East Asia 1997–8, Russia 1999, Brazil 1999, Turkey 2000–1 and Argentina 2001–2.

To promote capital-accumulation domestically, developing countries have continued to facilitate capital-inflows despite the resulting fragility for their economies. At the same time, to avoid the uncertainty and vulnerability caused by capital-flows, developing countries have altered macroeconomic policies. The main policy across the developing world has been to accumulate huge amounts of international reserves, mostly US-dollars. Accumulated foreign-exchange reserves have aimed at stabilising exchange-rates as well as protecting countries against sudden capital-outflows. World-reserves have risen from $1.2tr in January 1995 to more than $4tr in September 2005.[12]

9. Arrighi 2003; Harvey 2007 and Lapavitsas in this volume.
10. See Lapavitsas in this volume.
11. IMF 2008.
12. European Central Bank International Relations Committee 2006, p. 7.

By the same token, expanding capital-inflows into developing countries has inevitably changed the approach of the latter toward monetary policy. Developing countries have typically opted for contractionary monetary policy, with near-exclusive focus on price-stability, especially at the end of 1990s. Several developing countries have started to adopt inflation-targeting, which was first introduced by developed countries, such as New Zealand, Canada, and the United Kingdom.[13] Inflation-targeting consists of five components: absence of other nominal anchors, such as wages, exchange-rate or nominal GDP; an institutional commitment to price-stability; absence of fiscal dominance; policy-instrument independence; and policy-transparency and accountability.[14]

The adoption of inflation-targeting has had severe implications for the governments of developing countries that seek to attract inflows of foreign capital. In short, it has forced developing countries to adopt a series of restrictive monetary and fiscal policies. These include a balanced budget, retrenched fiscal expenditures, and an *ex ante* commitment to high real interest-rates. Thus, indirect market-based policy-instruments, such as short-term interest-rates, have become favourite tools of monetary policy.[15] The critical element has been *ex ante* commitment to high real interest-rates, which have been a tool for attracting foreign capital-flows into developing countries. In this context, it can be asserted that a key reason for adopting inflation-targeting together with accumulating huge reserves has been to attract capital-inflows.

In addition to its role of regulating capital-flows, inflation-targeting has also served as a mechanism for lowering labour-wages, thus allowing developing countries to compete globally and accelerating accumulation. This is one of the specific components of the so-called non-inflationary growth-policy that has been dominant among developing countries in recent years. This policy has relied on deregulated labour-markets (including flexibility in employment-protection legislation and indexing wage-increases to price-levels) as well as product-market competition through multilateral trade-agreements.[16]

---

13. Developing countries that have adopted inflation-targeting include Israel, Czech Rep., Poland, Brazil, Chile, Colombia, South Africa, Thailand, Korea, Mexico, Hungary, Peru, the Philippines, Slovak Republic, Indonesia, Romania, and Turkey.

14. Rose 2007; Mishkin 1999; Petturson 2000.

15. Epstein and Yeldan 2006.

16. Montgomerie 2008, p. 10.

In this context, inflation-targeting has had a significant impact on the productive structure of developing countries. All in all, inflation-targeting has played a critical role in shaping the process of capital-accumulation in developing countries in the era of financialisation.

Using Turkey as a case study, this chapter examines the results of inflation-targeting on middle-income developing countries. It is shown that, contrary to what is often asserted, inflation-targeting was certainly implemented in the interests of finance but also in line with requirements posed by capital-accumulation in the course of the global integration of the Turkish economy. The integration of Turkey into the global economy has parallels with other middle-income developing countries in the era of financialisation. This process started in the 1980s and has reached a peak in the 2000s. In the wake of the crisis of 2000–1, Turkey implemented inflation-targeting and a set of other reforms thus entering a period of growth. However, it is shown below that this growth-path has been unstable and increased the fragility of the economy. Not surprisingly, Turkey has been among the most vulnerable countries in the world-crisis that started in 2007.

The chapter proceeds as follows. Section 2 considers the implementation of inflation-targeting and its results on the economy. Sections 3, 4, 5, and on macroeconomic aspects of the economy, aiming to reveal the dynamics of capital-accumulation as Turkey entered a process of global integration. Sections 7, 8, and 9 consider changes in the financing of the real sector, in the structure of the banking sector, and in the activities and indebtedness of individuals throughout this period. These three sections offer evidence of how the actors of the economy – the productive sector, the financial sector and individuals – have been affected by the process of financialisation. They offer insight into new patterns of integration between the productive sector and the financial system of middle-income developing countries in the current period.

2. Changing monetary policy: the adoption of inflation-targeting

Combating inflation has been the main objective of macroeconomic policy in Turkey since end of 1990s, similarly to many other developing countries. The main policy-approaches were disinflation and 'Transition to a Strong Economy', which had a very specific meaning for the Turkish economy. In particular, 'Transition to a Strong Economy' included structural reforms that aimed at strengthening the global integration of the economy. This process had already started in the 1980s but was intensified in the 2000s.

Disinflation and macroeconomic restructuring were launched as a three-year (2000–2) programme by the Turkish government in 1999. The programme was essentially exchange-rate-based stabilisation supplemented by fiscal adjustment and structural reforms, including agricultural reform, pension-reform, fiscal-measurement transparency, and administration of tax-policy.[17] The mains goals included maintaining a primary surplus by means of reducing public expenditure and increasing public income as well as indexing public wages to an *ex ante* inflation-rate.

The disinflation-programme initially appeared successful, but in 2000 it started to run into problems. After a few months, it became clear that the programme was not viable and the currency-peg had to be abandoned in February 2001, replaced by a régime of free-floating exchange-rates on the advice of the IMF.[18] The government then adopted the 'Transition to Strong Economy', in order to eliminate 'the confidence-crisis' and financial instability. The 'Transition to Strong Economy' programme was essentially the name of structural reforms associated with the post-Washington consensus, which are known as the Kemal Derviş laws in Turkey, after the name of their main author.

There were three pillars to structural reforms, namely banking, public and private sector. The first pillar was restructuring of the banking sector. This involved deep restructuring of public banks as well as of failed banks that had come under public administration. It also involved strengthening the private banking system and improving banking regulation and supervision. The second pillar was improvements in public governance, including public-administration reform and pursuing further reforms in managing public expenditure. The third pillar was private-sector reforms, including privatisation, corporate governance, easier entry of foreign capital, and reducing bureaucracy in order to promote investment.

Fundamental to the entire approach, however, was the orientation of monetary policy toward fighting inflation. The most important elements of monetary policy were to restructure the banking sector, change the Central

---

17. Kibritçioğlu 2005.
18. Akyüz and Boratav 2005.

Bank Law and adopt inflation-targeting.[19] Turkey adopted inflation-targeting implicitly in 2002, following the 2000–1 crisis, and shifted to explicit inflation-targeting in 2006. Following adoption of implicit inflation-targeting, the Turkish economy witnessed rapid growth. The average annual growth-rate of GDP reached 7% in the period after 2001. But, despite this rapid growth, jobs were not created and unemployment has increased. This has been called 'jobless growth' in the literature.

During the same period, there have been enormous foreign capital-flows. The high rate of interest has pulled foreign capital into the country and, as a consequence, there has been relative abundance of foreign exchange, leading to overvaluation of the Turkish lira. Lower foreign exchange-rates in turn caused increases in imports. Paradoxically, exports also increased. The export/GDP ratio was 10.5% in 2000, 15.6% in 2002, and 16.3% in 2007. But the rate of increase of imports was faster than exports. The ratio of imports to GDP was 20.5% in 2000, 22.4% in 2002, and reached 25.9% in 2007. Overvaluation of the lira and import-increases, not surprisingly, manifested themselves in large current-account deficits.

At the same time, Turkey's international reserves have also increased, along similar lines to other developing countries. The central bank has invested its reserves mostly in US-Treasury bonds. Reserve-accumulation in Turkey has been very high, judging by the ratio of reserves to short-term foreign debt, which comprises the so-called Greenspan-Guidotti rule of reserve-adequacy. The ratio of reserves to short-term debt in Turkey currently stands at the very high level of 1.81. According to Aydoğuş and Türkler,[20] reserves of this size have imposed costs on the Turkish economy (income-losses) that are close to 1% of GDP.

Thus, recent trends in the Turkish economy have included rapid growth without rising employment, increases in exports and imports, high current-account deficits, finance-account surpluses, huge reserve-accumulation and rising external debt. How was the Turkish economy able to sustain this growth-rate after the 2000–1 crisis, which was the worst economic crisis that

---

19. The Central Bank Law was amended on April 2001, and instrument-independence of the Central Bank was introduced. The primary goal of the Bank was determined to be maintaining price-stability.

20. Aydoğuş and Türkler 2006.

Table 1 Selected Main Economic Indicators

	2000	2001	2002	2003	2004	2005	2006	2007
GDP Growth-rate %	6.8	−5.7	6.2	5.3	9.4	8.4	6.9	4.6
Export (fob)/GDP %	10.5	15.9	15.6	15.5	16.2	15.2	16.2	16.3
Import (cif)/GDP %	20.5	21.0	22.4	22.8	25.0	24.2	26.5	25.9
Current account/ GDP %	−3.7	1.9	−0.3	−2.5	−3.7	−4.6	−6.1	−5.7
Unemployment-Rate (%)	6.5	8.4	10.3	10.5	10.3	10.3	9.9	9.9
Inflation-Rate – CPI (2003=100) %	39.0	68.5	29.7	18.4	9.4	7.7	9.7	8.4
Real Exchange-Rate Index (1987=100)	140.35	152.04	123.05	137.75	151.74	162.08	179.57	198.96
External Debt/GDP %	44.7	57.8	56.2	47.3	41.2	35.1	39.5	36.1
Long Term/GDP %	34.0	49.4	49.1	39.8	33.0	27.4	31.4	30.0
Short Term/GDP %	10.7	8.4	7.1	7.5	8.2	7.8	8.0	6.1
CB Reserves (million $)	22.172	18.787	26.807	33.616	36.009	50.518	60.912	73.317
CB Reserves/Short Term Debt	0.78	1.14	1.63	1.46	1.12	1.36	1.44	1.81
CB Reserves/GDP %	8.4	9.5	11.6	11.0	9.2	10.5	11.5	11.1

Source: estimated from Republic of Turkey Prime Ministry Undersecretariat of Treasury 'Economic Indicators', available at: <www.hazine.gov.tr>; Turkey Republic Prime Ministry State Planning Organisation 'Main Economic Indicators', available at: <www.dpt.gov.tr>; Turkish Industrialists and Businessmen Association 2007, Yılına Girerken Türkiye Ekonomisi, pp: 11–12.

the Turkish Republic has experienced since its foundation in 1923?[21] How did the Turkish economy handle the surging capital-inflows? And how has financialisation affected the country?

The performance of the economy is captured in a series of macroeconomic indicators presented in Table 1. In a sense, these capture the dynamics of the capital-accumulation régime, and the requirements imposed on it in the process of global integration. To examine these and answer the questions asked above, analysis in the following section turns first to the transformation of the structure of production and the behaviour of exports and imports.

---

21. As a result of the 2000–1 crisis, GDP dropped by 9.5% and government-debt increased by more than 40% of GDP. The lira depreciated by 30% within six months, and inflation picked up very rapidly to reach 70% by the end of 2001. See Taymaz and Yılmaz 2008, p. 6.

3. Transformation of the structure of production

3.1. *Changes in export-performance*

The appreciation of the Turkish currency has had a negative effect on the export-performance of the manufacturing sector, which is the mainstay of Turkish exports. Nonetheless, in recent years, Turkey's export-performance has remained strong despite an overvalued currency. The rate of total exports to GDP was 10.5% in 2000, but rose to 16.3% in 2007. This strong performance took place in what might be called the investment-goods sectors, which include electrical machinery, motor-vehicles, communication-equipment, televisions and radios. The annual average increase of exports by these sectors reached 31.8% in 2003–7, making them the most dynamic sectors across the economy as far as exports are concerned. Specifically, the share of these sectors in total exports was 15.5% in 1996, rose to 25.8% in 2001, reached 36.7% in 2007.

At the same time, exports by agriculture and mining have stagnated. The most interesting figures refer to consumer-goods, which include traditional export-products, such as textiles, ready-to-wear, food, and so on. Consumer-goods exports lagged behind overall exports, and started to become less important. Thus, while their share of the total was 49.7% during 1996–9, it declined to 33.5% during 2003–7.[22] This was contrary to the expectations at the start of the 1980s, when it was thought that the consumer-goods sector would be the engine of growth as the economy turned toward the world-market.

To recap, Turkey experienced a structural change as its exports have shifted from consumer-goods to investment-goods in recent years. In other words, exports have changed from conventional and relatively unskilled labour-intensive sectors to more technologically-intensive sectors requiring highly skilled labour. In this light, the sustainability of export-growth is not immediately apparent.[23]

---

22. Yükseler and Türkan 2008, pp. 24–6.
23. Aysan and Hacıhasanoğlu 2007.

Table 2   Export-Structure (2000–7), $mn

Years	Total Export	Agriculture Products	Mining Products	Manufacturing-Industry Products				Others
				Total	Consumption-Goods	Inter-mediate Goods	Invest-ment-Goods	
2000	25.775	1.684	400	25.518	12.810	6.118	6.589	173
2001	31.334	2.006	349	28.826	13.369	7.384	8.073	153
2002	36.059	1.806	387	33.702	15.287	8.512	9.902	165
2003	47.253	2.201	469	44.378	19.335	10.609	14.434	204
2004	63.167	2.645	649	59.579	22.865	15.756	20.959	294
2005	73.476	3.468	810	68.813	25.669	18.312	24.833	384
2006	85.535	3.611	1.146	80.246	26.754	23.076	30.416	531
2007	107.154	3.882	1.661	100.966	31.604	30.041	39.320	645

Source: Yükseler, Zafer and Ercan Türkan 2008, Türkiye'nin Üretim ve Dış Ticaret Yapısında Dönüşüm, Turkish Industrialist's and Businessmen's Association, p. 25.

3.2. Changes in import-volumes and patterns

Dramatic increases also took place in Turkey's imports, as was mentioned above. While the rate of annual increases in imports was 2.8% during 1997–2002, it became 27% during 2003–7. The ratio of imports to GDP was 20.5 in 2000, but climbed to 25.9 in 2007. As a result of increases in imports, Turkey's foreign-trade deficit rose continuously: from $26.7bn in 2000, it became $65bn in 2008.

It is notable that the share of consumer-goods in aggregate imports has regressed, in a similar way to the share of consumer-goods in exports. While the share of consumer-goods within total imports was 10.1% in 1996–9, it declined to 8% during the period of 2003–7. However, imports of intermediate and investment-goods have increased. The share of intermediate goods within aggregate imports was 30% during 1996–9, but rose to 37.1% during 2003–7.[24] An important aspect of this increase has been the deployment of large volumes of imported intermediate goods in the high-performance export-sectors.

Furthermore, regional trade has contributed to the rise in imports, particularly the growing competitive power of Asia. Two factors have been important in this respect. First, the Asian region has been the most important area

---

24. Yükseler and Türkan 2008, p. 38.

Table 3 Import-Structure (cif-$mn)

Years	Total Import	Agriculture-Products	Mining Products		Manufacturing-Industry Products				Others
			Total	Petrol & Natural Gas	Total	Consumption-Goods	Interme-diate Goods	Invest-ment Goods	
2000	54.503	2.125	7.097	6.196	44.198	4.237	17.280	22.681	1.083
2001	41.399	1.410	6.577	6.076	32.686	3.839	14.434	14.413	726
2002	51.554	1.704	7.192	6.193	41.383	5.359	18.405	17.619	1.275
2003	69.340	2.538	9.021	7.766	55.690	6.633	25.133	23.923	2.092
2004	97.540	2.765	10.981	9.366	80.447	8.232	35.067	37.148	3.346
2005	116.774	2.826	16.321	14.140	94.208	9.087	42.818	42.303	3.419
2006	139.576	2.935	22.034	19.220	110.379	10.617	51.713	48.049	4.228
2007	169.987	4.671	25.311	21.782	133.879	13.061	65.138	55.680	6.126

Source: Yükseler, Zafer and Ercan Türkan 2008, Türkiye'nin Üretim ve Dış Ticaret Yapısında Dönüşüm, Turkish Industrialists' and Businessmens' Association, p. 35.

of production globally relying extensively on its cheap labour-force. Second, a high foreign exchange-rate has allowed Turkey to import cheaply.

Turkey has exported mostly to Europe, which has become a very important market for Turkish products since the Custom Union Agreement (gradual accession-process into the EU).[25] This pattern of trade has thus become known as 'Buy from Asia, sell to Europe'. The strategy of Turkey in order to maintain its competitive power within these chains of trade has been to keep its own labour cheap. Faced with intensifying competitive pressure and loss of competitiveness due to a high exchange-rate, the productive sector has compensated by restricting employment and keeping wages low.

It is striking aspect of Turkish trade that imports and exports involve similar commodities. This kind of trade indicates a high-level integration of Turkey into global markets through importing intermediate goods to be used in producing and exporting final products. The production-structure of Turkey has become intertwined with international production-chains mostly due to the overvalued Turkish lira. The high exchange-rate has increased pressure on the productive sector to lower real wages and raise productivity. At the same time, it has increased purchasing power over imports, creating a

25. The top ten export-destinations in 2006 were Germany, UK, Italy, US, France, Spain, Russia, Netherlands, Romania, U. Arab Emirates. See Aydın, Saygılı and Saygılı 2007, p. 26.

Table 4 Industrial Production (Annual Average Growth-Rate %) and Technology

Technology-Class			Low			High – Medium	Medium		High	
Years	Total Industry	Manufacturing-Industry Sector	Food, beverage-products	Textile-products	Clothing	Chemical Products	Basic metal-industry	Motor-vehicles	Metal-products	Electrical-machinery apparatus
2002	9.5	10.9	2.8	12.5	3.3	14.2	10.0	27.1	0.6	11.5
2003	8.7	9.3	7.7	2.1	1.8	8.8	11.9	47.7	3.2	2.8
2004	9.8	10.4	-0.5	-1.5	3.5	16.1	11.6	53.3	9.4	-4.6
2005	5.3	4.7	6.0	-11.8	-12.6	5.5	3.4	9.6	31.6	16.7
2006	5.8	5.5	6.0	-1.0	-4.8	6.3	10.7	9.7	18.9	20.4
2007	5.2	4.4	2.9	2.5	2.3	8.1	10.9	6.4	14.2	25.4

Source: tabulated from Turkish Industrialists' and Businessmens' Association 2007, 2008 Yılına Girerken Türkiye Ekonomisi, p. 34 and classified according to Saraçoğlu and Suiçmez, see Saraçoğlu, Bedriye and Halit Suiçmez 2006, Türkiye İmalat Sanayinde Verimlilik, Teknolojik Gelişme ve Yapısal Özellikler ve 2001 Krizi Sonrası Reel Değişmeler, National Productivity Center.

Table 5   Manufacturing-Industry Production-Increase – Main Sectors

	Total Amount Manufacturing Industry	Consumption-Goods	Intermediate Goods	Investment-Goods
Weighted average production-increase (%) – 1998/2005	4.07	1.02	4.06	7.58

Source: Yükseler, Zafer and Ercan Türkan 2008, Türkiye'nin Üretim ve Dış Ticaret Yapısında Dönüşüm, Turkish Industrialists' and Businessmens' Association, p. 58.

preference over domestic inputs. This has led to extensive use of imported intermediate and investment-goods.[26]

3.3. *Transformed production*

Thus, Turkish production witnessed structural transformation after the 2000–1 crisis, due in part to the Customs Union with the EU, but also to removal of agricultural support, restructuring of finance, and further migration from rural areas into the cities. Export-oriented production has become even more prominent than before.

Production rose significantly in sectors in which technological intensity has been above average. Competitive advantage and productivity have been strong in the sectors of electrical machinery and motor-vehicles, leading to increases in exports. Overall, for sectors in which technological intensity is above average, the share in output stood at 17% in 1997, but rose to 31% in 2006. However, in sectors in which technological intensity is below average, such as textiles, apparel, food and tobacco, both production and exports rose at rates below average.[27]

To recap, production-increases in the several sectors of manufacturing industry have presented significant variations during 1998–2007. The annual average-increase in the manufacturing industry as a whole was 4.1%, representing 1.0% in consumer-goods, 4.1% in intermediate goods, and 7.6% in investment-goods. Moreover, the rate of growth of manufacturing industry accelerated during 2003–7. Production intensified especially in the sectors which use a high ratio of imported (direct and indirect) inputs. In contrast,

---

26. Narin 2008b, p. 48.
27. Turkish Industrialists' and Businessmens' Association 2007, p. 35.

the rate of growth for consumer-goods stayed low, at 0.7%. Thus, the transformation in the composition of manufacturing production raised both the direct and indirect use of imported inputs.[28]

It is apparent that production of technology-intensive and investment-goods has gained weight in Turkey in recent years, even though overall production is still heavily skewed toward intermediate and consumer-goods. This has been the basis on which Turkish capital has become increasingly internationalised. Yet, this transformation has not included creation of capacity to produce producer-goods, and this can be understood as a peculiarity of late development. Turkish capital has relied on obtaining its input requirements from abroad because that has been comparatively cheaper than relying on domestic inputs.[29] In this sense, the policy of maintaining a high exchange-rate has facilitated the integration of domestic capital in world-markets. It is shown below that this structural transformation has also brought important changes in the financing of the productive sector, thus intensifying the process of financialisation.

4. Wages and productivity

Strong growth in the economy did not create corresponding gains in employment. The unemployment-rate increased from 6.5% in 2000 to 9.6% in 2008.[30] This tendency can also be observed in several other developing countries and is often called jobless growth. This phenomenon is hardly surprising in view of the changes in the structure of production outlined above. Increases in production have been strong in technology-intensive investment-goods, thus substituting capital for labour. This development has been behind the rise in the unemployment-ratio, as well as signifying an intensification of the exploitation of labour.

However, wage- and productivity-levels have also changed significantly during this period; above all, real wages have declined. The value of the real-wages index for the manufacturing sector was 111.3 in 2000, but fell to 93.7 in 2007. In sharp contrast, the productivity-index in the manufacturing sector

---

28. Yükseler and Türkan 2008, p. 59.
29. See Narin 2008b for a critical analysis.
30. The real unemployment-rate is probably higher than the official ratio. According to Sönmez the real unemployment-rate in Turkey is around 20%. Sönmez 2008, p. 101.

Table 6 Industrial Production, Real Wages, Workers' Productivity-Indexes (Manufacturing Industry-Per Hour Worked) and Inflation-Rate (CPI)

	2000	2001	2002	2003	2004	2005	2006	2007
Industrial-Production Index	103.4	94.4	103.3	112.4	123.4	130.0	137.6	145.0
Real-Wages Index	111.3	95.1	90.0	88.3	90.5	92.3	93.1	93.7
Index of Production-Workers	89.1	81.7	82.2	83.7	85.4	84.8	84.2	86
Partial Productivity-Index	115.7	116.9	126.9	136.1	146.1	154.8	162.2	169.4
CPI (2003=100)	39.0	68.5	29.7	18.4	9.4	7.7	9.7	8.4

Source: Republic of Turkey Prime Ministry Undersecretariat of Treasury, available at: <www.hazine.gov.tr>.

rose from 115.7 in 2000 to 169.4 in 2007. The trend is clear in Table 6. Even more important, labour-costs declined during 2000–7, as estimated by Yükseler and Türkan.[31] In short, productivity-increases in the manufacturing sector were secured by reducing employment. Rising productivity and low wages have been the driving force of the global competitiveness of Turkey.

The reduction of labour-costs has been essential to increasing profitability as well as sustaining exports.[32] In this context, the policy of inflation-targeting has acted as a mechanism for squeezing wages. By indexing the rate of wage-increases to an *ex ante* rate of inflation, wages have been kept low.

Export-performance has also benefited from technological advance. During the 1980s, Turkish exports relied predominantly on raw-material and labour-intensive products, but this has changed dramatically in recent years. The intensity of research and development (high and leading-edge technology) in manufacturing exports has risen sharply, especially in the most globally integrated sectors, such as telecommunications and automobiles. On the other hand, and as was mentioned earlier, the share of raw-material and agriculture-intensive sectors has fallen substantially.[33]

In sum, the structure of production has witnessed a remarkable technological transformation after the crisis of 2000–1. Technical progress and productivity-growth have accelerated, as is evidenced by increases in investment- and intermediate-goods production, typically of medium-level technology.[34] At the same time, production in labour-intensive sectors has been much

---

31. Yükseler and Türkan 2008, p. 75.
32. See CBRT; Aydın, Saygılı and Saygılı 2007.
33. Aydın, Saygılı and Saygılı 2007, p. 22; Aysan and Hacıhasanoğlu 2007, p. 27.
34. Narin 2008a.

Table 7   Classification of Exports by Factor-Intensity
(Turkey, % share in total exports)

	High-tech-intensive	Raw-material-intensive	Labour-Intensive	Capital-intensive	Agriculture-intensive
1980–9	6.0	16.9	30.6	9.3	24.2
1990–6	6.9	5.5	42.7	14.8	17.7
1997–2000	12.0	3.7	44.3	12.8	13.0
2001–4	18.0	3.9	39.4	16.0	8.8

Source: Aydın, Faruk, Hülya Saygılı and Mesut Saygılı 2007, 'Empirical Analysis of Structural Change in Turkish Exports', Research and Monetary Policy Department Working Paper No: 07/08, The Central Bank of the Republic of Turkey, p. 22.

less successful. Consequently, production has expanded without creating employment.

But working hours have not declined, despite improvements in technology. On the contrary, working hours have lengthened, particularly through unpaid overtime. Meanwhile, real wages have declined. In short, rising production and competitiveness have relied on the intensification of labour (absolute surplus-value) as well as on increasing profitability through technical progress (relative surplus-value).[35]

5. The sources of growth and fixed investment

Exports aside, the rapid growth of the economy as a whole has been mostly driven by consumption, as is clear from Table 8. The growth in private consumption has stemmed from the expansion of credit, particularly consumer-credit and credit-related purchases.[36]

The surge in capital-inflows has also been associated with a boom in consumption, while reducing household-savings and raising indebtedness. These trends have been vital to the financialisation of the Turkish economy.

Nevertheless, the volume of fixed investment and its contribution to growth have also increased. While gross fixed-capital formation was (Turkish lira) YTL22.783 (thousands) in 2001, it rose to YTL46.373 (thousands) in 2007. This tendency is also apparent in the index of fixed-capital investment, which stood at 66 in 2001, but rose to 138 in 2007. The private sector, especially manu-

---

35. Narin 2008a.
36. Bağımsız Sosyal Bilimciler 2008, p. 86.

Table 8   Sources of the Growth (= 1987 Prices, Thousands YTL)

	2000	2001	2002	2003	2004	2005	2006
Consumption	91.084	82.786	84.834	89.559	97.645	105.579	111.528
Private Consumption	80.774	73.356	74.894	79.862	87.897	95.594	100.584
Gov. Cons. Exp.	10.310	9.430	9.940	9.697	9.748	9.985	10.944
Gross Fixed Capital Formation	33.281	22.783	22.532	24.782	32.802	40.683	46.373
Public Sector	8.630	6.733	7.325	6.482	6.180	7.778	7.760
Private Sector	24.651	16.050	15.207	18.300	26.622	32.904	38.614
Change in Inventories	3.082	−1.699	6.121	9.714	11.145	7.770	4.750
Exports of goods & services	39,198	42,097	46,787	54,264	61,033	66,235	71,857
Imports of goods & services	−47,498	−35,700	−41,350	−52,541	-65,515	−73,066	−78,259
GDP	118.789	109.885	118.612	125.485	136.693	146.781	155.732

Source: Turkey Republic Prime Ministry State Planning Organisation 'Main Economic Indicators', available at: <www.dpt.gov.tr>.

Table 9   Fixed-Capital Investment-Index (1997=100)

	2000	2001	2002	2003	2004	2005	2006	2007
Total	96	66	63	70	91	114	130	138
Public	132	93	103	97	91	125	131	134
Private	85	58	52	62	91	111	129	139
– Manufacturing Industry	98	63	67	107	167	203	238	250
– Transportation	110	63	62	49	79	90	98	100
– House	56	38	25	25	32	46	54	63

Source: Bağımsız Sosyal Bilimciler 2008, 2008 Kavşağında Türkiye, p. 93, available at: <www.bagimsizsosyalbilimciler.org>.

facturing, rapidly increased fixed investment, taking advantage of the strong exchange-rate and abundant external financing facilities.

6. External debt

A further important result of the direction adopted by Turkey in recent years has been the increase in the absolute levels of external debt but, more significantly, a change in its composition. External debt stood at $130bn in 2002 but rose to $263bn in 2008Q1, due to increases in both public- and private-sector debt. But the increase has been driven mostly by the private sector, especially the non-financial private sector. The external debt of the non-financial private sector was $25bn in 2002 but rose to $87bn, as is shown in Table 10.

Table 10   Composition of External Debt ($mn)

	2002	2003	2004	2005	2006	2007	2008Q1
External Debt-Stock	129.721	144.319	160.835	168.849	205.548	247.094	262.934
Short-Term	16.424	23.013	31.880	37.103	40.354	41.810	44.550
A. CBTR	1.655	2.860	3.287	2.763	2.563	2.282	2.357
B. Deposit Money Banks	6.344	9.692	14.529	17.741	18.275	14.657	15.028
C. Other Sectors	8.425	10.461	14.064	16.599	17.766	22.708	24.829
D. General Government	0	0	0	0	1.750	2.163	2.336
Medium and Long Term	113.297	121.306	128.955	131.746	165.194	205.283	218.385
A. Total Public	63.619	69.507	73.813	68.215	69.840	71.272	72.009
B. CBRT	20.340	21.504	18.114	12.654	13.115	13.519	14.233
C. Private	29.338	30.295	37.028	50.877	82.239	120.492	132.143
1. Financial	4.728	5.168	8.451	15.954	29.134	42.712	45.048
a. Banks	3.030	3.142	5.757	12.244	22.068	30.479	32.307
b. Nonbanking	1.698	2.026	2.694	3.710	7.066	12.233	12.741
2. Nonfinancial	24.610	25.127	28.577	34.923	53.105	77.780	87.095

Source: Turkey Republic Prime Ministry State Planning Organisation, 'Main Economic Indicators', available at: <www.dpt.gov.tr>.

In contrast to private debt, the rate of increase of external public debt has slowed down over the last few years. Fundamental to this tendency has been the reduction of IMF-debt due to raising the primary surplus and also reducing public investment.[37] Historically, the external debt of Turkey has been associated with the state, as is typical of late-developing countries. It is a sign of how times have changed that the recent increase in the non-financial-sector external debt has been due to changes in the financing of the productive sector. These changes can be seen in both long-term and short-term debt, but the increase in long-term debt has been particularly striking. The cause of this increase is obviously the financing of investment by the productive sector. Private enterprise borrows from abroad to sustain growth in fixed capital, as is explained in the next section.

7. Transformation in the financing of the productive sector

There have been dramatic changes in finance for the Turkish productive sector in recent years, reflecting the rising production of import-dependent

---

37. Sönmez 2008, p. 72.

Table 11   YTL-FX Cash-Credits Used in Bank-Mediation (2004–6) – Selected Sectors

Sectors	Share of Sectors	YTL-FX Credit-Shares						Percentage-Increase		
		2004		2005		2006		2005 2006		2005 2006
		YTL %	FX %	YTL %	FX %	YTL %	FX %	YTL % Increase		FX % Increase
Agriculture	0.3	49.9	50.1	47.3	52.7	45.6	54.4	34.6	15.8	49.2	24.0
Manufacturing	55.4	22.3	77.7	26.8	73.2	31.2	68.8	51.8	56.0	18.8	26.1
Electricity	7.8	3.6	96.4	4.6	95.4	3.4	96.6	25.9	−1.6	−0.7	31.8
Construction	6.2	23.9	76.1	29.1	70.9	40.6	59.4	62.3	57.4	24.5	−5.7
Trade	15.9	35.6	64.4	43.7	56.3	47.4	52.6	71.8	37.3	22.5	18.0
Transportation and Communication	3.9	30.4	69.6	36.2	63.8	57.7	42.3	158.9	273.8	99.2	55.2
Real Estate, Hiring	6.3	22.0	78.0	15.9	84.1	8.5	91.5	−2.6	24.7	44.8	152.9
Total	100	22.7	77.3	27.8	72.2	31.7	68.3	57.4	58.0	20.2	31.1

Source: Central Bank of the Republic of Turkey, 2007, 'Sector Balance Sheet Analysis (2004–2006)', p. 12, available at: <www.tcmb.gov.tr>.

investment-goods. The productive sector has been forced to seek cheap finance in foreign currency, and this has meant borrowing abroad. The turn to foreign lenders has been greatly facilitated by the policy of high domestic interest-rates and strong exchange-rates as part of inflation-targeting.

The Central Bank's *Sectoral Balance Sheet Analysis Report,* based on information from 7,308 enterprises, shows that industrial enterprises furnished their rising foreign-exchange requirements generally from foreign sources. Table 11 shows that the bulk of foreign cash-credits were taken up by the manufacturing sector, while the share of manufacturing in total credit stood at 55.4% during 2004–6. The transportation- and communication-sectors were the second largest users of credit after the manufacturing sector.[38]

The same point can be seen in terms of the credits received by the productive sector as a whole. Table 12 shows that credits received from abroad were $26bn in 2003 but rose to $87bn in the third quarter of 2008. Credit from abroad has consistently exceeded domestic credit for the productive sector throughout this period.

---

38. CBRT 'Sector Balance Sheet Analysis (2004–2006)', available at: <www.tcmb.gov.tr>.

Table 12   Non-Financial Enterprises Foreign-Exchange Assets and Liabilities ($mn)

	2003	2004	2005	2006	2007–12	2008–03
ASSETS	30.980	38.659	45.701	63.426	77.864	80.832
Deposits	19.958	24.565	30.890	45.452	54.834	55.377
Domestic Banks	8.578	10.598	12.636	18.756	24.402	24.051
Overseas Banks	11.385	13.967	18.254	26.696	30.432	31.326
Securities	920	1.306	1.035	933	830	898
Government-Debt Securities	808	1.175	790	632	573	622
– Issued internally*	271	379	96	83	61	106
– Issued externally	536	797	693	549	512	516
Overseas Portfolio-Investments	112	131	245	301	257	276
Export-Receivables	5.158	7.005	6.721	9.584	12.009	14.154
Direct Capital-Investments Abroad	4.945	5.783	7.056	7.467	10.191	10.403
LIABILITIES	50.759	59.006	72.383	100.047	138.843	154.584
Cash-Credits	44.204	49.603	61.348	88.275	124.250	138.905
Credits Derived Domestically	18.158	20.457	26.429	34.804	46.305	51.666
Credits Derived from abroad	26.046	29.146	34.919	53.471	77.964	87.239
Import-Debt	6.555	9.403	11.035	11.772	14.593	15.679
Net Foreign-Exchange Position	−19.778	−20.347	−26.682	−36.621	−60.979	−73.752

Source: Central Bank of Republic of Turkey, 2008a, 'Firmaların Döviz Pozisyonu Göstergeleri', available at: <www.tcmb.gov.tr>.

However, the burden of debt on the productive sector has declined, reflecting the lower rates of interest on foreign debt. It is instructive to consider the distribution of net value according to factor-income for the top 500 industrial enterprises. The ratio of interest-payments stood as 33.4% in 2000 but it declined to 8.8% in 2005.

To recap, external borrowing became prevalent during this period, although the financing of the productive sector has continued to rely heavily on domestic bank-loans. It is also probable that non-bank sources of funding have also increased. These changes reflect the impact of financialisation on the productive sector that is directly related to the process of internationalisation of domestic capital. The productive sector has been able to compete globally by squeezing wages and increasing productivity. It has been able to obtain investment-goods necessary for production through imports. Thus, a strong exchange-rate has become a facilitating factor in the changing finances of the productive sector.

Years	2000	2001	2002	2003	2004	2005
Top 500 Industrial Enterprises	33.4	93.5	30.4	13.3	11.7	8.8
Second Top 500 Industrial Enterprises	28.5	78.2	34.7	17.3	13.6	13.8

Table 13   Interest-Payments of Industrial Enterprises

Source: Istanbul Chamber of Industry, available at: <www.iso.org.tr>.

8. Transformation of the banking sector

During this period, a transformation has also occurred in the structure and activities of the banking sector. Penetration by foreign banks has intensified, and their market-share reached 39.7% in 2007.[39] The Turkish banking sector, especially after 2005, became one of the most attractive markets for foreign banks. In 2005–7, fifteen domestic banks were bought by foreigners partially or wholly (one of those sales has not been fully ratified). The reasons for foreign bank-entry are both international and national, typically discussed as 'push and pull factors' in mainstream-economics. Historically, the entry of foreign banks reflects the internationalisation of capital. As huge international capital-flows were directed toward developing countries in recent years, foreign banks also entered to explore profit-opportunities and increase their market-share.

The crisis of 2000–1 made Turkish banks more attractive to foreign banks as mergers and acquisitions led to rationalisation of branches and personnel.[40] The restructuring of the Turkish banking system also encouraged foreign banks because the banking sector was strengthened. The total assets of the banking sector increased from $132.2bn in 2002 to $501.7bn in 2007. Deposits and credits increased in parallel. The ratios of deposits to GDP and of credits to GDP were, respectively, 17.2% and 35.1% in 2003, but rose to 42% and to 34.6%, respectively, in 2007. The ratio of credits to deposits rose from 49% in 2003 to 83% in 2007.[41] These structural changes motivated foreign banks to acquire domestic banks. In addition, the Turkish market seemed to have strong growth potential as the ratio of bank-assets to GDP in 2007 was 76%, well below the average of the EU, which stood at more than 300%.[42]

---

39. Banking Regulation and Supervision Agency 2007.
40. Aysan and Ceyhan 2008, p. 94.
41. Central Bank of Republic of Turkey 2008, p. 36.
42. Kutlay 2008, p. 4.

From the standpoint of domestic banks, or the conglomerates that own them, there were several reasons to sell to foreigners, wholly or partially. Returns from sales were typically high. Moreover, domestic banks have increased their credibility and are increasingly able to seek alternative credit-facilities in international markets. By the same token, the large conglomerates that typically own private Turkish banks have acquired a lot more flexibility in obtaining funding.

It is important to note that foreign banks have directed their attention particularly toward the sector of consumer-credit. Their expectation appeared to be that the growth of the consumer-credit market was likely to be high, even in comparison with EU-countries. To this purpose, foreign banks have been able to acquire consumer-databases by buying domestic banks or becoming their partners.

In a similar spirit, domestic banks have also shifted their activities towards individuals rather than the industrial sector. The supply of consumer-credit, such as housing, education, and automobile, has increased rapidly. The total volume of individual credits rose phenomenally, from $4bn billion in 2002 to $81.9bn in 2007. The proportion of individual credits within the aggregates similarly rose from 13.4% in 2002 to 33.3% in 2007. The bulk of the increase was in housing credit – private mortgages emerged for the first time as a significant economic phenomenon in Turkey.

Table 14   GDP, Assets and Credit-Indicators (2002–7), $bn

	2002	2003	2004	2005	2006	2007
GDP	230.5	304.9	390.4	481.5	526.4	658.8
Total Assets	132.2	183.0	234.8	303.2	355.5	501.7
Total Credits	29.9	47.5	74.4	116.6	155.9	246.4
– Commercial and Institutional Credits	25.9	38.3	54.4	80.1	103.3	164.4
– Individual Credits	4.0	9.2	20.0	36.5	52.6	81.9
Percentage of commercial credit in total credit %	86.6	80.6	73.1	68.6	66.2	66.7
Percentage of individual credit in total credit %	13.4	19.4	26.9	31.4	33.8	33.3
Total Credits/GDP	13.0	15.6	19.1	24.2	29.6	37.4
Total Assets/GDP	57.3	60.0	60.1	63.0	67.5	76.2

Source: Banking Regulation and Supervision Agency 2007, Financial Market Reports, December 2007, p. 54, available at: <www.bddk.org.tr> and estimation.

Foreign banks have pioneered the transformation of activities of the banking system as a whole. As they moved aggressively into the consumer-credit market, they increased competitive pressure across the entire sector, and pulled domestic banks behind them. Foreign banks have had major advantages in technology and banking experience. But domestic banks have tried to improve their competitive strength through differentiated consumer-loans and rapid adoption of technological innovation.[43]

9. Rise in individual indebtedness

The inevitable result of banks orienting themselves toward consumer-credit was has been accelerated indebtedness of individuals. Consumption-expenditures have also risen, financed through consumer-credit and credit-cards. The ratio of household-debt to household-disposable income rose extremely rapidly: from 7.5% in 2003, it became 29.5% in 2007.

Consequently, the proportion of interest-payments out of household disposable income has also increased dramatically. The ratio of interest-payments to disposable income rose from 2.1% in 2003 to 4.6% in 2007. These interest-payments represent a direct transfer of disposable income from individuals to the financial system. Moreover, the increase of individual indebtedness implies that finance has acquired greater control over the economic and social life of individuals.

Finally, increasing individual indebtedness has meant that individual insolvencies have also risen. Individuals were encouraged to spend in excess of normal practices by means of consumer-credit and credit-cards, eventually finding that they could not pay back their loans. The number of people who could not meet credit-card bills and consumer-loans rose from 38,538 in 2002 to 203,736 in 2006.[44]

---

43. See Ergüneş 2008 for a detailed study of the transformation of the Turkish banking sector.
44. Yükseler and Türkan 2008, p. 12.

Table 15   Household Disposable Income, Indebtedness and Interest-Payments

	2003	2004	2005	2006	2007
Interest-Payments/Disposable Income (%)	2.1	3.2	4.2	4.1	4.6
Household-Debt/Disposable Income	7.5	12.9	20.9	25.1	29.5

Source: Central Bank of the Republic of Turkey 2008b, Financial Stability Report May 2008, p. 22; Central Bank of the Republic of Turkey 2006, Financial Stability Report December 2006, p. 11.

10. Conclusion

It is often said that the Turkish economy turned the 2000–1 crisis into an opportunity, entering a period of rapid growth. Undoubtedly this has been based on the weakness of the working-class movement during this period. Turkish capital became even more globally integrated, while the country has been opened to the full impact of financialisation. This was a strategic choice by the Turkish ruling class, but it was also necessary for domestic capital, if it was to succeed globally. Financialisation has manifested itself as growing capital-inflows, affecting all aspects of the economy.

Inflation-targeting has been an important mechanism shaping capital-accumulation during this period. Inflation-targeting has made it easier to attract capital-inflows into the country, while contributing to keeping wages low. Depressed wages have been vital to the competitive strength of the productive sector, which has been particular notable in the export-sector. The productive sector has financed the expansion of import-dependent production by means of external borrowing.

These developments reflect the integration of Turkey as a middle-income developing country into the world-economy under conditions of financialisation. They also point to new types of vulnerability that have emerged for these countries, which became clearer as the crisis of 2007–9 unfolded. The main blow fell on the productive sector, presumably the motor of development during the last decade. The risks to the banking sector have been less pronounced as banks have restructured since 2000–1 in ways explained above.

That is not to say that banks are immune to danger, particularly as consumer-lending has increased so rapidly. Still, Arzuhan Yalçındağ, the chairwoman of the Turkish Industrialists' and Business Association, succinctly expressed the main dangers facing the current accumulation-strategy:

We ought to assume that private sector external debt, the amount of which has reached $140 billion, is an important risk factor. The deterioration of external financing that has affected the private sector would also interrupt the growth process. It is obvious that the sources that have featured in private sector investment during 2001–7 would be restricted during the current global financial crisis.[45]

Not surprisingly, the first enterprise that stopped production when the crisis of 2007–9 to hit Turkey was the textile-firm of Sönmez Filament, the largest fibre-producer in the country. The traditional sectors of the Turkish economy have lost competitive strength during the period of financialisation. Denteks Textile followed, another large enterprise in this sector and major fabric-producer in the Denizli Industrial Zone. Other textile-firms also stopped production in late 2008, including Atakan, Atak, Irem, Bordo, and Türkmar.

Rapid financialisation since 2001 has left Turkey with import-dependent production, a huge current-account deficit, large public and private debts, increasing unemployment and indebted individuals. The path of Turkey – national specificities aside – has been characteristic of middle-income developing countries under the new conditions. The crisis of 2007–9 has revealed the weaknesses of the accumulation-strategy adopted by the Turkish ruling class. The ability of the country to cope with the impact of the crisis in the coming years remains to be seen.

---

45. Yalçındağ 2008.

References

Agenor Pierre-Richard 2001, 'Monetary Policy under Flexible Exchange Rates: An Introduction to Inflation-Targeting', Working Paper no. 124, Central Bank of Chile.

Aglietta, Michel and Régis Breton 2001, 'Financial Systems, Corporate Control and Capital Accumulation', *Economy and Society*, 30, 4: 433–66.

Akers, Douglas, Jay Golter, Brian Lamm, and Martha Solt, 2005, 'Overview of Recent Developments in the Credit Card Industry', *FDIC Banking Review*, 17, 3: 23–35.

Akyüz Yilmaz 1992, 'On Financial Openness in Developing Countries', Working Paper Series, unpublished manuscript, Geneva: UNCTAD.

—— 2008a, 'Managing Financial Instability in Emerging Markets: a Keynesian Perspective', *Third World Perspective*, Penang: Malaysia, available at: <http://www.twnside.org.sg/title2/ge/ge12.pdf>.

—— 2008b, 'Financial Instability and Countercyclical Policy', paper prepared for UNDESA, available at: <http://www.un.org/esa/policy/wess/wess2008files/wso8backgroundpapers/akyuz_aug08.pdf>.

—— and Korkut Boratav 2005, 'The Making of the Turkish Financial Crisis', in *Financialisation and the World Economy*, edited by Gerald Epstein, Cheltenham: Edward Elgar Publishing.

Allen, Franklin and David Gale 2001, *Comparative Financial Systems: A Survey*, Wharton: Centre for Financial Institutions, Working Paper 01–15.

—— and Anthony M. Santomero 1997, 'The Theory of Financial Intermediation', *Journal of Banking and Finance*, 21, 11–12: 1461–85.

—— 2001, 'What Do Financial Intermediaries Do?', *Journal of Banking and Finance*, 25, 2: 271–94.

Barclays 2008, *Annual Report 2007*, London: Barclays plc.

Ammons, Lila 1996, 'The Evolution of Black-Owned Banks in the United States, 1880s to 1990s', *Journal of Black Studies*, 26, 4: 467–89.

Anderson, Jenny and Vikas Bajaj 2007, 'Wary of Risk, Bankers Sold Shaky Debt', *New York Times*, December 6: A1.

Anderson, Perry 2007 [2008], 'Jottings on the Conjuncture', *New Left Review*, II, 48: 5–35.

Arestis, Philip and Murray Glickman 2002, 'Financial Crisis in Southeast Asia: Dispelling Illusion the Minskyan Way', *Cambridge Journal Economics*, 26, 2: 237–60.

—— and Malcolm Sawyer, 2006, 'Inflation-targeting: A Critical Appraisal', available at: <www.levy.org/pubs/wp.388.pdf>.

Arrighi, Giovanni 2003, 'The Social and Political Economy of Global Turbulence', *New Left Review*, II, 20: 5–71.

Autor, David, Frank Levy and Richard Murnane 2003, 'The Skill Content of Recent Technological Innovation: An Empirical Investigation', *Quarterly Journal of Economics*, 118, 4: 1279–333.

Aybar Sedat and Laurence Harris 1998, 'How Credible Are Credibility Models of Central Banking', in *The Political Economy of Central Banking*, edited by Philip Arestis and Malcolm Sawyer, Cheltenham: Edward Elgar.

Aydın, Faruk, Hülya Saygılı and Mesut Saygılı 2007, 'Empirical Analysis of Structural Change in Turkish Exports', Research and Monetary Policy Department Working Paper 07/08, The Central Bank of the Republic of Turkey.

Aydoğuş, İsmail and Harun Öztürkler 2006, 'Merkez Bankası Döviz Rezervlerinin Sosyal Maliyeti', in Afyon Kocatepe Üniversitesi İ.İ.B.F. Journal.

Aysan, Ahmet Faruk and Fatih Bektaş, 2007 'Export Competitiveness of Turkey: The New Rising Sectors in Turkey Comparison with Eastern European Countries', Boğaziçi University Research Papers, ISS/EC.

—— and Yavuz Selim Hacıhasanoğlu 2007, 'Investigation on Determinants of Turkish Export-Boom in 2000s', *The Journal of International Trade and Diplomacy*, 1, 2: 159–202.

Bagehot Walter, 1978 [1873], 'Lombard Street', in *The Collected Works of Walter Bagehot*, Volume 9, edited by Norman St John-Stevas, London: The Economist.

Bağımsız Sosyal Bilimciler 2007, 'IMF Gözetiminde On Uzun Yıl: 1998–2008: Farklı Hükümetler Tek Siyaset', available at: <www.bagimsizsosyalbilimciler.org>.

—— 2008, '2008 Kavşağında Türkiye', available at: <www.bagimsizsosyalbilimciler. org>.

Bair, Sheila 2005, *Low-Cost Payday Loans: Obstacles and Opportunities*, Isenberg School of Management, University of Massachusetts, Amherst.

Ball Laurence and N. Niamh Sheridan 2003, 'Does Inflation-Targeting Matter?', IMF Working Paper 03/129, Washington DC.: IMF.

Bank of Japan (BOJ) 2008, Bank of Japan Statistics, available at: <http://www.boj. or.jp/en/type/stat/boj_stat/index.htm>.

Banking Regulation and Supervision Agency 2007, Financial Market Reports 2007, available at: <www.bddk.org.tr>.

Bannock, Manser and William Graham, 2003 [1989], *International Dictionary of Finance*, London: The Economist Series.

Baron, Harold 1985, 'Racism Transformed: The Implications of the 1960s', *Review of Radical Political Economics*, 17, 3: 10–33.

Bauer, Otto 2000 [1906], *The Question of Nationalities and Social Democracy*, Minneapolis: University of Minnesota Press.

Bean Charles 2003, 'Asset Prices, Financial Imbalances and Monetary Policy: Are Inflation Targets Enough?', *Revue d'Economie Politique*, 110, 6: 787–807.

Bear, Sterns 2007, *Form 10–Q*, United States Securities and Exchange Commission, available at: <http://www.bearsterns.com/includes/pdfs/investor_relations/proxy/ 3q_10q_07.pdf>.

Benston, George 1981, 'Mortgage Redlining Research: A Review and Critical Analysis', *Journal of Bank Research*, 12: 8–23.

Berman, Dennis K., Carrick Mollenkamp, and Valerie Bauerlein 2006, 'Wachovia Strikes $26 Billion Deal for Golden West', *Wall Street Journal*, May 8: A1.

Berger, Allen, Leora Klapper and Groegort Udell 2001, 'The Ability of Banks to Lend to Informationally Opaque Small Business', *Journal of Banking and Finance*, 25: 2127–67.

—— and Loretta J. Mester, 2003, 'Explaining the Dramatic Changes in Performance of U.S. Banks: Technological Change, Deregulation, and Dynamic Changes in Competition', *Journal of Financial Intermediation*, 12, 1: 57–95.

—— and Gregory Udell 1995, 'Relationship Lending and Lines of Credit in Small Firm Finance', *Journal of Business*, 68, 3: 351–81.

Bernanke Ben 2003, 'Constrained Discretion and Monetary Policy', Remarks by Governor Ben Bernanke before the Money Marketeers of New York University, available at: <www.federareserve.gov/Boarddocs/2003/20030203/default.htm>.

—— 2004, 'The Great Moderation', Remarks by Governor Ben S. Bernanke at the meetings of the Eastern Economic Association, Washington, DC February 20, available at: <www.federareserve.gov/Boarddocs/2004>.

—— 2005, 'The Global Saving Glut and the U.S. Current Account Deficit', Remarks by Governor Ben Bernanke at the Sandridge Lecture, available at: <http://www. federalreserve.gov/boarddocs/speeches/2005/200503102/default.htm>.

—— and Mark Gertler 1999, 'Monetary Policy and Asset Price Volatility', *Federal Reserve Bank of Kansas City Economic Review*, 4: 18–51.

—— and Frederic Mishkin 1997, 'Inflation-Targeting: A New Framework for Monetary Policy?', *Journal of Economic Perspectives*, 11, 2: 97–116.

——, Thomas Laubach, Adam Posen and Frederic Mishkin 1999, *Inflation-Targeting: Lessons from the International Experience*, Princeton: Princeton University Press.

Bessler, Wolfgang 1999, 'Equity Returns, Bond Returns, and the Equity Premium in the German Capital Market', *The European Journal of Finance*, 5, 3: 186–201.

BIS 2007a, 'Financial Stability and Local Currency Bond Markets', Committee on the Global Financial System Papers, no. 28, Basle: BIS.

—— 2007b, 'Foreign Exchange and Derivatives Market Activity in 2007', Triennial Central Bank Survey, Basle: BIS.

Black, Fischer and Myron S. Scholes 1973, 'The Pricing of Options and Corporate Liabilities', *Journal of Political Economy*, 81, May/June: 637–59.

Blackburn, Robin 2006, 'Finance and the Fourth Dimension', *New Left Review*, II, 39: 39–70.

Blundell-Wignall, A. 2007, 'Structured Products: Implications for Financial Markets', *Financial Market Trends*, 2, 93: 27–57.

Boddy Radford and James Crotty 1975, 'Class Conflict and Macro Policy: The Political Business Cycle', *Review of Radical Political Economics*, 7, 1: 1–19.

Boratav, Korkut 2007, 'Dünya Ekonomisinde Değişimler ve Türkiye'ye Yansımaları', available at: <http://www.bagimsizsosyalbilimciler.org/Yazilar_Uye/Boratav_Mayis07.pdf>.

Bordo Michael, Michael Dueker, and David Wheelock 2000, 'Aggregate Price Shocks and Financial Instability: A Historical Analysis', Federal Reserve Bank of St. Louis, Working Paper 2000–005B.

—— and David Wheelock 1998, 'Price Stability and Financial Stability: The Historical Record', *Federal Reserve Bank of St. Louis Review*, 80, 4: 41–62.

Borio, Claudio and Philip Lowe 2002, 'Asset Prices, Financial and Monetary Stability: Exploring the Nexus', Bank of International Settlements, Working Paper 114, Geneva: BIS.

Boston Consulting Group 2003, *Navigating the Maze, Asset Management 2003*, Boston: Boston Consulting Group.

Bowles, Samuel L. 1982, 'The Post-Keynesian Capital-Labor Stalemate', *Socialist Review*, 65: 44–72.

—— and Robert Boyer 1989, 'Labor Discipline and Aggregate Demand', *American Economic Review*, 78, 2: 395–400.

—— and Herbert Gintis 1982, 'The Crisis of Liberal Democratic Capitalism: The Case of the United States', *Politics and Society*, 11: 51–93.

—— David Gordon and Thomas Weisskopf 1989, 'Business Ascendancy and Economic Impasse: A Structural Retrospective of Conservative Economics, 1979–1987', *Journal of Economic Perspectives*, 3, 1: 107–34.

Boyer, Robert 2000, 'Is a Finance Led Growth Regime a Viable Alternative to Fordism: A Preliminary Analysis', *Economy and Society*, 29, 1: 111–45.

Brenner, Robert 1998, 'The Economics of Global Turbulence', *New Left Review*, I, 229: 1–264.

—— 2002, *The Boom and the Bubble: The US in the World Economy*, London: Verso.

Brewer III, Elijah and Thomas H. Mondschaen 1992, 'The Impact of S&L Failures and Regulatory Changes on the CD Market, 1987–1991', *Working Paper Series WP-92-93*, Federal Reserve Bank of Chicago, December.

British Petroleum 2008 Annual Report and Accounts, available at: <http://www.scribd.com/doc/23308756/BP-Annual-Report-Accounts-2008>.

Brooks, Rick and Ruth Simon 2007, 'As Housing Boomed, Industry Pushed Loans to a Broader Market', *Wall Street Journal*, December 3: A1.

Bryan, Dick and Mike Rafferty 2007, 'Financial Derivatives and the Theory of Money', *Economy and Society*, 36, 1: 134–58.

Brynjolfsson, Erik and Lorin Hitt 2000, 'Beyond Computation: Information Technology, Organizational Transformation and Business Performance', *Journal of Economic Perspectives*, 14, 4: 23–48.

—— and Lorin Hitt 2003, 'Computing Productivity: Firm-Level Evidence', *MIT-Sloan Working Paper* 4210–01.

Bukharin, Nikolai 1972 [1915], *Imperialism and World Economy*, London: Merlin.

Buiter Willem 2008, 'Can Central Banks Go Broke?', *Policy Insight*, no. 24, London: Centre for Economic Policy Research.

Buiter Willem and Anne Sibert 2007, 'The Central Bank as the Market-Maker of Last Resort: From Lender of Last Resort to Market-Maker of Last Resort', in *The First Global Financial Crisis of the 21st Century*, edited by Andrew Felton and Carmen Reinhart, London: Centre for Economic Policy Research.

Business Week 2002, 'The Besieged Banker: Bill Harrison Must Prove J.P. Morgan Chase Wasn't a Star-Crossed Merger' (cover story), April 22.

Bussière, Matthieu and Christian Mulder 1999, 'External Vulnerability in Emerging Market Economies: How High Liquidity Can Offset Weak Fundamentals and the Effects of Contagion', IMF Working Papers, no. 99/88, Washington, DC.: IMF.

California Reinvestment Coalition 2001, *Inequities in California's Subprime Mortgage Market*, San Francisco: California Research Coalition.

California Reinvestment Coalition, Community Reinvestment Association of North Carolina, Empire Justice Center, Massachusetts Affordable Housing Alliance, Neighborhood Economic Development Advocacy Project, Ohio Fair Lending Coalition and Woodstock Institute 2008, 'Paying More for the American Dream: The Subprime Shakeout and Its Impact on Lower-Income and Minority Communities'.

Calomiris, Charles W. 2008, 'The Subprime Turmoil: What's Old, What's New, and What's Next', Working Paper, American Enterprise Institute, October.

——, Charles M. Kahn and Stanley D. Longhofer 1994, 'Housing-Finance Intervention and Private Incentives: Helping Minorities and the Poor', *Journal of Money, Credit and Banking*, 26, 3 (part 2): 634–74.

Calvo, Guilhermo and Carmen Reinhart 2000, 'Fear of Floating', NBER Working Paper Series, n. 7993, Cambridge, MA.: National Bureau of Economic Research.

Canner, Glenn B., Wayne Passmore and Elizabeth Laderman 1999, 'The Role of Specialized Lenders in Extending Mortgages to Lower-Income and Minority Homebuyers', *Federal Reserve Bulletin*, November: 709–23.

Carare Alina and Mark Stone 2003, 'Inflation-Targeting Régimes', IMF Working paper, 03/9, Washington, DC.: IMF.

Carney, Mark 2004, 'The New International Monetary Order', Speech to the Toronto Society of Financial Analysts, available at: <http://www.bankofcanada.ca/en/review/winter04–05/carney04–05.pdf>.

Caruana, Jaime, 2007. 'Global Financial Market Risk – Who is Responsible for What?', Keynote Adress at the conference on Financial Stability, Berlín Heinrich Böll Foundation/German Association of Banks, 30 May 2007. Mimeo: IMF, Available [26/02/2008] at: <http://www.imf.org/external/np/speeches/2007/053007.htm>.

Cecchetti Stephen and Michael Ehrmann 1999, 'Does Inflation-Targeting Increase Output Variability? An International Comparison of Policymakers' Preferences and Outcomes', NBER Working Paper No. 7426, Cambridge, MA.: National Bureau of Economic Research.

Central Bank of the Republic of Turkey 2006, Financial Stability Report, December 2006, Ankara.
—— 2007, 'Sector Balance Sheet Analysis (2004–2006)', available at: <www.tcmb.gov.tr>.
—— 2008a, 'Firmaların Döviz Pozisyonu Göstergeleri', available at: <www.tcmb.gov.tr>.
—— 2008b, Financial Stability Report, May 2008, Ankara.
Chang, Ha-Joon, Hong-Jae Park, and Chul Gyeu Yoo, 1998, 'Interpreting the Korean Crisis: Financial Liberalization, Industrial Policy, and Corporate Governance', Cambridge Journal Economics, 22, 6: 735–46.
—— and Ilene Grabel 2004, Reclaiming Development: An Alternative Economic Policy Manual, London: Zed Books.
Chang, Roberto and Andres Velasco 1998, 'The Asian Liquidity Crisis', Federal Reserve Bank of Atlanta, Working Paper, no. 98–11, July.
—— and Andres Velasco 1999, 'Liquidity Crises in Emerging Markets: Theory and Policy', NBER Working Paper Series, no. 7272, Cambridge, MA.: National Bureau of Economic Research.
Chen, Hsuan-Chi and Jay Ritter 2000, 'The Seven Percent Solution', Journal of Finance, 55, 3: 1105–31.
Chesnais, François 1999, La mundialización financiera. Génesis, costo y desafíos, Buenos Aires: Losada.
Corbett, Jenny and Tim Jenkinson 1996, 'The Financing of Industry, 1970–1989: An International Comparison', Journal of the Japanese and International Economies, 10, 1: 71–96.
—— 1997, 'How Is Investment Financed? A Study of Germany, Japan, the United Kingdom and the United States', Papers in Money, Macroeconomics and Finance, The Manchester School Supplement, 65: 69–93.
Cornford, Andrew, 2005, 'Reflections on the Prediction, Management and Measurement of (Primarily Financial) Risk', Paper preparé pour la 4ème Rencontre Internationale Ethique, Finance Responsabilité, Château de Bossey (September 30 October 1, Geneva, available at: <http://www.networkideas.org/featart/mar2006/Reflections.pdf>.
Corsetti, Giancarlo, Paolo Pesenti, and Nouriel Roubini, 1998, 'Paper Tigers? A Model of the Asian Crisis', NBER Working Paper Series, no. 6783, Cambridge, MA.: National Bureau of Economic Research.
Crotty, James 2005, 'The Neoliberal Paradox: The Impact of Destructive Product Market Competition and "Modern" Financial Markets on Nonfinancial Corporation Performance in the Neoliberal Era', in Financialization and the World Economy, edited by Gerry Epstein, Cheltenham: Edward Elgar.
D'Aristá, Jane 2004, 'U.S Debt and Global Imbalances', International Journal of Political Economy, 36, 4: 12–35.
Dash, Eric 2007, 'American Home Mortgage Says It Will Close', New York Times, August 3.
Debelle Guy, Paul Masson, Miguel Savastano, Sunil Sharma 1998, 'Inflation–targeting as a Framework for Monetary Policy', Economic Issues, No. 15, Washington, DC: IMF.
Debelle Guy and Stanley Fisher 1996, 'How Independent Should a Central Bank Be?', in Goals, Guidelines, and Constraints Facing Monetary Policy Makers, edited by Jeffrey Fuhrer: Federal Reserve Bank of Boston Conference Series 38.
DeBrunhoff Susanne 1976, The State, Capital and Economic Policy, London: Pluto Press.
DeGrauwe Paul 2007, 'There Is More to Central Banking than Inflation-Targeting', in The First Global Financial Crisis of the 21st Century, edited by Andrew Felton and Carmen Reinhart, London: Centre for Economic Policy Research (CEPR).
DeLong, J. Bradford and Konstantin Magin 2007, 'The U.S. Equity Return Premium: Past, Present and Future', unpublished manuscript, University of California Berkeley.

De Vroey, Michel 1984, 'Inflation: A Non-Monetarist Monetary Interpretation', *Cambridge Journal of Economics*, 8, 4: 381–99.

Dickens, Edwin 1990, 'Financial Crises, Innovations and Federal Reserve Control of the Stock of Money', *Contributions to Political Economy*, 9, 1: 1–23.

—— 1999, 'A Political-Economic Critique of Minsky's Financial Instability Hypothesis: The Case of the 1966 Financial Crisis', *Review of Political Economy*, 11, 4: 379–98.

Dodd, Randall 2007, 'Subprime: Tentacles of a Crisis', *IMF Finance and Development*, 44, 4: 15–19.

Downey, Kirstin 2006, 'Mortgage Lender Settles Lawsuit: Ameriquest Will Pay $325 Million', *Washington Post*, January 24: D01.

Dymski, Gary A. 1992, 'Towards a New Model of Exploitation: The Case of Racial Domination', *International Journal of Social Economics*, 19, 7/8/9: 292–313.

—— 1996a, 'Exploitation and Racial Inequality: The US Case', *Research in Political Economy*, 15: 111–38.

—— 1996b, 'Economic Polarization and US Policy Activism', *International Review of Applied Economics*, 10, 1: 65–84.

—— 2002, 'U.S. Housing as Capital Accumulation: The Contradictory Transformation of American Housing Finance, Households and Communities', in *Housing Finance Futures: Housing Policies, Gender Inequality and Financial Globalization on the Pacific Rim*, edited by Gary Dymski and Dorene Isenberg, Armonk: M.E. Sharpe.

—— 2006, 'Discrimination in the Credit and Housing Markets: Findings and Challenges', in *Handbook on the Economics of Discrimination*, edited by William Rodgers, Cheltenham: Edward Elgar.

—— 2008, 'Financial Risk and Governance in the Neoliberal Era', mimeo, University of California Center: Sacramento.

—— and Dorene Isenberg 1998, 'Housing Finance in the Age of Globalization: From Social Housing to Life-Cycle Risk', in *Globalization and Progressive Economic Policy*, edited by Dean Baker, Gerald Epstein and Robert Pollin, Cambridge: Cambridge University Press.

—— and Dorene Isenberg (eds.) 2002, *Seeking Shelter in the Pacific*, Armonk: M. E. Sharpe.

—— and John M. Veitch 1996, 'Financial Transformation and the Metropolis: Booms, Busts and Banking in Los Angeles', *Environment and Planning A*, 28, 7: 1233–60.

—— and John M. Veitch, and Michelle White 1991, 'Taking It to the Bank: Race, Poverty, and Credit in Los Angeles', in *United States Senate, Committee on Banking, Housing, and Urban Affairs. Report on the Status of the Community Reinvestment Act: Views and Recommendations. Vol. II, September.* Washington, DC.: US Government Printing Office.

Duffie, Darrell and Kenneth Singleton 2003, *Credit Risk*, Princeton: Princeton University Press.

Dumenil, Gérard 2007, 'Neo-Liberalism under US Hegemony: The Crisis of the late 2000s', Paper presented in the conference, 'A Crisis of Financialisation?' SOAS, 30 May 2008, available at: <www.soas.ac.uk/events/event43769>.

—— and Dominique Lévy 2004, *Capital Resurgent: Roots of the Neoliberal Revolution*, Cambridge, MA.: Harvard University Press.

Economist, 2007a, 'Fannie and Freddie Ride Again', July 5.

—— 2007b, 'At the Risky End of Finance', August 21.

—— 2007c, 'Sold Down the River Rhine', August 11.

Eichengreen, Barry, Michael Mussa, Giovanni Dell'Ariccia, Enrica Detragiache, Gian Maria Milesi-Ferretti, and Andrew Tweedie 1998, 'Capital-Account Liberalization: Theoretical and Practical Aspects', IMF Occasional Papers, no. 172, Washington DC: IMF.

——, Michael Mussa, Giovanni Dell'Ariccia, Enrica Detragiache, Gian Maria Milesi-Ferretti, and Andrew Tweedie 1999, 'Liberalizing Capital Movements: Some Analytical Issues', *IMF Economic Issues*, no. 17, Washington DC.: IMF.

Emm, Ekaterina and Gerald D. Gay 2005, 'The Global Market for OTC Derivatives: An Analysis of Dealer Holdings', *The Journal of Futures Markets*, 25, 1: 39–77.

Emmanuel, Arghiri 1972, *Unequal Exchange*, New York: Monthly Review Press.

Epstein Gerald 1992, 'Political Economy and Comparative Central Banking', *Review of Radical Political Economics*, 24, 1: 1–30.

—— 2002, 'Financialization, Rentier Interests and Central Bank Policy', Paper prepared for PERI conference on 'Financialization of the World Economy', 7–8 December 2001, University of Massachusetts, Amherst.

—— 2003, 'Alternatives to Inflation Targeting Monetary Policy for Stable and Egalitarian Growth: A Brief Research Summary', Working Paper Series 62, PERI, Amherst, MA.: Political Economy Research Institute.

—— 2005, 'Introduction: Financialization and the World Economy', in *Financialization and World Economy*, edited by Gerald Epstein, Cheltenham: Edward Elgar.

—— and Thomas Ferguson 1984, 'Monetary Policy, Loan Liquidation and Industrial Conflict: The Federal Reserve and the Open Market Operations of 1932', *Journal of Economic History*, 44, 4: 957–83.

—— and Arjun Jayadev 2005, 'The Rise of Rentier Incomes in OECD Countries: Financialization, Central Bank Policy and Labor Solidarity', in *Financialization and the World Economy*, edited by Gerry Epstein, Cheltenham: Edward Elgar.

—— and Juliet Schor 1986, 'The Political Economy of Central Banking', Harvard Institute for Economic Research, Discussion Paper No.1281.

—— and Juliet Schor 1988, 'The Determinants of Central Bank Policy in Open Economies', in *Monetary Theory and Central Banking*, edited by Bruno Jossa and Carlo Panico, Naples: Liguori Press.

—— and Juliet Schor 1989, 'The Divorce of the Banca D'Italia and the Italian Treasury: A Case Study of Central Bank Independence', in *State, Market and Social Regulation: New Perspectives on the Italian Case*, edited by Peter Lange and Marino Regini, Cambridge: Cambridge University Press.

—— and Juliet Schor 1990, 'Macropolicy and the Rise and Fall of the Golden Age', in *The Golden Age of Capitalism: Reinterpreting the Postwar Experience*, edited by Stephen Marglin and Juliet Schor, Oxford: Oxford University Press.

—— and Erinç Yeldan 2006, 'Developing Policy Alternatives to Inflation Targeting, The New Facade of Neoliberal Conditionality: an Introduction', available at: <http://www.bagimsizsosyalbilimciler.org/Yazilar_Uye/EpYeDec06.pdf>.

Ergüneş, Nuray 2008, 'Transformation of Turkish Banking Sector within the Financialisation Process of Turkish Economy', unpublished manuscript.

Ersel, Hasan and Fatih Özatay 2007, 'Fiscal Dominance and Inflation Targeting: Lesson from Turkey', available at: <http://fatih.ozatay.etu.edu.tr/ersel_ozatay.pdf>.

Erturk, Ismail and Stefano Solari 2007, 'Banks as Continuous Reinvention', *New Political Economy*, 12, 3: 369–88.

European Central Bank International Relations Committee 2006, 'The Accumulation of Foreign Reserves', Occasional Paper Series 43, February.

Farrel, Diana, Susan M. Lund and Alexander Maasry 2007, 'Mapping the Global Capital Markets', *The McKinsey Quarterly*, available at: <http://www.mckinseyquarterly.com/Mapping_the_global_capital_markets_January_2007_Europe_rising_1899>.

Fine, Ben 2008, 'From Financialisation to Neo-Liberalism, Engaging Neo-Liberalism', unpublished manuscript.

——, Costas Lapavitsas and Dimitris Milonakis 1999, 'Analysing the World Economy: Two Steps Back', *Capital and Class*, 67: 21–47.

Fisher, Irving 1933, 'The Debt-Deflation Theory of Great Depressions', *Econometrica*, 1, 1: 337–57.

Frey, Laure and Gilles Moëc 2005, 'US Long-Term Yields and Interventions by Foreign Central Banks', *Banque de France Monthly Bulletin Digest*, May, No. 137.

Friedman Milton and Anna Schwartz 1963, *A Monetary History of the United States 1867–1960*, Princeton: Princeton University Press.

Foster, John Bellamy 2007, 'Financialization of Capitalism', *Monthly Review*, 58, 11, available at: <http://www.monthlyreview.org/0407jbf.htm>.

—— 2008, 'The Financialization of Capital and the Crisis', *Monthly Review*, 59, 11, available at: <http://www.monthlyreview.org/080401foster.php>.

Froud, Julie, Colin Haslam, Sukhdev Johal and Karel Willams 2001, 'Financialisation and the Coupon Pool', *Gestao & Producao*, 8, 3: 271–88.

Furnace, David 2004, 'Why Overdraft Income Is Growing for Financial Institutions?', *Kentucky Banker Magazine*, March 2004, Lousiville: Kentucky Bankers Association.

Garcia, Pablo and Claudio Soto 2004, 'Large Hoarding of International Reserves: Are They Worth It?', Working Papers Central Bank of Chile, no. 299, Santiago: Central Bank of Chile.

General Accounting Office 2002, 'Electronic Transfers: Use by Federal Payment Recipients Has Increased but Obstacles to Greater Participation Remain', *Report to the Subcommittee on Oversight and Investigations, Committee on Financial Services, U.S. House of Representatives. Report Number GAO-02–913*. Washington, DC.: General Accounting Office, September.

Gill, Louis 2002, *Fundamentos y límites del capitalismo*, Madrid: Trotta.

Gittelsohn, John 2007, 'How Subprime Lending All Started in O.C.', *Orange County Register*, December 30.

Glyn, Andrew 2006, *Capitalism Unleashed: Finance, Globalization and Welfare*, Oxford: Oxford University Press.

——, Alan Hughes, Alain Lipietz and Ajit Singh 1988, 'The Rise and Fall of the Golden Age', *Cambridge Working Papers in Economics*, No. 884, University of Cambridge.

Goldstein, John 1986, 'Mark-Up Variability and Flexibility: Theory and Empirical Evidence', *Journal of Business*, 59, 4: 599–621.

Goldstein, Steve 2007, 'HSBC Restructures Two SIVs', *Wall Street Journal*, November 26.

Grahl, John 1998, 'Emergency Changes in Monetary Policy', in *Adjustment, Convergence and Economic Policy: Essays in Macroeconomics in Honour of Bernard Corry and Maurice Pesto*, edited by Philip Arestis, Sami Daniel and John Grahl, Cheltenham: Edward Elgar.

Goodhart, Charles 2008, 'The Background to the 2007 Financial Crisis', *International Economics and Economic Policy*, 4: 331–46.

—— and Michel Persaud 2008, 'The Crash of 2007–08 Has Laid Bare the Poverty of the Current Regulatory Philosophy', *Financial Times*, 31 January.

Gordon, Robert 1999, 'Has the "New Economy" Rendered the Productivity Slow-Down Obsolete?', *Working Paper*, Northwestern University, mimeo.

—— 2004, 'Why Was Europe Left at the Station when America's Productivity Locomotive Departed?', Working Paper 10661, NBER, Cambridge, MA.: National Bureau of Economic Research.

Gosselin, Peter 2004, 'The Poor Have More Things Today – Including Wild Income Swings', *Los Angeles Times*, 12 December.

Gourinchas, Pierre and Helene Rey 2005, 'From World Banker to World Venture Capitalist: US External Adjustment and the Exorbitant Privilege', NBER Working Papers No. 11653, Cambridge MA.: National Bureau of Economic Research.

Green, Francis 2006, *Demanding Work: The Paradox of Job Quality in the Affluent Economy*, Princeton: Princeton University Press.

—— and Tsitsianis Nikolaos 2004, 'Can the Changing Nature of Jobs Account for National Trends in Job Satisfaction?', *Studies in Economics 0406*, Department of Economics, University of Kent.

—— and Tsitsianis Nikolaos 2005, 'An Investigation of National Trends in Job Satisfaction', *British Journal of Industrial Relations*, 43, 3: 401–29.

Greenspan Commission 1983, *Report of the National Commission on Social Security Reform*, Washington, DC.: Social Security Administration.

Gruben, William P. and Robert C. McComb 1997, 'Liberalization, Privatization, and Crash: Mexico's Banking System in the 1990s', *Federal Reserve Bank of Dallas Economic Review*, First Quarter: 21–30.

Hagerty, James R. and Karen Richardson 2007, 'Countrywide Shows Even Prime Loans Are Beginning to Sour', *Wall Street Journal*, 25 July: C1.

Harvey, David 2007, 'In What Ways Is "the New Imperialism" Really New?', *Historical Materialism*, 15, 3: 57–70.

Henriques, Diana B. and Lowell Bergman 2000, 'Profiting from Fine Print with Wall Street's Help', *Wall Street Journal*, 15 March.

Herbert, Bob 2007, 'A Swarm of Swindlers', *New York Times*, 20 November.

Hilferding, Rudolf 1981 [1910], *Finance Capital*, London: Routledge & Kegan Paul.

Hobson, John, 1938, *Imperialism*, 3rd ed., London: George Allen & Unwin.

Holmes, Andrew, and Paul Horvitz 1994, 'Mortgage Redlining: Race, Risk, and Demand', *Journal of Finance*, 49, 1: 81–99.

Housing and Economic Rights Advocates and California Reinvestment Coalition 2007, 'Foreclosed: The Burden of Homeownership Loss on City of Oakland and Alameda County Residents', December.

HSBC 2007, *Annual Report 2006*, London: HSBC Holdings plc.

Hviding, Ketil, Michael Nowak, and Luca Ricci 2004, 'Can Higher Reserves Help Reduce Exchange-Rate Volatility?', IMF Working Paper, n. 04/189, Washington DC: IMF.

International Energy Annual (IEA) 2005, 2006, 2007, 2008, Energy Information Administration Official Energy Statistics from the US Government.

International Financial Services London 2007, IFSL Pension Reform, available: <www.ifsl.org.uk>.

IMF 2007, 2008a, *Global Financial Stability Report*, April, September, October, Washington DC.: IMF.

—— 2008b, *World Economic Outlook*, April, Washington: IMF.

International Finance Corporation 2008, *Annual Report 2007*, Washington, DC.: World Bank Group.

Investment Company Institute 2006, '401(k) Plan Asset Allocation, Account Balances and Loan Activity in 2005', *Research Perspective*, 12, 1: 1–20.

—— 2007, *2007 Investment Company Fact Book, 47th Edition*, available at: <www.icifactbook.org>.

Itoh, Makoto 2000, *The Japanese Economy Reconsidered*, Houndmills: Palgrave.

—— 2006, *Capitalism in the Era of Disillusionment* [in Japanese], Tokyo: Otsuki-shobo.

—— and Costas Lapavitsas 1999, *Political Economy of Money and Finance*, London: Macmillan.

Japan Cabinet Office, Policy Planning Room 2007, 'The Background and the Influence of the Subprime Housing Loan Problem', in *Tide in the World Economy* [in Japanese], Fall.

Jorgenson, Dale and Kenneth Stiroh 2000, 'Raising the Speed Limit: US Economic Growth in the Information Age', *Brookings Papers on Economic Activity*, 1: 125–211.

Kaneko, Masaru and Andrew DeWit 2008, *The World Financial Crisis* [in Japanese], Tokyo: Iwanami-shoten.

Katkov, Neil 2002, *ATMs: Self-Service for the Unbanked*, Tokyo: Celent Communications.

Kelly, Kate, Serena Ng and David Reilly 2007, 'Two Big Funds At Bear Stearns Face Shutdown As Rescue Plan Falters Amid Subprime Woes, Merrill Asserts Claims', *Wall Street Journal*, 20 June: A1.

Kindleberger, Charles 1989, *Manias, Panics, and Crashes: A History of Financial Crises*, Revised Edition, New York: Basic Books.

—— and Robert Aliber 2005, *Manias, Panics, and Crashes – A History of Financial Crises*, Fifth Edition, Hoboken: John Wiley & Sons, Inc.

King, Mervyn 2006, 'Reform of the International Monetary Fund', Speech by Mervyn King, Governor of the Bank of England, at the Indian Council for Research on International Economic Relations (ICRIER), New Delhi.

King, Stephen 1999, 'Bubble Trouble: The US Bubble and How It Will Burst', HSBC Economics & Investment Strategy, July, London: HSBC.

Kneeshaw J.T. and P. van den Bergh 1989, 'Changes in Central Bank Money Market Operating Procedures in the 1980s', BIS Economic Papers, no. 23. Available at: <http://www.bis.org/publ/econ23.htm>.

Kregel, Jan 1999, 'Yes, "It" Did Happen Again – A Minsky Crisis Happened in Asia', Working Paper Series no. 234, Annandale-on-Hudson: The Jerome Levy Economics Institute.

Krinsman, Allan N. 2007, 'Subprime Mortgage Meltdown: How Did It Happen and How Will It End?', Journal of Structured Finance, 13, 2: 13–19.

Krugman, Paul 1998, 'What Happened to Asia?', MIT Department of Economics, available at: <http://web.mit.edu/krugman/www/DISINTER.html>.

—— 2007, 'Henry Paulson's Priorities', New York Times, 10 December.

Lang, William W., Loretta Mester and Todd A. Vermilyea 2007, 'Competitive Effects of Basel II on U.S. Bank Credit Card Lending', Federal Reserve Bank of Philadelphia Working Paper, 07–9, Philadelphia: Federal Reserve Bank of Philadelphia.

Lapavitsas, Costas 1991, 'The Theory of Credit Money: A Structural Analysis', Science & Society, 55, 3: 291–322.

—— 1997a, 'Two Approaches to the Concept of Interest–Bearing Capital', International Journal of Political Economy, 27, 1: 85–106.

—— 1997b, 'The Political Economy of Central Banks: Agents of stability or Sources of Instability?', International Papers in Political Economy, 4, 3: 1–52.

—— 2000, 'On Marx's Analysis of Money Hoarding in the Turnover of Capital', Review of Political Economy, 12, 2: 219–35.

—— 2003, Social Foundations of Markets, Money and Credit, Routledge: London.

—— 2006, 'Relations of Power and Trust in Contemporary Finance', Historical Materialism, 14, 1: 129–54.

—— 2007, 'Information and Trust as Social Aspects of Credit', Economy and Society, 36, 3: 416–36.

—— 2009, 'Financialised Capitalism: Crisis and Financial Expropriation', Historical Materialism, 17, 2: 114–48.

—— and Paulo Dos Santos 2008, 'Globalization and Contemporary Banking: On the Impact of New Technology', Contributions to Political Economy, 27: 31–56.

Lazonick, William and Mary O'Sullivan 2000, 'Maximizing Shareholder Value: A New Ideology for Corporate Governance', Economy and Society, 29, 1: 13–35.

Leamer, Edward 2007, 'Housing is the Business Cycle', NBER Working Paper 13428, Cambridge, MA.: National Bureau of Economic Research.

Levine, Ross 1996, 'Foreign Banks, Financial Development, and Economic Growth', in International Financial Markets: Harmonization versus Competition, edited by Claude Barfield, Washington, DC.: The AEI Press.

Liebowitz, Stan J. 2008, 'Anatomy of a Train Wreck: Causes of the Mortgage Meltdown', Independent Policy Report, Oakland: The Independent Institute, 3 October.

Lenin, Vladimir 1964 [1916], Imperialism, the Highest Stage of Capitalism, in Collected Works, Volume 22, Moscow: Progress.

Leyshon, Andrew and Nigel Thrift 1997, Money/Space, London: Routledge.

Luxemburg, Rosa 1951 [1913], The Accumulation of Capital, London: Routledge & Kegan Paul.

MacKenzie, Donald 2003, 'Long-Term Capital Management and the Sociology of Arbitrage', Economy and Society, 32, 3: 349–80.

—— 2004, 'The Big, Bad Wolf and Rational Portfolio Insurance, the 1987 Crash and the Performativity of Economics', Economy and Society, 33, 3: 303–34.

—— and Yuval Millo 2003, 'Constructing a Market, Performing Theory: The Historical Sociology of a Financial Derivatives Exchange', *American Journal of Sociology*, 109, 1: 107–45.

Marx, Karl 1991 [1861–3], *Karl Marx and Frederick Engels: Collected Works*, Volume 33, London: Lawrence and Wishart.

—— 1976 [1867], *Capital*, Volume I, London: Penguin/New Left Review.

—— 1978 [1885], *Capital*, Volume II, London: Penguin/New Left Review.

—— 1981 [1894], *Capital*, Volume III, London: Penguin/New Left Review.

Masson, Paul, Miguel A. Savastano and Sunil Sharma 1997, 'The Scope for Inflation Targeting in Developing Countries', IMF Working Paper, WP/97/130, Washington DC.: IMF.

Mathieson, D.J. and Liliana Rojas-Suárez 1992, 'Liberalisation of the Capital-Account: Experiences and Issues', IMF Working Paper, no. 92/46, Washington DC: IMF.

McCoy, Patricia and Elvin Wyly 2004, 'Special Issue on Market Failures and. Predatory Lending: Guest Editorial', *Housing Policy Debate*, 15, 3: 453–66.

McGee, Robert 2000, 'What Should a Central Bank Do?', Department of Economics, Florida State University, mimeo.

McGrath, Kathryn B. 1989, 'Legislative and Regulatory Update: Banks and Mutual Funds', Speech given to 1989 American Bankers Association by SEC Director of Investment Management, 6 February, Washington, DC.: Securities and Exchange Commission.

McKinnon, Ronald 1973, *Money and Capital in Economic Development*, Washington DC.: Brookings Institution.

—— 1991, *The Order of Economic Liberalisation: Financial Control in the Transition to a Market Economy*, Baltimore: John Hopkins University Press.

McKinsey 2008, *Mapping Global Capital Markets*, 4th Annual Report, McKinsey Global Institute, available at: <http://www.mckinsey.com/mgi/publications/Mapping_Global/slideshow/slideshow_1.asp>.

Meltzer, Allen 2007, 'Let 'Em Fail', *Wall Street Journal*, 21 July: A6.

Merton, Robert C. 1973, 'Theory of Rational Option Pricing', *Bell Journal of Economics and Management Science*, 4, Spring: 141–83.

Mester, Loretta 1997, 'What Is the Point of Credit Scoring?', *Federal Reserve Bank of Philadephia Business Review*, September–October: 3–16.

Meyer Thomas 2003, 'The Monetarist Policy Debate: An Informal Survey', Department of Economics, Working Paper, 03–9, University of California, Davis.

Millo, Yuval and David MacKenzie 2007, 'Building a Boundary Object: The Evolution of Financial Risk Management', unpublished manuscript.

Mishkin Frederic 1996, 'Understanding Financial Crises: A Developing Country Perspective', NBER Working Paper Series, No. 5.600, Cambridge, MA.: National Bureau of Economic Research.

—— 1999, 'Inflation Experiences with Different Monetary Policy Régimes', *Journal of Monetary Economics*, 43, 3: 579–605.

—— 2002, 'Structural Issues for Successful Inflation Targeting in Transition Countries', presentation at the National Bank of Poland's Annual International Conference Monetary Policy in the Environment of Structural Change, available at: <http://www.nbp.pl/konferencje/falenty2002/pdf_en/mishkin.pdf>.

—— 2008, 'The Federal Reserve's Tools for Responding to Financial Disruptions', Speech delivered at the Tuck Global Capital Markets Conference, Tuck School of Business, Dartmouth College, Hanover, New Hampshire, available at: <www.federalreserve.gov/newsevents/speech/mishkin20080215a.htm>.

—— and Claus Schmidt-Hebbel 2001, 'One Decade of Inflation-Targeting in the World: What Do We Know and What Do We Need to Know?', NBER Working Paper, 8397, Cambridge, MA.: National Bureau of Economic Research.

Mizuho Research Institute 2007, *The Subprime Financial Crisis* [in Japanese], Tokyo: Nihonkeizai-shibunsha.

Mollenkamp, Carrick, Deborah Solomon, Robin Sidel and Valerie Bauerlein 2007, 'How London Created a Snarl in Global Markets', *Wall Street Journal*, 18 October: A1.

Morera, Carlos 1998, *El capital financiero en México y la globalización : límites y contradicciones*, México: Ediciones Era.

—— 2002, 'La nueva corporación trasnacional en México y la globalización', in *Globalización y alternativas incluyentes para el siglo XXI*, edited by Dolores de la Peña, Marisol Simón, Carlos Morera. México: UNAM (FE, CRIM, IIEc, DGAPA) UAM–Azcapozalco.

—— and José Antonio Rojas 2007, 'Notas sobre los cambios en la naturaleza del trabajo y la reorganización productiva y financiera mundial', IIEc, UNAM, en prensa.

—— and José Antonio Rojas 2008, 'Mercado mundial de dinero y renta petrolera', in *La guerra del fuego*, edited by Guillaume Fontaine and Alicia Puyana, Facultad Latinoamericana de Ciencias Sociales (FLACSO) y Ministerio de cultura.

Montgomerie, Johnna 2008, '(Re)Politicizing Inflation Policy: A Global Political Economy Perspective', Centre for Research on Socio-Cultural Change, Working Paper 53, Manchester: Manchester University.

Morrison, Alan D. and William J. Wilhelm 2007, *Investment Banking, Institutions, Politics, and Law*, Oxford: Oxford University Press.

Moseley, Fred 2007, 'Is the US Economy Headed for a Hard Landing?', available at: <http://www.mtholyoke.edu/~fmoseley/>.

Munck Ronaldo 2002, *Globalización y Trabajo: La nueva gran transformación*, Madrid: El viejo topo.

Narin, Özgür 2008a, 'Bügünü Anlamamak: Üretimde Teknoloji Artıyor Ama Çalışma Saatleride, İşsizlikte Artıyor', Karaburun Bilim Kongresi, 4–7 Eylül 2008.

—— 2008b, *Teknolojik Değişim: Türkiye'de Üretim Araçları Üretimi (1996–2005)*, unpublished PhD thesis, Marmara Üniversitesi.

Neely, Christopher J. 1995, 'Will the Mutual Fund Boom Be a Bust for Banks?', *Federal Reserve Bank of St Louis Regional Economist*, October.

Neumann, Manfred and Jurgen von Hagen 2002, 'Does Inflation-Targeting Matter?', *Federal Reserve Bank of St. Louis Review*, 84: 149–53.

New York Times 2002, 'Round Table: Wall Street's Prescriptions in a Convalescing Economy', 2 January.

OECD 2007a, *Closing the Pensions Gap: The Role of Private Pensions*, Paris: OECD.

—— 2007b, 2008, 2009, *Economic Outlook*, issues no. 80. 82, 84, 86, Paris: OECD.

Oliner, Stephen and Daniel Sichel 2000, 'The Resurgence of Growth in the Late 1990s: Is Information Technology the Story?', *Journal of Economic Perspectives*, 14, 4: 3–22.

—— and Daniel Sichel 2002, 'Information Technology and Productivity: Where Are We Now and Where Are We Going?', *Economic Review*, Federal Reserve Bank of Atlanta, Third Quarter: 15–44.

Onaran, Özlem 2006, 'Speculation-Led Growth and Fragility in Turkey: Does EU Make a Difference or Can It Happen Again?', Vienna University, Department of Economics Working Paper Series, 93.

Oppel, Jr., Richard A. and Patrick McGeehan 2000, 'Citigroup Announces Changes to Guard Against Abusive Loan Practices', *New York Times*, 8 November.

Orhangazi, Ozgur 2007, 'Financialization and Capital Accumulation in the Non-Financial Corporate Sector: A Theoretical and Empirical Investigation of the US Economy: 1973–2003', PERI, Working Paper, no. 149, Amherst: Political Economy Research Institute.

—— 2008, 'Financialization and Capital Accumulation in the Non-Financial Corporate Sector: A Theoretical and Empirical Investigation of the US Economy, 1973–2004', *Cambridge Journal of Economics*, 32, 6: 863–86.

Orozco, Manuel 2004, *The Remittance Marketplace: Prices, Policy and Financial Institutions*. Washington, DC.: Pew Hispanic Center.

Persaud, Avinash 2002, 'Liquidity Black Holes', UNU-WIDER, DP 2002/31.

Petruno, Tom 2007, 'Loan Fix Requires Investors to Yield', *Los Angeles Times*, 8 December.

Petursson, Thorarinn G. 2000, 'Exchange Rate or Inflation Targeting in Monetary Policy', *Monetary Bulletin* 2000/1, available at: <http://www.sedlabanki.is/uploads/files/mb001_6.pdf>.

Pittman, Mark 2007, 'Moody's, S&P Understate Subprime Risk, Study Says (Update2)', *Bloomberg News Service*, May 3, available at: <http://www.bloomberg.com/apps/news?pid=newsarchive&sid=aETDs1PMKDG8>.

——— and Bob Ivry 2008, 'U.S. Pledges Top $7.7 Trillion to Ease Frozen Credit', Bloomberg, 24 November, available at: <http://www.bloomberg.com/apps/news?sid=an3k2rZMNgDw&pid=20601109>.

Poiret, P. 2001, 'New Horizons and Policy Challenges for Foreign Direct Investment in the 21st Century', OECD Global Forum on International Investment, Mexico City.

Pollin, Robert 2007, 'Resurrection of the Rentier', *New Left Review*, II, 46: 140–53.

Rose, Andrew K. 2007, 'Are International Financial Crisis a Barbarous Relic? Inflation Targeting as a Monetary Vaccine', Centre For Economic Policy Research, Policy Insight, 1, available at: <http://www.voxeu.org/index.php?q=node/199>.

Reinhart, Carmen M. and Kenneth S. Rogoff 2008, 'Is the 2007 U.S. Sub-Prime Financial Crisis So Different? An International Historical Comparison', *Working Paper*, Department of Economics, University of Maryland, College Park.

Rodrik, Dani 2006, 'The Social Cost of Foreign Exchange Reserves', *International Economic Journal*, 20, 3: 253–66.

Saad-Filho, Alfredo 2000, 'Inflation Theory: A Critical Literature Review and a New Research Agenda', in *Research in Political Economy. Value, Capitalist Dynamics and Money*, 18: 335–62.

——— and Maria Mollo 2002, 'Inflation and Stabilization in Brazil: A Political Economy Analysis, *Review of Radical Political Economics*, 34, 2: 109–35.

Sapsford, Jathon, Laurie Cohen, Monica Langley and Robin Sidel 2001, 'J.P. Morgan Chase to Buy Bank One', *Wall Street Journal*, 14 January.

Saraçoğlu, Bedriye and Halit Suiçmez 2006, Türkiye İmalat Sanayinde Verimlilik, Teknolojik Gelişme ve Yapısal Özellikler ve 2001 Krizi Sonrası Reel Değişmeler, report, National Productivity Center.

Saunders, Anthony and Linda Allen 2002, *Credit Risk Measurement*, New York: John Wiley & Sons.

Schor Juliet 1985, 'Wage Flexibility, Social Wage Expenditures and Monetary Restrictiveness', in *Money and Macro Policy*, edited by Mark Jarsulic, Boston: Kluwer-Nijhoff.

——— and Samuel Bowles 1987, 'Employment Rents and the Incidence of Strikes', *Review of Economics and Statistics*, 59, 4: 584–92.

Schwartz, Anna 1988, 'Financial Stability and the Safety Net', in *Restructuring Banking and Financial Services in America*, edited by William Haraf and Rose Marie Kushmeider, Washington, DC.: American Enterprise Institute for Public Policy and Research.

——— 1998, 'Why Financial Stability Depends on Price Stability', in *Money, Prices and the Real Economy*, edited by Geoffrey Wood, Cheltenham: Edward Elgar.

Shaikh, Anwar 1997, 'The Challenge of Marxian Economics to Neoliberal Economic Theory', Paper presented at the Conference on Contemporary Economic Theory: Critical Perspectives, Athens University of Economics and Business, 6–7 October.

Shaw, Edward 1973, *Financial Deepening in Economic Development*, Oxford: Oxford University Press.

Shiller, Robert J. 2008, *The Subprime Solution*, Princeton: Princeton University Press.

Siconolfi, Michael 2007, 'Did Authorities Miss a Chance To Ease Crunch?', *Wall Street Journal*, 10 December, C1.

Siklos, Pierre. 2002, *The Changing Face of Central Banking: Evolutionary Trends Since World War II*, Cambridge: Cambridge University Press.

Sinkey Jr., Joseph F. 1981, *Problem and Failed Institutions in the Commercial Banking Industry*, Greenwich, Conn.: JAI Press.

Smith, Adam 1950 [1776], *The Wealth of Nations*, 6th ed., London: Methuen.

Skott, Peter and Soon Ryoo 2008, 'Macroeconomic Implications of Financialisation', *Cambridge Journal of Economics*, 32, 6: 827–62.

Sönmez, Mustafa 2008, 2008 Dünya Krizi ve Türkiye, report, Petrol-iş Yayınları.

Squires, Gregory D. (ed.) 1993, *From Redlining to Reinvestment*, Philadelphia: Temple University Press.

State Planning Organization, 'Main Economic Indicators', available at: <www.dpt.gov.tr>.

Staten, Michael E. and Anthony M. Yezer 2004, 'Introduction to the Special Issue: Subprime Lending: Empirical Studies', *Journal of Real Estate Finance and Economics*, 29, 4: 359–63.

Steuart, James 1995 [1767], *Principles of Political Economy*, in *Collected Works of James Steuart*, London: Routledge/Thoemmes.

Stockhammer, Engelbert 2004, 'Financialisation and the Slowdown of Accumulation', *Cambridge Journal of Economics*, 28, 5: 719–41.

—— 2007, 'Some Stylised Facts on the Finance-Dominated Accumulation Régime', PERI, Working Paper, no. 142, Amherst: Political Economy Research Institute.

Stone, Mark and Ashok Bhundia 2004, 'A New Taxonomy of Monetary Régimes', IMF Working Paper, 04/191.

Svensson, Lars E.O. 2007, 'Inflation Targeting', in *The New Palgrave Dictionary of Economics*, edited by Larry Blum and Steven Durlauf, 2nd Edition, Houndmills, Basingstoke: Palgrave MacMillan.

Takumi, Mitsuhiko 1994, *The Great Global Crisis* [in Japanese], Tokyo: Ochanomizu-shobo.

—— 1998, *The Great Crash* [in Japanese], Tokyo: Koudan-sha.

Taylor, Lance 1998, 'Capital Market Crises: Liberalisation, Fixed Exchange-Rates and Market Driven Destabilisation', *Cambridge Economic Journal*, 22, 6: 663–76.

Taymaz, Erol and Kamil Yılmaz 2008, 'Integration with the Global Economy, The Case of Turkish Automobile and Consumer Electronics Industries', Working Paper 0801, TUSIAD-Koc University Economic Research Forum.

Toporowski, Jan 2000, *The End of Finance: Capital Market Inflation, Financial Derivatives and Pension Fund Capitalism*, London: Routledge.

Treasury Undersecretariat, 'Economic Indicators, Financial Markets', available at: <www.treasury.gov.tr>.

Triplett, Jack and Barry Bosworth 2001, 'What's New about the New Economy? IT, Economic Growth and Productivity', *International Productivity Monitor*, 2: 19–30.

—— and Barry Bosworth 2003, ' "Baumol's Disease" Has Been Cured: IT and Multifactor Productivity in the US Services Industries', *Brookings Economics Papers*, September.

Tully, Shawn 2007, 'Wall Street's Money Machine Breaks Down: The Subprime Mortgage Crisis Keeps Getting Worse – And Claiming More Victims', *Fortune*, 12 November.

Turkish Industrialists and Businessmen Association 2007, 2008 Yılına Girerken Türkiye Ekonomisi, Istanbul.

UNCTAD 1999, *World Investment Report 1999, Foreign Direct Investment and the Challenge of Development*, New York and Geneva: published by the United Nations.

—— 2002, *World Investment Report 2002: Transnational Corporations and Export Competitiveness*, New York and Geneva: published by the United Nations.

—— 2003, *World Investment Report 2003: FDI Policies for Development: National and International Perspectives*, New York and Geneva, published by the United Nations.

—— 2005, *World Investment Report 2005: Transnational Corporations and the Internationalization of R&D*, New York and Geneva: published by the United Nations.

—— 2006, *World Investment Report 2006: FDI from Developing and Transition Economies: Implications for Development*, New York and Geneva: published by the United Nations.

US Treasury 2008, *Report on Foreign Portfolio Holdings of U.S. Securities*, available at: <http://www.treas.gov/tic/fpis.shtml>.

Vives, Xavier 2008, 'Bagehot, Central Banking and the Financial Crisis', in *The First Global Financial Crisis of the 21st Century*, edited by Andrew Felton and Carmen Reinhart, London: Centre for Economic Policy Research (CERP).

Wade, Robert 1998, 'From "Miracle" to "Cronyism": Explaining the Great Asian Slump', *Cambridge Economic Journal*, 22, 6: 693–706.

Walsh, Lynn 2008, 'A Global Shock to the System', *Socialism Today*, 115, February, available at: <http://www.socialismtoday.org/115/economy.html>.

—— 2008, 'Bear Stearns Bail-Out', *Socialism Today*, 117, April, available at: <http://www.socialismtoday.org/117/bailout.html>.

Watson and Wyatt 2007, 'The World's 500 Largest Asset Managers', available at: <www.watsonwyatt.com/research/deliverpdf.asp?catalog=PI_500_Analysis_2007>.

Weisskopf, Thomas 1988, 'The Analysis of a Neo-Marxian Crisis Theory', *The Economic Review*, 39, 8: 193–208.

Warnock Francis and Veronica Warnock 2005, 'International Capital-Flows and US Interest-Rates', International Finance Discussion Papers, September, No. 840.

Williamson, John and Molly Mahar 1998, A Survey of Financial Liberalisation, Princeton: International Finance Section, Department of Economics, Princeton University.

World Bank 2006, *Global Development Finance*, Washington, DC.: World Bank.

Wray, L. Randall 2007, 'Lessons from the Subprime Meltdown', Working Paper no. 522, Levy Economics Institute of Bard College.

Yalçındağ, Arzuhan 2008, 'Küresel Kapitalizmin Geleceği ve Türkiye', Conference, Opening Speech, 10 October, available at: <http://www.ku.edu.tr/ku/images/EAF/desifre_10102008.pdf>.

Yeldan, Erinç 2006, 'Patterns of Adjustment under the Age of Finance: The Case of Turkey as a Peripheral Agent of New-Imperialism', paper prepared for presentation at the annual meeting of URPE (Union for Radical Political Economy).

—— 2006, 'Neoliberal Global Remedies: From Speculative-Led Growth to IMF-Led Crisis in Turkey', *Review of Radical Political Economics*, 38, 2: 193–213.

Yükseler, Zafer and Ercan Türkan 2008, Türkiye'nin Üretim ve Dış Ticaret Yapısında Dönüşüm, report, Turkish Industrialist's and Businessmen's Association, available at: <http://www.tcmb.gov.tr/yeni/iletisimgm/TUSIAD_aciskonus.pdf>.

—— and Ercan Türkan 2008, Türkiye'de Hanehalkı: İsgücü, Gelir, Harcama ve Yoksulluk Açısından, report, Turkish Industrialist's and Businessmen's Association, available at: <http://www.tusiad.org.tr/FileArchive/2008.03.21-Turkiyede HanehalkiRaporuOzetBulguları.pdf>.

Index